LEVIATHANS AT THE GOLD MINE

LEVIATHANS AT THE GOLD MINE

Creating Indigenous and Corporate Actors in Papua New Guinea

Alex Golub

Duke University Press
DURHAM AND LONDON
2014

Printed in the United States of America on acid-free
paper ∞
Typeset in Minion Pro and Officina Sans by Graphic
Composition, Inc.

Library of Congress Cataloging-in-Publication Data
Golub, Alex.
Leviathans at the gold mine : creating indigenous and
corporate actors in Papua New Guinea / Alex Golub.
p. cm
Includes bibliographical references and index.
ISBN 978-0-8223-5494-9 (cloth : alk. paper)
ISBN 978-0-8223-5508-3 (pbk. : alk. paper)
1. Ipili (Papua New Guinean people)—History.
2. Gold mines and mining—Papua New Guinea—
Porgera. 3. Porgera (Papua New Guinea)—History.
I. Title.
DU740.9.P66G655 2014
333.8'541099563—dc23
2013026444

Duke University Press gratefully acknowledges the
Department of Anthropology Publication Grant
at the University of Hawaii, Manoa, which provided
funds toward the publication of this book.

CONTENTS

PREFACE

Before we begin, here are some quick points on terminology and language use.

In this book I use highly racialized language to distinguish between "black," "white," and "mixed-blood" or "half-caste" people. These terms are drawn from the lifeworld I encountered in Porgera. Papua New Guineans regularly use terms like these because Australian colonialism has left in its wake an extremely racialized imagination of difference. Please understand them as local terms, not my endorsement of some bizarrely racist ideology.

There is also the issue of describing the differences between Ipili culture and the culture of Europe and its settler colonies. Benjamin Whorf's term "Standard Average European" does well but is awkward. The term "the West" is problematic for reasons now known from decades of scholarship on Eurocentrism. A frequent alternative, "the global North" is unpalatable in the context of Papua New Guinea, where the white metropole is below Papua New Guinea on a map and Australians leaving Papua New Guinea are said to "go south." "Euroamerican" is frequently used by Melanesianists as a substitute for "white," but this is a mere fig leaf and makes no sense in the context of Australian colonialism, since Australia is neither American nor European. I have opted for the more accurate "Euro-christian," which is a nonraced and frankly more accurate way to designate those societies importantly shaped by the culture of Latin Christendom.

Most anthropologists will recognize the specialized kinship terminology I employ. The exception is the term "enate," which some readers of the manuscript did not know. Following Peter Lawrence's definition in *The Garia* (1984, 256), I use this term to refer to a person connected to a cognatic stock through a female. Lawrence got the term from Meyer Fortes, who got it from Justinian.

There is a standard orthography for Ipili developed by the linguist and missionary Terry Borchard. However, few Ipili people use it. Throughout this book I have spelled Ipili names as their owners spell them. Other terms are spelled as I encountered them in the valley. They all sound pretty much as you'd expect—*t* and *r* tend to be tapped.

Over time, the government office responsible for overseeing matters relating to mining has undergone several name changes. Throughout this book I refer to it as the Department of Mining, since that was what it was called during my time here. Throughout, I refer to Papua New Guinea as a colony of Australia, despite the fact that many Australians consider their activity in Papua New Guinea a form of "imperial administration" rather than settler colonialism. I follow here the wider, academic use of the term "colony" to subsume all of these activities.

Many of my respondents asked that I use pseudonyms to identify them. Some, however, did not, and some were insistent that their proper names be used so that their fame and fortune would increase. Some are public figures, elected officials, or government employees who are well known and not entitled to anonymity. In this book I have decided to handle this complex mix of publicity, privacy, and desire for recognition by using pseudonyms to refer to all living participants in the Yakatabari negotiations—even the ones who requested that their actual names be used. This will appear ridiculous to many in Papua New Guinea, who will hardly be deceived about the identity of the people I discuss. Nevertheless, I believe consistency in the use of pseudonyms is ultimately the best policy. The names of ethnic groups and institutions have not been changed.

The Yakatabari negotiations and much of the other action described here took place in a context that was almost exclusively, if not totally, male. Some Porgerans have opinions about and engage in conduct towards women which may not agree with the sentiments of my readers. I would like, therefore, to emphasize that the focus on men's lives in this book is the result of the situation I described rather than any gender chauvinism on my part.

Finally, a note on terminology: throughout this book, *Leviathan* refers to the book by Thomas Hobbes, Leviathan to the mythological chaos beast of ancient Near Eastern political theology, and leviathan to any sort of black-boxed corporate entity.

ACKNOWLEDGMENTS

After I presented an early version of a chapter in this book at Jonathan Friedman's seminar in Paris, one of the students asked: "You talk about Leviathans, but aren't you making your own mythology?" He was right, of course. But the difference between corporations and scholars is that we academics acknowledge the networks out of which we are composed.

This book began as a dissertation at the University of Chicago, where Marshall Sahlins, Michael Silverstein, Danilyn Rutherford, and Manuela Carneiro da Cunha generously served on my dissertation committee. Ira Bashkow, Rupert Stasch, Lise Dobrin, Tom Strong, and Debra McDougall helped me both prepare for the field and live in it. Ken Hopper taught me institutional politics, Jim Nitti taught me the art of the short con, and AKMA taught me agape. Thank you all.

My account of Yakatabari could never have been written if both sides of the negotiations had not wanted me to tell their story. My thanks to Jeffrey, Kurubu, Jonathan, Graham M., Graham T., Ken, Craig, Fritz, Mel, Ila, Evert, Daniel, Koeka, Pakiru, Guy, and Sam.

I particularly wish to thank Anginape Mapia, Sawa Yawini, Jordan Iso, Andrew K., Kambo Olape, and the rest of Waiwa *yame* for hosting me.

My fellow Porgera-ists deserve special thanks for their generosity and collaborative spirit—not all anthropologists have the opportunity to share a valley with such amicable colleagues. Thanks to Glenn Banks and Jerry Jacka. Special thanks go to Aletta Biersack, the senior scholar in my area. When I first met Aletta, I found her incredibly intimidating. In the years that have passed since then I've discovered her to be a model of professional ethics: demanding, judicious, impartial—and intimidating.

Several sources funded this research. I thank the US Department of Education for the Fulbright-Hayes Doctoral Dissertation Research Abroad Fellowship P022A990042, which made my dissertation fieldwork possible. Follow-up research was made possible by a Research Relations Grant from the University Research Council of the University of Hawaii at Manoa and a CIBER Interdisciplinary Research Grant.

There are worse things in life than shuttling between Honolulu and Paris. Thanks to Marie Salaun, Jonathan Friedman, and Albin Bensa for hosting me at the École des Hautes Études en Sciences Sociales where a good portion of this book was revised. In Marseille, Laurent Dousset and Serge Tcherkézoff were very kind hosts.

In Port Moresby, I'd like to thank Greg Anderson and the staff of the Papua New Guinea Chamber of Mining and Petroleum, Jephat Kol and Miriam Supuma, and Paul Barker and the Institute for National Affairs.

Special thanks to Eleanor Kleiber, Stu Dawrs, and the rest of the staff of the Pacific Collection at the Hamilton library here at UH Mānoa for allowing me free access to the material that formed a central part of chapter 4. Kathy Creely helped support an early trip to the Melanesian Collection at the University of California San Diego, which was in part supported by a small grant from the Friends of the Library there. Thanks also to all the archivists and librarians at the National Archives of Papua New Guinea, the National Library of Australia, and the National Archives of Australia.

I never sweat the small stuff and, unfortunately, I seem never to sweat the medium-sized stuff either. Thanks so much to the three (!) hard-working editors who turned my manuscript into a readable book: Melinda "From Ohio" Eakin, Jeanne Ferris, and Sara Leone. Thanks also to the Robert S. and Mary M. E. Lingley Charitable Foundation for Childcare for allowing me the free time necessary to polish the manuscript in the congenial environs of the Bangor public library. And thanks, obviously, to Kate for being so supportive.

All the errors in this book are my own.

INTRODUCTION

"A set of principles necessarily includes a political attitude," Henri said. "And on the other hand, politics is itself a living thing."

"I don't think so," Lambert replied. "In politics, all you're concerned with are abstract things that don't exist—the future, masses of people. But what is really concrete is the actual present moment, and people as separate and single individuals."

"But each individual is affected by collective history," Henri said.

"The trouble is that in politics you never come down from the high plateau of history to the problem of the lowly individual," Lambert said. "You get lost in generalities and no one gives a damn about particular cases."

—Simone de Beauvoir, *The Mandarins*

How does a discipline that studies "what is really concrete in the actual present moment" come to understand "abstract things"? How do we move from our experience of "people as separate and single individuals" to the "high plateau of history"? These were crucial questions for de Beauvoir's characters as they struggled to rebuild postwar France. But these are our questions as well: anthropology today oscillates uneasily between two different imaginations of our contemporary situation that are only tenuously linked. On the one hand, there is a Foucauldian scrutiny of global regimes of governance that grow ever more panoptic, neoliberal technologies of subjectification that shape individuals ever more strongly, and lives that appear increasingly proscribed, described, and inscribed in proliferating technoscientific imaginaries. On the other hand, there is a Deleuzian enthusiasm for evanescent assemblages of actors, an enthusiasm which discerns trajectories of hope

and desire that gainsay the pretension to omnipotence that currently structures our world. Whatever the ties between Foucault, Deleuze, and other
authors might have been, I cannot help feeling that there is something incoherent about an anthropological vision that sees the world as both more
controlled and less controlled than it has ever been before. Is there a better
way to do justice to a contemporary scene characterized by both spontaneity and regime?

This book attempts to answer this question by examining the relationship between two entities that, with differing degrees of success, attempt to
transform themselves from a collection of "separate and single individuals"
into "abstract things": the Porgera gold mine and the Ipili-speaking people
on whose land the mine is located. In 1939 the Ipili were one of the last major
ethnic groups to be contacted by the Australian administration of what was
then the Trust Territory of New Guinea. Gold was discovered on that initial
patrol, and after fifty years of prospecting and small-scale alluvial mining,
the third largest gold mine in the world opened in Porgera. It has been in
operation ever since, and Porgerans have gone from a world without metal
or textiles to one in which trucks carrying hundreds of tons of rock operate
nonstop in a huge open pit that was once their mountain. Since its establishment in 1962, the Porgera government station has been transformed from
a remote airstrip to a bustling "wild West" boomtown with—if the census
can be believed—roughly 20,000 inhabitants (Government of Papua New
Guinea 2002). The valley's past is littered with spectacular industrial accidents, large-scale civic unrest, and one particularly well-remembered be-
heading. In sum, Porgera fulfills every stereotype of Papua New Guineans'
living "10,000 years in a lifetime" (Kiki 1968), and going "from stone to steel"
(Salisbury 1962) or "from the stone age to the jet age" (Biersack 1992) in one
generation.

Porgera is both easy and hard to understand. It is easy to understand
because it is the kind of place that people like to tell stories about. Anthropologists and activists, for instance, like to tell stories of global capital destroying untouched cultures and pristine environments, and of valiantly re-
sisting, agentive indigenes. Mining companies and development agencies,
on the other hand, like to tell stories of progress and development, of the
benefits that mining brings to its Third World stakeholders. But Porgera is
also hard to understand because neither of these narratives fit very well with
the reality of life in the valley—or perhaps because they both do, but simultaneously and in unexpected ways. In this book my goal is to do justice to
Porgera by complicating the stories that are told of it, not out of an obscu-

2

rantist impulse to confound or an ideographic insistence that cases cannot be generalized, but because Porgera deserves a story that will do justice to its complex reality.

Simplicity in narrative, the rhetorician Kenneth Burke might have noted, is best achieved by keeping the number of characters small. One of the reasons that stories about Porgera are so straightforward is that they usually feature only two actors: the mine and the Ipili. These stories have simple plots with obvious heroes and villains. In this book, in contrast, I seek to describe the morally ambiguous reality of life in the valley by crafting a narrative that examines the proliferation of actors in valley politics.

Who, specifically, acts in the name of "the mine" and "the Ipili"? By what semiotic and political processes are these abstractions made to appear unproblematically as actors? What sorts of conflicts occur as people vie to become spokespeople for these groups, challenging each other's right to speak in their name? How does recognition of corporate identity claims affect people's entitlement not only to money and resources, but also to dignity? It is with this perspective, with identities unstuck, that I will examine the relationship between "the mine" and "the Ipili."

Finding answers requires asking some of the oldest questions about human social life: How do individuals come to represent groups? How is action coordinated across time and space? How do macro orders of determination interface with micro levels of human interaction? How do human beings form social totalities, and how do the methods that are used today compare with those of the past? This book does not pretend to solve the constitutive problems of social science, but I do at least hope to provide answers to these questions that will help us make sense of Porgera and possibly other similar places as well.

In this book, I attempt to answer these questions by analyzing two topics that are normally treated separately: the creation and maintenance of a large corporation (and, by extension, global capital) on the one hand, and the creation and maintenance of an ethnic group (and, by extension, indigenous identity) on the other hand. Each topic has its own massive body of literature, yet studies of the corporations (Welker, Partridge, and Hardin 2011) and of kinship (Carsten 2000) rarely interact with each other (the one great, and largely-unread, exception being Smith, M.G. 1975). Neither of these literatures articulates with studies of the cultural construction of the state (for an overview, see Sharma and Gupta 2006) despite the fact that such studies have done much to clarify how de Beauvoir's "abstract things" are created "in the actual present moment."

And yet all three of these literatures are converging around a similar set of issues. 1990s bedazzlement with the inscrutability of global capitalism has given way to a movement which is "directly engaging with the global as a specific cultural formation and unpacking the global ethnographically from its black box" (Ho 2005, 88; see also Knorr Cetina and Preda 2005; Rajak 2011; Downey and Fischer 2004). The study of the state has transitioned from James Scott's (1998) image of the state as a monolithic knower of facts to an anthropology that examines the "repetitive re-enactment of everyday practices" through which "the coherence and continuity of state institutions is constituted and sometimes destabilized" (Sharma and Gupta 2006, 13, see also Feldman 2008, Hull 2012b). In the Pacific, studies of indigenous identity have moved beyond the literature on the invention of tradition and the concept of *kastom* (Lindstrom 2008) and alternate modernities (Knauft 2002). Instead, they have developed accounts of social change that focus on political innovation (Hviding and Rio 2011), a new native cultural studies which holds that identity is always contingent and achieved (Diaz and Kauanui 2001; Clifford 2013), and most importantly for this book, a powerful account of social organization and land tenure as it interacts with governmental forms (Weiner and Glaskin 2007). In the study of business, government, kinship, and indigeneity, then, scholars are examining how larger, stable social units are made in social processes that extend across time and space.

Although these literatures do not always talk to one another, I hope to develop a framework that can subsume them all. This is not a new move. The literature is littered with different terms for the sort of entities "the mine" and "the Ipili" hope to become: collective subjects, social persons, social totalities, macro actors, mass collectivities, and so forth. In recognition of the antiquity of these phenomena, I will refer to all of those kinds of collective entities as leviathans and attempt to understand how, generally, they come to be "concrete in the actual present moment," represented by particular people in particular offices and particular boardrooms—how, in other words, "the mine" can sign an agreement given the fact that, strictly speaking, it has no hands.

But before this complexity, exposition: who are these two leviathans I am about to unknit?

The Mine

Mention mining in the Third World, and people's imaginations will often conjure haunting images of sulfur mining in Indonesia and gold rushes

4

in Brazil: stark portraits of primitive, dangerous conditions and Third Worlders whose lives are shaped by the backbreaking misery of mining. Porgera is nothing like that.

Porgera is an enormous, technologically sophisticated, and highly mechanized operation. It is also a world-class mine: in 1992—its second year of production—it produced 1,485,077 ounces of gold, making it the third most productive gold mine on the planet and the most productive outside of South Africa (Banks 1997, 121). In 2000—the ethnographic present of this book—it produced 910,434 ounces of gold (Placer Dome Asia Pacific 2001, 1). Porgera is an open-cut mine: huge excavators dig away at the side of the mountain, moving roughly 200,000 tons of earth daily. Ore is dumped into an enormous crusher and then gradually refined and treated in enormous autoclaves. Over 95 percent of the ore becomes tailings (residue), which are discharged into the Pongema River. The rest becomes gold bars. In this way what was once a mountain has become a giant pit.

The mine is owned by the Porgera Joint Venture (PJV). The financial arrangements of the joint venture are complex, but during my fieldwork shares in the PJV were basically owned by Placer Dome (a transnational mining company based in Vancouver, Canada), the national government of Papua New Guinea, the Enga provincial government, and local landowners. Placer, the main shareholder, has a history in Papua New Guinea that goes back to the 1930s (Healy 1967); in 2000 it operated two properties in Papua New Guinea, the Misima and Porgera gold mines. Placer had been a key partner in prospecting and exploration in Porgera even before the mine opened, and after twenty years in the valley its name has become synonymous with the mine. Thus although employees of the Porgera Joint Venture wear uniforms with "PJV" on them, in the minds of most Porgerans "PJV" and "Placer" were synonymous. Although Placer was purchased by Barrick in 2006, this book will continue to refer to Placer, since this is the company that was operating the mine when the events recounted in this book took place.

In 2000, Placer described itself as "the world's gold leader" and employed 12,000 people at fifteen mining operations in six countries on five continents; its shares were traded on the Toronto, New York, Swiss, and Australian stock exchanges. In Porgera, the PJV employed 1,972 people, of whom 1,724 were citizens of Papua New Guinea and 248 were expatriates. Roughly half (1,046) of the "national" workers were drawn from points of hire within Porgera itself, while 182 came from elsewhere in Enga Province and 496 from other areas of Papua New Guinea (Placer Dome Asia Pacific 2001, 12). The result was a multiethnic, if stratified, workforce. Senior management

positions (including that of mine manager) and highly specialized technical positions were held by white expatriates (typically from Europe, Australia, or other Commonwealth countries), while most midlevel positions
that require education and expertise were filled by Papua New Guineans
from outside of Enga—typically people with experience working in other
mines in the country. The bulk of the staff members who operated equip-
ment and provided custodial services are hired in Porgera, although—as we
shall see—whether or not this means that they are "Porgeran" is a constant
topic of debate (Placer Dome Asia Pacific 2001, 12).

The person most centrally responsible for the mine was the mine manager.
Like the captain of an eighteenth-century ship, the mine manager was given
considerable latitude by his distant superiors in managing his operations,
and in many ways he was single-handedly responsible for the safety of thousands of employees and an operating budget that runs into the hundreds of
millions of US dollars. The position of mine manager is often a stepping-
stone for senior management jobs at the national, regional, or even international level. This seems to be particularly the case for Porgera. Before its acquisition by Barrick, four of the nineteen members of Placer Dome's senior
management in Vancouver had been involved in Porgera, and two had been
mine managers. As one member of senior management told me, there was
a strong informal sense in the company that "if you could survive Porgera,
you were ready for anything." In fact, the person who was mine manager
during the majority of my time in the valley eventually became the executive
vice president of operations for Placer Dome—essentially the second most
powerful person in the company's global organization.

The mine and its manager were just one node in a network of sites that together made up Placer's global organization. As the senior official living on
site in Porgera, the mine manager reported to Placer Niugini, the branch of
Placer Dome incorporated in Papua New Guinea whose offices were located
in Port Moresby. The Port Moresby office was headed by the managing director, who is responsible for Placer's activities in the country at the national
level. Two other senior executives in that office—chosen for their experience and connections—specialized in relationships with industry and government representatives. People in this office reported back to both Placer
Dome Asia Pacific (whose headquarters was in Sydney) and the company's
international headquarters in Vancouver.

At the mine site itself, a small group of senior managers were in charge of
overseeing different aspects of the mine's operations. Most of these people
did not directly deal with the Ipili in any capacity other than as coworkers.

The two branches of the mine that dealt with the Ipili community in Porgera were loss control, which includes site security, and community affairs, whose staff members served as the interface between the mine and the Ipili. The director of community affairs oversaw a group of roughly five people who are in charge of different units. One man, for instance, was responsible for relations with groups downstream of the mine, which he visited by helicopter. Another was in charge of the office where Ipili complaints about land and compensation were handled. Although the director of community affairs had an office in the mine's main administration building, which requires security clearance to enter, most other community affairs officers had publicly accessible offices and thus became the people who most frequently represented "the mine" to Porgerans.

A central theme of this book is the logistical difficulty of keeping a mine like Porgera up and running. The mine is a complex sociotechnical system made up of a variety of human and nonhuman actors—employees, autoclaves, and of course the mountain itself—and maintaining its operations requires an extraordinary amount of coordination. Most central to the mine's operations were two "lifelines" critical for its continued operation: first, a seventy-eight-kilometer power line that supplied electricity from a natural gas plant in a neighboring province; and second, the road on which semitrailers take two days to wind their way up from the coastal city of Lae, carrying containers full of supplies (Lavu 2007). The mine's operations could have been easily disrupted if the road or power line were damaged, either by natural incidents like landslides or by disgruntled Papua New Guineans cutting down the guy wires that supported the power line. The mine was powerful, influential, and important—but it was also vulnerable.

Thus the mine has a dual existence: as an engineering project digging away at the side of a mountain, it deals with the most brute of brute facts, and is hostage to the material conditions required to operate it. At the same time, however, "the mine" is a remarkable semiotic accomplishment. Defining who "the mine" is can be ambiguous and tricky. If a security guard shoots an Ipili trespasser in the back, has "the mine" or "an employee" shot someone? Do community affairs officers speak for "the mine"? Does the mine manager? The country manager in Port Moresby? Even "the facts" about the mine can be contentious: does the price of gold merit large royalty payments or small ones from the company to the government? Does the answer differ if the question comes from a shareholder in Canada instead of a minister in Port Moresby? Are the tailings that are released into the river toxic? How much does it cost to produce an ounce of gold? Logistics require semiotic

7

work to clarify and coordinate the complex technical work of the mine—and to use ambiguity and uncertainty to the mine's advantage.

The Ipili

Just as the stereotypes of mud-smeared miners emerging from rough-hewn pits fail to capture the sophistication of the Porgera mine's engineering, preconceptions of the Ipili as ecologically noble savages (Buege 1996) who are trampled on and degraded by global capitalism do not capture the complexity of Porgera's politics. Gold was discovered in Porgera in the late 1930s, and both outsiders and Porgerans had been working the alluvial deposits for decades before a large-scale mine seemed feasible at Porgera. It was at this point, in the 1980s, that the copper mine in Bougainville closed in the face of massive community unrest. The loss of revenue from Bougainville left a massive hole in the government's budget, and Porgera was quickly seized on as a solution. At the same time, the failure of the Papua New Guinea Defense Force to keep Bougainville open demonstrated that the government lacked the capacity to operate a mine in the face of local opposition. The result was a moment of opportunity that the Ipili seized, becoming one of the most active and successful groups in pressing claims against the state and transnational capitalism. Indeed, so thoroughgoing were Ipili attempts to extract benefits from the mine that Timothy Andambo, a Porgeran mining engineer, has described the tangle of trust funds, equity companies, and committees that manage the Ipili's numerous investments as "social technology to extract rent from the Porgera lode" (2002). The benefits package the Ipili negotiated with the government and the company has now been exceeded by other landowning groups in Papua New Guinea such as those at Lihir (Bainton 2010), but Porgera set the standard. In the beginning, then, Porgerans welcomed a mine—provided that it agreed to their terms.

Who should receive benefits from the mine? What sort of assent is needed for the mine to claim that it has a social license to operate in Porgera? Answering these questions means deciding who counts as "the Ipili" or, to be more exact, that subset of them known as "landowners."

Linguistically and culturally, the Ipili are part of a wide ethnic galaxy that includes the Huli (to the south) and the Enga (to the east), both of which are larger in population than the Ipili by an order of magnitude or more (for regional overviews, see Biersack 1995a, Wiessner, Tumu, and Pupu 1998; for Porgera itself, see Jacka 2003). In practice, boundaries between ethnic groups are not clearly defined in the area, and the Ipili are a "hinge" or "intermediate" group wedged between the two much larger groups. Like their neighbors, the Ipili prefer to live in dispersed homesteads and practice mounded sweet potato agriculture. Ipili culture—like that of many other groups in Papua New Guinea—is preoccupied with fertility and wealth: one of the best-known symbols of Ipili identity is the bullhorn-shaped wigs that young men make out of their own hair (for more on fertility, ritual, and beautification among the Ipili, see Biersack 1998). Very roughly, we can say that their kinship system is cognatic, similar to that of the Huli described by Robert Glasse (1969) and the Garia described by Peter Lawrence (1984). In contrast to the more corporate-minded Enga or the Hagen people of Western Highlands Province, the Ipili believe that anyone with a single Ipili grandparent has a good claim to affiliate with the cognatic stock with which that grandparent is affiliated, as long as the descendant demonstrates some sort of solidarity with other members of the stock through work and consociation. As in other areas in Papua New Guinea, affines and nonconsanguines are often incorporated into local groups that are theoretically based on descent (Langness 1964).

Beyond these generalizations, it is not easy to separate "Ipili culture" from "the mine." Decades of mining in Porgera have made kinship and landownership contested topics, even in areas not directly affected by mining. Ipili speakers live in two adjacent valleys, the Porgera and the Paiela. Although the Porgera Valley has been transformed by the mine, the Paiela Valley to its west has felt the impact only indirectly, and lack of access to direct benefits from the mine is often a source of resentment. Many people in Paiela pin their hopes on the potentially large Mt. Kare gold deposit in the south of their valley, but until this project pans out, Paielans will remain the country cousins of Porgerans. To the east of Porgera, near the road that runs out of the valley, is the hamlet of Tipinini. The inhabitants are known as the East Ipili, and have been studied by Jerry Jacka (2003). This group is in many ways transitional between the Ipili speakers of Porgera proper and the Western Engans from the area around Laiagam. The East Ipili's dialect is slightly different from that of people in Porgera, and intermarriage between East Ipilis and Engans is common. Downstream of the mine, the people of the Lower Porgera remember when their area was a hotbed of alluvial mining, dream of returning to their former prominence in valley affairs, and attempt to cope with the bright red water discharged from the mine that now flows through their territory (Biersack 2006). Paiela, Tipinini, and the Lower Porgera receive a number of spin-off benefits from the Porgera mine, but see these benefits less as perks and more as bitter reminders of the mine-

arbitrary
fluke of
geography

no consent
needed

derived affluence that an arbitrary fluke of geography has bestowed on their relatives nearby.

The question of benefits—which "mine" the mine belongs to—is central. Legally, the subsoil gold is the property of the national government, while the land above it is under the customary title of seven landowning clans. Under Papua New Guinea's Land Act, Ipili land is inalienable, may not be sold, and must be safeguarded for future generations. However, the government may issue a lease to outsiders if it decides that such a lease is in the best interest of its citizens—whether they consent or not. Thus the clearest definition of "Ipili landowners" is the people whose land is the subject of the special mining lease (SML) on which the mine operates: land the Ipili own but cannot sell or legally prevent the government from leasing to others.

Relations between the SML landowners, the national and provincial governments, and the mine are regulated by a series of legal agreements. The first is a compensation agreement—required by law—between the mine and landowners. This describes the price the mine must pay for land and plants damaged by its activities. An additional set of agreements called the Porgera Agreements were signed by the Ipili landowners and representatives of the Enga provincial government and the national government. These agreements obliged the national government to include certain clauses in the Mineral Development Contract that regulates the relationship between the government and the mine. Thus the Porgera Agreements effectively represent concessions made by the mine and the national government to the Enga provincial government and the Ipili, even though the mine is not party to the Porgera Agreements. These agreements were without precedent and arose largely from the initiative of the Porgera landowners and the Enga provincial government. The strength of the Ipili position, along with the government's desire to do the right thing, created a situation in which for the first time the state signed an agreement with landowners who permitted the state to issue a special mining lease to a developer. The Porgera Agreements were thus both unprecedented (a new mining act was passed to ensure that they were technically legal) and extremely lucrative, and they are the source of many of the most important benefits that the SML landowners receive.

Measuring exactly how much compensation the Ipili have received from the mine is difficult because of the variety of benefit streams that affect the Ipili—everything from direct monetary compensation for damaged land to indirect economic activity generated from the mine's presence and the market value of the Ipili equity in the mine might be included under the rubric of "benefit." According to mine statistics, the Ipili have received K66,000,000—the currency of Papua New Guinea is the *kina*—in compensation for land lost from the mine's opening up to the time of my fieldwork—roughly, the mine's first decade (Placer Dome Asia Pacific 2001, 12). This is a difficult figure to appreciate due to the *kina*'s fluctuation in value: in the late 1980s a *kina* was worth US$1, but in 2001 it was worth less than US$0.25. In 2000 the mine estimates it spent roughly K20,000,000 on donations to groups within the valley for education and community infrastructure and K113,700,000 in wages and salaries—although what percentage of those wages went to ethnic Ipili is difficult to say. In addition, the Ipili own 2.5 percent of the PJV (Banks 2003, 226–29). They receive quarterly royalties from gold sales, and the government has given them a multitude of new services, including a hospital and roads. Indeed, the Ipili are not only the lessors of the special mining lease on which Placer operates the Porgera gold mine, but they also own the high-rise building in Port Moresby where Placer Niugini has its corporate headquarters (for data on economic benefits up to 2012 see Johnson 2012).

The Ipili also signed a relocation agreement with Placer. In the 1980s the future site of the Porgera gold mine was inhabited by landowners—indeed, when it became clear where the mine would be located, people quickly moved there and built houses and gardens in anticipation of future compensation. As a result, Placer undertook a relocation program that was without precedent in modern mining history—roughly 3,400 people were moved off the future mine site and into 420 new houses (Bonnell 1999; Banks 1999). For many people, new relocation houses made of tin and timber replaced homes based on traditional materials from the bush, and a relocation house was often the greatest benefit that a Porgera landowner would receive from the mine. These new nucleated "relocation communities" were built inside the special mining lease area, and each one was meant to be home to one of the seven landowning clans. Thus "villages" based on "clan ties" were created. Some of the mining operation is shielded by fencing, but much of it is not. In order to enter the open pit in 2000, for instance, Ipili landowners needed only to walk up the ridge on whose side their houses are built, cross to the other side, and then descend into the pit.

But even these people are not the epitome of the term "landowners." The benefits of mining have not been distributed equally, and an elite of "big men" has emerged in Porgera. It is composed of the people appointed to positions of power on the various boards of directors and those who receive lucrative contracts from the mine to provide security, janitorial, and other services. When people speak of "landowners," it is really these people who they have in mind—large, well-fed men with reputations for prodigality who drive Toyota Land Cruisers with windows tinted to make them opaque.

Despotic Assemblages and Other Assemblages

Both "the mine" and "the Ipili," then, share a common feature: at a distance they appear to be unproblematically existing actors, but the closer you come to them, the more their coherence and integrity begins to falter. For this reason, this book will repurpose the old trope of the Pacific Islands as laboratories (for a critique of this trope, see Terrell, Hunt, and Gosden 1997). Margaret Mead, for example, argued that New Guinea's "densest jungles" created "untouched societies" in which "the student of human nature was guaranteed one kind of laboratory" (1954, 6–8). Similarly, James Barnes wrote that the highlands of Papua New Guinea "could be seen to provide, as it were, laboratory conditions for the investigation" of "the general characteristics of human culture and social institutions" (1969, 3).

Rather than argue that the geography of Papua New Guinea creates ideal conditions for causal inference, I will claim that Porgera resembles the laboratory as revealed to us by science studies: the closer one approaches, the more one sees conditions of novelty and innovation, the proliferation of controversies, and—as Michel Callon (1980) would put it—struggles and negotiations to define what is problematic and what is not (for a similar argument see Mullaney 2011, 62). Or, to speak the language of ethnohistory, Porgera is a middle ground (White 1991), contact zone (Pratt 1992), or frontier, "a kind of 'interstitial space' in which some human enterprise, such as warfare, trade, or religious conversion, has extended beyond the effective control of established institutions" (Parker and Rodseth 2005, 23). Because "the Ipili" and "the mine" are still being fashioned in Porgera, the valley presents us with an opportunity to demonstrate the broader utility of a "sociology of associations" (Latour 2005, 13) by bringing the frontier to the laboratory.

Science studies is also a good place to begin tracing the work the figure of the Leviathan has done in our anthropological imaginations. Calling both "the Ipili" and "the mine" leviathans allows us to, as Callon and Latour put it, "unscrew" them (1981). Such unscrewing reveals a macro actor's ability to "translate" "all the negotiations, intrigues, calculations, acts of persuasion and violence, thanks to which an actor or force takes, or causes to be conferred on itself authority to speak or act on behalf of another actor or force"

(Callon and Latour 1981, 279). For Callon and Latour, a leviathan becomes a potent actor by "making many elements act as one" (Callon and Latour 1981, 213; Latour 1987, 131) within a "black box": "The more elements one can place in black boxes—modes of thoughts, habits, forces and objects—the broader the construction one can raise" (Callon and Latour 1981:285). As Larry Stucki (2009) points out, this sort of black boxing is central to the projects of large-scale companies in frontier situations—creating ultra-durable institutions requires routinization of this sort.

This notion is appealing because it captures the way in which leviathans "seem both real and illusory" (T. Mitchell 2006, 169) but does so without posing these two terms as incompatible. By now social analysts know that we must steer between two tendencies. First, we ought to avoid seeing "these composite institutions" as merely "giv[ing] off the impression of unified thinking, talking, acting subjects" (Welker, Partridge, and Hardin 2011, 4) and thus viewing them as epiphenomena of the real stuff of social life: individual agency and actors. Second, we ought to avoid taking leviathans so seriously that we reify them and treat them as actors whose existence is unproblematic. Callon and Latour's approach is useful because it understands leviathans as both potent and constructed—or, even better, potent because constructed.

Using the term "leviathan" to describe these sorts of macro actors is particularly appropriate because the term and its genealogy encompasses two ideal types of leviathans that correspond roughly to the two sorts of leviathans that the mine and the Ipili are.

The first is leviathan-as-bureaucracy. Callon and Latour's use of the concept of Leviathan is drawn, of course, from Hobbes. Hobbes believed that all humans had the ability to "personate," or "act, or represent himselfe, or an other" (1996, 112), and in *Leviathan* Hobbes sought to ground the legitimacy of the early modern state through such personation, arguing that people must "appoint one Man, or Assembly of men, to beare their Person; and to every one to owne, and acknowlege himselfe to be Author of whatsoever he that so beareth their Person shall Act . . . This is the Generation of that great LEVIATHAN, or rather (to speake more reverently) of that Mortall God, to which wee owe under the Immortal God, our peace and defence" (Hobbes 1996, 120).

It was the organizational superiority of the leviathan-sovereign that was important for Hobbes: at the center of his theory of social contract lies the ability of people to act in concert across space and time with greater efficacy than the disorganized factions found in the state of nature. Indeed, it is just

potent because constructed [why?]

[are things not constructed therefore impotent?]

Hobbes' humans must "personate" the modern state

time across space to punishe

contract social monopoly of force

this overwhelming retaliatory potential that inspires Hobbes's biblical imagery: free riders could be discouraged only through the use of an intense, Old Testament punitive force. This force's ties to the newly modernized bureaucratic states springing up around Europe were made clear to Hobbes by, among other things, the New Model Army that defeated his king, Charles I, and forced him to flee from England to France.

Leviathan here is the power of bureaucracy incarnate: professional, dedicated, and disciplined people acting in accordance with predetermined rules and regulations. Belief in the structuring force of rules makes such bureaucratically-organized macro actors feasible. And so it has been ever since, as dozens—perhaps hundreds—of books have borrowed Hobbes's terminology to describe any large, overwhelmingly powerful government. In all of them, it is the prescriptive and regimenting power of rules, bureaucracy, and order that give Leviathan power. Regimented, efficacious, expansive in its power, "leviathan" is an appropriate term for the Porgera gold mine and other manifestations of the corporate form.

Ironically, the second leviathan I wish to discuss here guaranteed social order in a radically different way from Hobbes. In Hobbes's Protestant imagination, the king was Leviathan, and a rational calculus of benefits and drawbacks of obedience would ground the early modern state. In the ancient Near East, where Leviathan was originally spawned, the sovereigns of the first complex states ruled not because they were Leviathan, but because they were "cosmocrats" (Sahlins 2010, 114)—monarchs whose reign exemplified the sociocosmic regime instantiated by their deity's defeat of Leviathan or a chaos monster like him (on the exegetical tradition between the redactors of the Hebrew Bible and Hobbes, see Malcolm 2007; on chaos beasts, see Day 1985, Gunkel 2006, Levenson 1988). Sovereign rule was legitimized by a wider cosmology in which "Yahweh the divine warrior-king parallels the human king ruling in Jerusalem" (M. Smith 2001, 157)—the historical metaphor, as it were, of a cosmological reality (Sahlins 1981). Thus while Hobbes's Leviathan was meant to ground the state at a time when divine order was going out of fashion, the original Leviathan was part of a political theology in which precisely such an order underwrote the legitimacy of ancient polities. Norman Yoffee points out that this sense of order was central to the formation of early states. Paradoxically, "what occurs in these 'complex societies' is a tendency toward standardization, legibility, and simplification" (2001, 768). Ironically enough, sociocosmic simplification enabled organizational complexity.

[significance of ancient states here?]

In this way Leviathan has become emblematic not just of bureaucracy but also of cosmology, a sense of what Yoffee and Jeffrey Baines call "order" (1998), or "a belief that truly significant actions recapitulate the primordial cosmogenesis or participate in a pattern established outside of the flux of ordinary events," which is part of the "very general human effort to relate the changing requirements of action to a permanent and unchanging order of things" (Lovin and Reynolds 1985, 1; see also von Benda-Beckmann and Pirie 2007).

Although they are far from the ancient Middle East, the Ipili have inherited the mantle of cosmology just as much as the mine has inherited the legacy of bureaucracy. In a story too well known to be rehearsed here, the West has always been haunted by the idea that someone somewhere longs to live life perfectly in accordance with a cosmological scheme. Even as Europe told itself that it had abandoned cosmology when it took up the new, more ink-stained leviathan of the modern state, it came to view its colonial others as authentically primordial executors of unchanged tradition. Victorian projects of comparative religion and jurisprudence (Maine 1963; W. Smith 1957; Stasch 2010, 49) fed into anthropology, where they would come to inform the social anthropological tradition. Kinship systems were conceived of as invisible but efficacious forces which regulated the conduct of individuals. This view continues to inform a variety of discourses today, ranging from First World legislation of indigenous rights to Fourth World postcolonial self-fashionings.

The Leviathan therefore lurks in the distant past of anthropology's culture concept. But even though anthropological theory has moved beyond the notion that cultural structure determines human action to a dynamic understanding of the relationship of cosmology to practice (Sahlins 1985), anthropologists continue to encounter less supple accounts of cosmology in the course of their fieldwork. As I will show in this book, a crucial part of personating the Ipili rests on the assumption—by politicians and others—that what they refer to as "customary law," "kinship," and "clan systems" are sufficiently unambiguous in formulation and efficacious enough in their regimentation of Ipili life that they can be codified into bureaucratic form when governments and corporations interface with the Ipili as the "customary landowners" of the Porgera Gold Mine. The rules that the Ipili "follow" about how kin should act toward one another could, for instance, be formalized in law and used as a basis for compensation payments. Cosmological beliefs about the relationship of land to corporate groups (including Ipili rights to land that exclude the claims of other ethnic groups) could be used in negotiations to demand recognition that "the true landowners" of the Porgera gold mine are "the Ipili." Conforming to cosmology—used here in the word's broadest sense—is what the Ipili are supposed to do. A major part of this book will involve showing how anthropological ideas articulate with these beliefs.

This is necessary because leviathans always leak, regardless of whether they are cosmological or bureaucratic. Both Bronze Age monarchs and the Porgera mine struggled to deal with frontiers and seal black boxes shut. Yoffee (2004) has demonstrated how official ideologies of royal power coexisted with the political power of local communities and elders, and, Daniel Fleming (2004) has shown that Bronze Age rulers such as Zimri-Lim at Mari often had to cope with nonsedentary groups that resisted clear labeling or interpellation in a hierarchical system of authority—a process similar to the frontier dynamics in Porgera. Zainab Bahrani (2008) points out that regimes in the ancient Near East used spectacular violence to enforce their reign on a level that Hobbes's sovereign would approve of. Contemporary bureaucracies, whether companies or governments, are of course fallible and dilatory. Indeed, much of the earlier anthropological work on bureaucracy worked at "laying bare the informal structures of bureaucracy" (Hull 2012a, 252) to reveal the reality and imperfection of bureaucratic operations.

Just as royal ideologies of order and harmony rode alongside political contestation and violence, so did Hobbes's work employ "strategies" (Bredekamp 2003) of persuasion that were as much aesthetic (A. Smith 2006) as they were rational. The famous frontispiece of *Leviathan* was meant to instill fear and awe in those who saw it, using affect to make Hobbes's argument seem more plausible to readers. At the same time, the majority of the book, often unread by anthropologists, focuses on creating a Christian commonwealth: a government in which rational actors riveted into place by incentives were also value-rational Christian subjects. Studying the ways in which leviathans become powerful thus involves analyzing the deep cultural structures which enable their pretensions to power. For that reason I hope this book will be a contribution to the emerging anthropological study of the "real-politics of the marvelous" (Sahlins 2010, 118).

Finally, it is important to recognize that it is not simply globalization and resource frontiers that lead to questions regarding the nagging intangibility yet doubtless efficacy of leviathans. Understanding the issues raised by de Beauvoir's mandarins—the coordination of action across time and space, and the attribution of that action to leviathans, as well as the way individual agency is amplified when one speaks for a leviathan—involves revisiting questions that have been asked and answered for a very long time. Indeed, I've chosen to use a Bronze Age concept as my central theoretical trope precisely to signal my awareness that the topics I cover in this book are as old as human politics. I cannot hope to point out my indebtedness to the tremendous number of authors who have touched on these issues. But in choosing a trope that stretches from the Psalms to science studies, I try to indicate my awareness of their depth.

Making the Ipili Feasible

How, then, can we analyze the fashioning of leviathans? Leviathans and the sociologists who help them often use what might be called "vertical" models of culture, in which people "on the ground" "reach up" to cosmological-cum-bureaucratic orders and "draw down" categories to use in practice. This spatial imagery is particularly appropriate in cosmological schemes oriented to the heavens, as well as to hierarchical diagrams such as organization charts and kinship diagrams in which the apical source of legitimacy is at the top of the page.

Here, I will focus more on what might be called the "horizontal" models of culture. Although I have discussed this approach in terms of science studies, it also encompasses the approaches used by authors such as Sahlins, Butler, and Deleuze. All three of these authors focus on the historical and contingent nature of existing structures, insisting on their reality and power while remaining intent on scrutinizing their genealogy and understanding the contingent and achieved nature of their application to any given event. Categories are, on these accounts, "behind" us rather than "above" us, a product of historical accumulation which ends up committing actors "to one particular alternative or set of alternatives out of many, and these commitments . . . inform subsequent evaluations of practice, and . . . practical judgment . . . but do not determine practice" (Lambek 2010: 39). In this way we can see leviathans as the emerging effects of the conjunctures they are assembled out of, and watch them (perhaps) eventually decompose (De Landa 2006; Sawyer 2005). Such an approach allows me to pursue a "natural history" of discourse about them (Silverstein and Urban 1995).

Interest in process is an old, perhaps constitutive, feature of anthropology in certain of its moods, and I do not want to dress up political anthropology's traditional focus on conflict, faction, and contention in newfangled theoretical apparel merely in the name of fashion. The question must always be: how, specifically, will a theoretical approach result in changed ethnographic practice? Using horizontal models of culture enables us to see patterns of life at work in the valley that more vertical models—the ones used by leviathans and their allies in the social sciences—gloss over when they attempt to disambiguate Porgera's resource frontier.

[concept of feasibility ?]

In this book, I approach this issue through the concept of "feasibility," a term that features a felicitous overlap between the jargon of the mining industry and theories of communicative practice. In the mining industry, a mine is "feasible" if a prospective body of ore will cost less to remove from the ground than its product will fetch on the market. Feasibility is the result of a complex network of variables including the cost of supplying a mine and refining the ore as well as the price of gold on the market. If all of these variables add up correctly, they are sufficient to trigger the massive organization of human labor that transforms an exploration camp into a fully functioning mine—a set of actions that range from obtaining capital from international financial markets to blasting away the overburden surrounding an ore body. Once a mine is operational, these calculations remain in play. If the cost of diesel fuel increases by one cent per gallon, thousands of tons of rock can be transformed from ore to waste rock, all without altering the material's physical properties one bit.

As Marshall Sahlins reminds us, while all actors deploy indexable macrocosmic order (for instance, what an older literature called "role expectations"), applying them in practice is a "great gamble" since we live in a world where "every implementation of cultural concepts . . . submits the concepts to some determination by the situation" (1985, 149). As Stasch (2011, 160) notes "action is the linking of specific times, spaces, and situations to more spatiotemporally expansive categorical types and norms, even when these categories are tacit, partial, plural, or unsettled." This means that all action is "tropic figuration" and "characterized by the tensions of the presence in concrete practice of spatiotemporal layers that are 'other' to that concreteness" (ibid., 160).

However, just because one wants to personify a leviathan does not mean that one will be able to do so in any particular circumstance. In linguistic anthropology, "feasibility" refers to the ways in which cultural categories are deployed in practice. "A judgment of practical feasibility," William Hanks writes, "is anything but timeless. Not only does it connect with changing circumstances, but it involves timing, knowing when to act, how long to maintain engagement, the rhythm with which to proceed, and how to deal with successive outcomes" (1996, 231). In this way semiotic casuistry ("I am a token of this type") is tied to political economy, and politics becomes "the struggle to entextualize authoritatively" (Silverstein and Urban 1995, 11). The history of mining is the history of exerting control over a mountain to make it "feasible," and the history of the Porgera Valley is a story of various people attempting to become feasible political actors. Politics in Porgera often consists of arguing about whether a specific person's actions are those of a leviathan that they represent or are merely a "frolic of his own" (Gaddis 1994). The ability to personate leviathans (as Hobbes would put it) or perform *[ugh)]* leviathanness (if you prefer a Butlerian formulation) is determined by the extent to which an individual's actions can be made to correspond to an invisible and legitimating order. Throughout this book I will examine a number of leviathans, including Australia's colonial government of Papua New Guinea, the Porgera Joint Venture (PJV), and the Enga provincial government. But pride of place and analytic focus will be on "the Ipili."

In the case of the mine or the government, personating leviathans requires a relatively straightforward appeal to a bureaucratic organization with standard operating procedures, a hierarchical structure, and defined roles and responsibilities. "The Ipili," on the other hand, needed to be identified as a collective whose will can be personified. Just as the gold in a mountain requires refining if it is to take a form suitable for circulation in national and international financial markets, so too the identities of Ipili people had to be refined and transformed in order to circulate in the national and international arenas of law, policy, and ideas that accompany and buttress transnational capitalism. Thus "the Ipili" needed to exist and have certain features if the legal and ethical requirements of the government and mine were to be met. As Basil Sansom put it, "Leviathan addresses not Aborigines but Aborigines Inc." (1985, 70). In this book I examine four dimensions of feasibility: the authorization of spokespeople, the disambiguation of kinship and ethnicity, pacification, and political agency.

One of the first things that needed to be fashioned were spokesmen. This need for delegation of authority in landowner communities produced "the twenty-three"—the twenty-three members of the Landowner Negotiating Committee who, authorized by their clansmen, capture the consensus of their community and represent this collective will in an official capacity, at least in theory. But there is more to it than this. Many of the controversies discussed in this book touch on what is real and what is not. As a result, feasibility is not solely a matter of successfully assuming a preexisting role as the representative of a leviathan. In the ambiguity of Porgera's resource frontier, many attempts to become feasible involve arguing, that new leviathans exist—for instance, when an Ipili man appearing at a government office is the "true landowner" of a contested piece of territory because he is the elder of the previously unknown leviathan-clan X, or when an Australian marched into a valley in 1948 and declared that he was "the government" come to put a stop to tribal fighting. Throughout this book I examine both sides of the struggle for feasibility: how people attempt to personate preexisting leviathans and how people empower themselves by creating new leviathans that they claim to represent. Entailment, then, is as much a political strategy as presupposition.

Another feature of feasibility was the creation not only of "the Ipili" as a group, but also of an entire system of ethnic difference. Since landownership in Papua New Guinea is tied to traditional tenure, "the Ipili" not only have to exist, but they have to own land in such a way that only a certain subset of them—the "landowning clans"—could lay claim to own the future home of the Special Mining Lease territory. This required a form of indigenous sociality composed of clearly delineated "traditional" units with clear ties to demarcated areas of land and rules for affiliation that resulted in unambiguous group membership. Only in this way could clans be associated with parcels of land and a list of individual "clan members" be created. These same principles could also be used to exclude individuals and groups from the category of "landowner." The creation of the mine thus requires the (sometimes literal) concretization of the unstable semiotic and geophysical resources of the valley.

In addition to this more abstract work, feasibility has a mundane dimension: the Ipili had to be made feasible in the sense of physically docile if the mine was going to function. Facilities such as workers' camps not only needed to be legally zoned and built, but they also needed to be defended: at a very basic level, the mine is in danger of being physically overrun and destroyed by the Ipili. Porgerans are not, in general, sufficiently organized to coordinate a highly organized military campaign carefully designed to bring the mine to its knees. What the mine really fears is some sort of spontaneous outburst that could disrupt it: the fragile complexity of its operations means that even a relatively small amount of disturbance could be crippling. Rolling a few logs across the road supplying the mine or cutting down the guy wires that support the pylons bringing electricity into the valley could be accomplished by anyone with an axe.

These are not idle fears. In 1988, while negotiations about establishing the mine were going on, a handful of people broke into the exploration camp and stole the safe containing the camp's entire cash supply as well as the passports of every expatriate employee of the mine (see chapter 2). In 1993 Porgerans rioted after police officers believed to be in the mine's pocket killed a young boy. Local people stormed the mine's barracks, overturned cars, and caused millions of dollars' worth of damage (Banks 1997, 260–65). Despite the presence of a well-maintained airstrip and an enormous market of cash-rich customers, no commercial airline has operated in Porgera since a pilot embroiled in a disagreement with customers was pulled out of his plane and chopped to death. In sum, although outbursts are few, they have occurred, and Ipili leaders have often suggested to mine officials that more could be arranged in the future if necessary.

A final, a more fascinating form of feasibility has arisen from the conjunction of these representational and pacificatory requirements. The semiotic requirements of bureaucratic actors have mixed with the valley's unpredictable nature to make "the Ipili" feasible political actors at the national level. As we have seen, the closing of the Bougainville copper mine during the period immediately preceding the creation of the Porgera gold mine left the national government desperate for money, while simultaneously demonstrating its inability to use its military to coerce local landowners into accepting a mine. The Ipili were in the right place at the right time, and they were not afraid to seize the opportunity. Today they continue to use their position to effect change at a national level. Ironically, attempts to make the Ipili compliant have ended up making them more politically efficacious, although by ensnaring them in structures that they can only partially manipulate. As we shall see in the afterword to this book, the price that was paid in this regard may have been too high.

The Plan of the Book

This book takes the form of a long zoom out. Chapter 1, in many ways the central focus of the book, is an extended case study (Buroway 1998; J. Mitchell 1956) of an eighteen-month-long negotiation between the mine and landowners that I call the "Yakatabari negotiations." These negotiations were ultimately unsuccessful, and in examining their conception, birth, and death I will present most of the major themes of this book: the way that leviathans are both presupposed and entailed by people in the course of their daily life, the blurred line between "the mine" and "the Ipili," and the nature of politics in the valley. As an analysis of the micropolitics of negotiation, it focuses on spokesmanship: the way leviathans must be represented by actual people if they are to be feasible—and vice versa.

Being plunged into the midst of the Yakatabari negotiations can give the reader a sense of culture shock—the welter of associations, acronyms, laws, agreements, and memoranda of understanding that are at play in valley politics can be disorienting. Certain aspects of the negotiations, particularly the way the biographies of the main players are intertwined, are also difficult to appreciate without a sense of the history of the valley. Chapter 2 provides the backstory for the Yakatabari negotiations by tracing the history of the valley from its discovery by whites in 1938 to the creation of the mine in the late 1980s. This historical approach provides a genealogy of the leviathans that eventually became "the mine" and "the Ipili." My focus here is on the decisions which established precedents which would shape the Yakatabari negotiations, and the network of actors who were central to valley life.

Throughout the Yakatabari negotiations, "clan politics," "traditional culture," and "Ipili kinship" were constant topics of debate. But what, exactly, are Ipili beliefs and practices about land rights, genealogy, and social organization? I attempt to answer this question in chapter 3. Shifting from history back to ethnography, I explore Ipili identity and sociality to understand how Porgerans lived "on the ground" in the ethnographic present of 2000. I claim that there are serious differences between the visible and clearly bounded Ipili clans described on paper and the actual ambiguities and imprecisions of everyday relation-making in Porgera. Rather than focus on the disjuncture between "false" paper representations and "real" life "on the ground," I explore how Ipili sociality and paper representations of it mutually inform one another. Just as Ipili sociality informs micro-level negotiations, so too do the bureaucratic instruments that are forged in these negotiations inform and shape Ipili sociality, becoming in effect contexts that individual Ipili must master if they are to become feasible actors in the "lowlevel" arenas of valley politics. A key point here is that, despite pretensions to a technically pure knowledge and highly efficient organization, bureaucratic practices on the ground are in many ways as ambiguous as Ipili kinship itself.

Chapter 4 pulls the camera back again, to examine national discourses about so-called grassroots Papua New Guineans: the subsistence farmers living in rural areas who are prototypical Papua New Guineans. Central to the feasibility of the Ipili, I argue, is a broad and deep national sentiment that grassroots Papua New Guineans have a fundamentally legitimate claim to ethical consideration. This sentiment is deeply tied to Papua New Guinea's national identity, which valorizes the rural and traditional over the modern and urban. The result is a double-bind: Papua New Guineans legitimate the grassroots in general, but disenfranchise specific Ipili when they fail to perform grassrootedness in a way that middle-class urban policy elites expect. I argue that this problem is not unique to Porgera but occurs at resource developments across the country. But it is not only the grassroots who find themselves in this double-bind. This valorization of the rural also forecloses possible futures for middle-class Papua New Guineans, who seek an authentically Papua New Guinean modernity even as they imagine authenticity as quintessentially traditional. I conclude by returning to the themes that began the book and offer a few thoughts about what their implications are for Papua New Guineans, and what relevance this volume may have for anthropology at large. Finally, in a brief afterword, I discuss the changes that have occurred in Porgera since my initial research there.

But first, I will begin at the beginning: the Yakatabari negotiations.

1 The Yakatabari Negotiations

"We may not have a mine, but Alex will have one hell of a dissertation."
—Community affairs officer, after a tough round of negotiations

The *Porgera Mine Sustainability Report: 2000* (Placer Dome Asia Pacific 2001) is a colorful twenty-page booklet full of statistics detailing the mine's metallurgical and financial doings for the year and pictures of smiling children benefiting from the mine's commitment to sustainable development. As Placer's most stylistically accessible and complete statement of what had happened in Porgera in 2000 its synoptic charts and nontechnical prose address everything from the mine-funded creation of a local branch of the Girl Guides (Placer Dome Asia Pacific 2001, 6) to the amount of steel-grinding media used as a reagent in operations (Placer Dome Asia Pacific 2001:16). On page five of the report is a box entitled "Yakatabari Waste Dump Negotiations—Failure or Foundation for the Future" (fig. 1.1).

In roughly four hundred words, eighteen months of intense, immensely important negotiations regarding the future of the valley was condensed into a single, authoritative, and anonymously voiced narrative. Distributed widely outside the valley—in fact, distributed mostly outside the valley—the report circulated farther and faster than any other account of the negotiations, including those of the Ipili themselves. Indeed, as a PDF available on Placer Dome's website, the *Porgera Mine Sustainability Report: 2000* became available to a global audience. In this chapter I examine what happens when we open this black box.

One by-product of the report's brevity is the number of leviathans tucked into its prose: "the PJV" negotiates with "landowners" while "stakeholder groups" and the "community" hover anxiously in the background. This black-boxing of actors in Porgera's political process is typical of narratives that circulate outside the valley and simplify the complexity of life inside it. This is ironic, since my detailed account of Yakatabari will exemplify something else: the multitude of struggles to create and maintain feasible actors in a context that constantly threatens to unravel them.

[but it's not ironic]

In this chapter I present a richly detailed case study of the Yakatabari negotiations in order to provide an introduction to valley politics and some of the wider ethnographic themes of this book: how easily the mine creates itself as a leviathan, how contested collectivity making is among the Ipili, and how ontologically uncertain various facts about international finance and the geology of the valley are. The negotiations bring issues of representation and personation to the fore by examining how the plans of leviathans always devolve on the individuals who represent them. In particular, the feasibility of individual actors hinges on their ability to successfully personate leviathans, just as the feasibility of leviathans hinges on their ability to be successfully personated. As we shall see, the Yakatabari negotiations were as much about the personalities of the negotiators as they were about the wider issues that faced the leviathans in whose name they claimed to speak.

Personating Leviathans

Leviathans are like totemism: once we doubt that it is possible to isolate certain phenomena and group them together as an objective institution, the actors who make them up appear refractory. Thus Diamond Jenness writes:

> Just as the Indians have their chiefs or leading men, so there are chiefs or "bosses" (to use a word from the lumber camps that the Indians themselves employ) among animals, birds and fish, even among the trees . . . The bosses are always larger than the other plants and animals of their kind, and in the case of birds, fish and animals, always white. Now and then the Indians see and kill them, but generally they keep out of sight of human beings. They are like the government in Ottawa, one old Indian

Yakatabari Waste Dump Negotiations—
Failure or Foundation for the Future

Planning for economic, social and environmental benefits.

PJV proposed a new waste dump site in 1999 and hoped to conclude negotiations with an agreed package of benefits for landowners during 2000. Consensus with the landowners was not achieved, and the proposal was withdrawn by PJV. The failed negotiations have had some positive outcomes and identified some important lessons not only for PJV but also for the community.

It had been hoped that the new dump would contribute to sustainability in the following ways:

Dump Plan Component	Sustainability Outcome
Reduced capital/operating costs of dump trucks. Shorter/lower gradient waste rock hauls. Compensation for use of land. Compensation for loss of housing. Stable low altitude dump.	Decreased operating costs—longer mine life at low gold prices. Continued local and national revenue streams. Reduced fuel and maintenance costs. Reduced CO_2 emissions. Purchase of alternative gardening land as part of a benefits package. Provision of new houses. Suitable for reclamation as agricultural land.

Factors contributing to failure of the plan include:
- Limited information and awareness on the interplay between reduced operating costs, increased stakeholder benefits, and shareholder expectations.
- High demands of some stakeholder groups.
- Late involvement of some government institutions in negotiations.
- Difficulties in identifying alternative gardening and housing sites.
- Difficulties in coordinating the provision of government services in relocated communities.
- Limited awareness and understanding of the long-term sustainable benefits offered by the plan.
- Group dynamics resulting in polarisation of views within and between stakeholder groups.
- Precedence of immediate issues and benefits over long-term principles and sustainable benefits.

Fig 1.1 (*above and opposite*) Part of Placer Dome Asia Pacific's *Porgera Mine Sustainability Report: 2000*.

Despite the failure of the negotiations many stakeholders and the PJV were in favour of a strategy to prolong mine life involving a new dump and package of social benefits. The failed negotiations increased awareness and understanding of the key issues of transparency, multilateral decision making, and the need to focus on long-term benefits rather than short-term windfalls. These are cornerstones of sustainability.

In November 2000 the PJV identified an alternative possibility, Anawe North, for a new dump site which still provides for significant economic benefits. Potential stakeholder options and discussions are taking into account earlier problems and include more flexible solutions to relocation housing and replacement gardening land to suit both individual and wider community needs.

remarked. An ordinary Indian can never see the "government." He is sent from one office to another, is introduced to this man and to that, each of whom sometimes claims to be the "boss"; but he never sees the real government, who keeps himself hidden. (1930, 61)

Leviathans can never negotiate about waste dumps by themselves. They need spokesmen who can represent them. Many of us are used to tightly black-boxed accounts of politics because we grew up in places where "the notion that there may be something in a collective, something more than the group, which somehow emerges from their interaction, yet is above and beyond any individual is so commonplace . . . that it seems wholly unremarkable" (Leach 2006, 8). But during Yakatabari, the situation was much more unsettled.

In early modern Europe, political actors faced a similar dynamic as they opened the black box of divine right kingship. As Edmund Morgan (1992) notes, "the idea of fundamental law or higher law or fundamental constitutions is an ancient one; and the idea of resting such superior law on the people themselves is at least as old as the sixteenth century. The problem has always been to differentiate "the people themselves" from their mere representatives." And indeed, although we tend to think of Hobbes as semiotically naive, it is important to note that Hobbes's account of covenanting emphasized the performative power of speech to make something—a powerful, punishing something. Before the social contract, there was only a multitude. After it, there is a commonwealth and a sovereign who personates it (Skinner 2007). In this way individual actors became "the state" by virtue of their personation of Leviathan, the "artificial person" created by (but not subject to) the covenant which imparts sovereignty.

As we will see, Yakatabari rendered problematic who was representing what: Did mine negotiators really have the ear of the mine manager? Were landowner representatives really personating the Ipili, or acting in their own self-interest? How many clans existed inside the special mining lease? Where should the line between clan and subclan be drawn? In the negotiations leviathans were "not silent things, but rather that provisional product of a constant uproar made by the millions of contradictory voices about what is a group and who pertains to what" (Latour 2005, 31), and whether "spokespersons are turned into subjective individuals or into objective representatives" (Latour 1987, 78) was one of the most important questions that negotiators were to ask.

In the event, the negotiations did not turn on who was recognized as a "subjective individual" and who objectively represented a leviathan. Rather, Yakatabari would rise or fall based on how subjective projects became interpellated into the negotiations. Marshall Sahlins would insist that cultural structures are always realized in particular times and particular places, and that this moment of instantiation subjects them to risk. In particular, some cultural systems amplify the agency of individuals by putting them in a position of sociohistorical importance (Sahlins 1991, 2004) by enabling them to personify social totalities (Rumsey 1999, 2000) or, as Hobbes would put it, personating leviathans. This personation devolves "larger" issues onto the personalities of the individuals involved, thus allowing history (or globalization), to be made "in the medium of people's projects" (Sahlins 2000a, 343). In these negotiations the fate of the valley hung on the micropolitics of recognition, as the ostensible issues of the negotiations became a forum for negotiators to argue about who was a competent negotiator and who was not, who was good and who was not, and how best to understand the history of colonialism in the valley.

What Yakatabari Was About

The Yakatabari negotiations were, fundamentally, about how the Porgera gold mine would spend its middle age. Like most mines, Porgera's early years were its best. The richest ore was mined first; the price of gold was high, hovering just above US$350 per ounce, and the price of production was low, roughly around US$75 per ounce. In the late 1990s, however, the richer stocks of ore were worked out, the price of gold fell, and production costs hit an all-time high in 1996 of US$250 per ounce. By 1999, when the Yakatabari negotiations began, the difference between production cost and gold price was a mere US$50 (Jackson and Banks 2002, 228–39, on which this and further discussion of the mine's operations and budgeting is based).

Engineering issues also played their part. As ore grades fell (that is, there was less and less gold in the ore), throughput was increased to keep production levels steady. In August 1992 the mine processed 4,000 tons of ore a day. In 1993 this number doubled. In 1994 a detailed study was undertaken to determine a long-term plan of operation that would extend through the rest of the mine's life. The result was stage 4B of the mine plan, which more than doubled capacity to 17,000 tons a day (Jackson and Banks 2002, 208–12). Increased mining meant more waste rock, and the question arose as to where it could be dumped. Much of the waste rock had previously been discarded in the Kogai dump, but this location was now unsuitable: it was located on the mountain range just slightly above the mine's open pit, and as the pit deepened, the cost of hauling waste rock up to the dump increased. The waste dump was literally becoming an insurmountable problem.

While finances and logistics squeezed the mine, the Ipili faced another set of problems. Social change had been sweeping through the valley since the mine's opening. Over the past decade, a privileged elite had coalesced out of a previously much more fluid scene by mastering the art of obtaining contract work, compensation, and other spin-off benefits from the mine. These men's (and they were all men) personal interests were no longer always unproblematically aligned with those of the majority of Porgerans. In general, average Porgerans were not unhappy with the existence of a privileged elite per se—they were merely unhappy that they were not part of it. Younger men clamoring to replace the established and now-aging members of the elite saw Yakatabari as a chance to parlay the support they had garnered in the more fluid and low-stakes realms of valley politics into a place at the big table—the black boxes being open, as it were, this was the chance for young aspirants to climb into them.

There were demographic changes as well. As birthrates rose and child mortality decreased, an entire generation was coming of age surrounded by a mine they had not chosen, and without the houses and other compensation their elders had received from the mine. Many Porgeran families had a group of Engan or Huli immigrants who were attached to them in a client-patron relationship, and these factors compounded the land shortage caused by the mine's presence to create a crisis of subsistence agriculture that led in

generational issue

turn to an increased reliance on money from the mine to purchase store-bought food (for more details of social change in Porgera, see Bonnell 1999; Banks and Bonnell 1997).

Finally, Ipili dissatisfaction was underwritten by cultural structures that ran deep. The history of mining in Porgera overlapped with a series of millennial movements, and the Ipili have a penchant for eschatology. As a result many considered the opening of the mine an apocalyptic moment ushered in by Jesus and an ancestral python spirit named Kupiane, and expected that mine-derived benefits would result in endless affluence and immortality (for more on this, see Golub 2006). Different people had different levels of belief in Kupiane, but it is undoubtedly the case that in 2000, all Ipili felt very disappointed in the mine. Ten years into what was supposed to be an age of effortless wealth and health, they felt cheated by what the mine had wrought and deeply entitled to more than they had received.

The Yakatabari dump was designed as a solution to all of these problems. It was named, like so many other features of Porgeran geography, after a mishearing of a local place name—in this case, the Yakitipali stream whose watershed would form the dump's basin. The plan was attractive to the mine because the proposed new dump site was below the open pit, near the mine's main plant, and was capacious enough not only to receive waste generated by the current mine plan but possibly even to extend the mine's life by lowering costs. The plan was also attractive to landowners, whose goal—however unintuitive it might seem—was to be displaced by the Yakatabari dump. Ipili saw relocation as a chance to acquire the millennial affluence they had missed out on in 1988 and as a chance to leave an area increasingly affected by pollution, land shortages, and overpopulation. Throughout the negotiations, the groups which would be displaced by the dump were also those who were the most eager for its construction, while those who would remain felt that they were getting the short end of the stick. As the difficulties of living inside the Special Mining Lease territory grew more and more intractable, compensation and relocation looked more and more like the solution to their problems.

The central question then becomes: even if the dump was technically feasible, was it socially feasible? Ethically, politically, and militarily the mine needed consent from landowners—a feat made extremely difficult by the fact that both who specifically the "special mining lease landowners" were and what counted as "consent" were extremely ambiguous. Officially, relationships between the mine and the Ipili were defined by the agreements of the late 1980s, and the terms of those agreements could be changed only if mine operations deviated significantly from the plans described in the Mineral Development Contract. Stage 4B had been extremely contentious because it had not triggered this sort of reconsideration, despite landowners' insistence that doubling of plant capacity and stockpiling ore was never envisaged in the contract. Landowners insisted that Yakatabari was the occasion to fundamentally rethink the politics of the valley. This was nothing new—Ipili make claims on the mine all the time—but if Yakatabari constituted a change from the original plan, then suddenly these claims would gain new legitimacy in Port Moresby.

Was the creation of Yakatabari a case of "stereotypic reproduction" of the relations in the valley, or did it represent an opportunity to transform those relations? Were these negotiations, in other words, a "structure of the conjuncture," in Sahlins's sense (1985, xiv), a time when several levels of determination combined to create a situation in which existing orders were put into play and could be reshaped by individual agency? Was Yakatabari "new"? This was a question the mine did not want asked, much less answered. It sought to implement Yakatabari without creating instability in the valley that could threaten its operations. To this end, the mine's representatives settled on a two-pronged approach. First, they submitted a document—called the Porgera Vision Plan—to the government explaining the Yakatabari waste dump and the changes that it would entail. Second, they began negotiating a new agreement—known as the Yakatabari Agreement—with the landowners that would give more lucrative benefits to those affected by the new dump than were provided for under existing agreements.

The Porgera Vision Plan left the question of Yakatabari's novelty ambiguous. It described not just Yakatabari, but the rest of the mine's life, its impact on the valley and the nation, and life in the valley after the mine closed. These plans—the most comprehensive to date in Papua New Guinea—were meant to demonstrate the mine's concern with sustainability and social change in the valley as a responsible company committed to partnering with the government to achieve maximum stakeholder benefits through best practices. Compensation for landowners was described as part of the mine's goal of supporting and embracing sustainable development with the Porgeran community and not—of *course*—as a cynical quid pro quo for a new waste dump. The mine thus portrayed itself as an exemplary corporate citizen—so exemplary, in fact, that there would be no point in mucking about in the details of the Mineral Development Contract. By focusing on the future rather than the past, the mine sought to keep the question of its compliance with older plans as far from people's minds as possible.

The mine was not totally Machiavellian in all this. The Yakatabari negotiations occurred at a time when Placer Dome officially embraced sustainable development as part of its global strategy and began producing reports like the one I described at the start of this chapter. Moreover, I firmly believe that mine executives and senior managers in Porgera would have found it repulsive to bulldoze people's homes and forcibly relocate them to make way for a new waste dump. Senior managers had a genuine desire to do the right thing—as long as this was compatible with the imperatives of business. As the negotiations progressed, the mine became more and more desperate to find ways to convince itself that profitable decisions were also the morally correct ones.

Another important consideration for the mine was to keep the negotiations from spilling out of the valley. If landowners were quiescent, then other leviathans would not question the deal. Indeed, the exact status of what had been agreed on could be developed later to suit the legal and rhetorical requirements of other stakeholders. But if landowners were not satisfied, chances were that the government would not be either. By providing a suitably generous settlement, the mine hoped to satisfy the Ipili and prevent Yakatabari from getting out of hand. Indeed, there were hopes that the advantages of Yakatabari (increased mine life and hence more money for landowners) and the changes in landowner communities might even make possible a better and fairer relationship between the mine and the Ipili as supposedly "uncorrupted" younger leaders replaced older, "corrupt" ones.

Time was a final—and key—feature of the negotiation. Once the mine reached a certain point in its operations, it would be forced to invest in the fleet of larger trucks so the existing mine plan could be carried out, and the window of opportunity for Yakatabari would close. Even though negotiations began a year before this point would be reached, the most important and intensive part of the negotiations would happen under enormously important deadlines. As we shall see, this pressure was augmented by landowner-induced crises that threatened to close the mine even sooner and thus forced the PJV to act quickly.

The Peoples and Places of the Negotiations

The original offer for the Yakatabari waste dump was made on 17 April 1999, with the formal reinstatement of meetings between the Landowner Negotiating Committee and mine representatives. The Landowner Negotiating Committee, also known as the LNC or simply "the twenty-three" (because they were representatives of the twenty-three subclans that lived inside the special mining lease territory), was the top organization of landowners who had signed the 1989 agreements that essentially established the mine's right to be in the valley. Across the table from them were the men employed as section heads in the mine's community affairs office (who I refer to here as "community affairs officers"). Many of these men had formerly been *kiaps*— government officers during Papua New Guinea's colonial period—who had retired and gone into the private sector. Although it is not unusual for kiaps to work in community affairs in the resource industry in Papua New Guinea (Banks and Ballard 1997), Porgera was unusual for the large number of kiaps it employed, mostly because the community affairs office had been created out of the informal personal network of its founder, who was himself a retired kiap. This situation had its advantages and its drawbacks. The community affairs officers had spent decades working with Papua New Guineans, often in the highlands and occasionally even in Porgera itself. This meant that they were familiar with Papua New Guinean cultures, spoke Tok Pisin, and were less likely to be cowed by the force and power of Ipili negotiating tactics.

Not all of the negotiators had been kiaps, but even the ones who hadn't still had a background in Papua New Guinea's colonial past. A good example of this sort of personal history can be seen in the man who headed up the day-to-day negotiations, an outside consultant named Geraint. A former *didiman* (agricultural extension officer), he had worked for years in Enga Province and had visited Porgera on at least one occasion in the 1970s. He also served on the team of consultants that produced the socioeconomic impact study as part of the mine's feasibility statement, and he was then retained by the mine to plan and implement the relocation of landowners living on the mine site. Geraint's extensive personal experience meant that he would be very familiar to the group of landowners he would be negotiating with. For some people, such as the Pulumaini representatives with whom he had worked closely in the past, he was a trusted and known quantity. Other members of the LNC, however, considered Geraint to be not only responsible for, but also guilty of, creating the institutional arrangements they had lived with for a decade, the man personally responsible for what they considered to be the injustices visited on them.

As a result, Yakatabari became more than a negotiation about a waste dump carried out between two leviathans. It became a referendum on the identities of people who personated the leviathans: were the mine representatives cruel colonizers or well-intentioned people attempting to develop

33

Papua New Guinea? Were "the twenty-three" unlettered bumpkins with delusions of sophistication, or proud and free members of an independent country who had taken on global capitalism and won? Or, as most people thought, were both somewhere in between? This was a classic case of what Sahlins calls "historical melodrama" (2004, 169) where large-scale differences between leviathans originate in small-scale and historically particular differences between the people who personate them.

Like all historically particular events, the Yakatabari meetings had to take place somewhere, and that somewhere was a building called the *haus win*— a largish (roughly nine meters across) round building made out of timber with a *kunai* (dried grass) roof, a wood floor, and walls entirely covered with louvered glass windows. Community affairs staff members believed that the haus win was "like a native building" and more comfortable for Ipili negotiators than a more formal conference room. At the far end of the room a small table was set up, behind which the chief mine negotiators, translators, and government representatives sat. Ipili participants sat on the other side of the room on chairs (or the floor, if there were too many of them for the available chairs) arranged across the back of the room. The meetings followed *Robert's Rules of Order* (Robert and Robert 2011). A chairman (almost always the same person) was elected, minutes were produced, and some system of managing who got the floor was also followed, although motions were almost never passed. This system was taken seriously—these rules were followed even in the secret landowner meetings that I attended (but do not describe in this book). After each meeting a light lunch was served, and landowner representatives were paid a small fee for attending (less than K50, and at that time the kina was worth roughly US$0.36).

The haus win was in Suyan, the compound where mine employees were housed. After the riot of 1995 in which Porgerans stormed Suyan, overturned trucks, and damaged buildings, security around the compound had been reinforced. By the time of the Yakatabari negotiations it was one of the more heavily fortified areas in the valley, with barbed-wire fences, security cameras, and a security checkpoint at the entrance. Holding the meetings in Suyan meant that access to them was highly restricted—although it also meant that the meetings were held in a less sensitive area than the main administrative building of the mine, where Ipili negotiators might have wandered into the mine manager's office or gone to one of the flotation mills or another industrial facility.

For some Ipili, access to the haus win was easy: members of the landowner elite simply drove their tinted-glass Toyota Land Cruisers to Suyan and obtained day passes from the security guards there, who had been pro-vided with a list of names of those allowed to enter. The less august boarded a special bus at the community affairs compound in Yokelama (which was open to the public) and were driven to Suyan. The ambitious, curious, and unauthorized attempted to worm their way into the personal entourage of powerful landowners, while less well-connected aspirants would attempt to inveigle their way onto the bus. In fact, kicking people off the bus to Suyan was an inevitable preliminary phase of any meeting. De-busing people was emotionally and physically intense: at one point, for example, an Ipili man pushed past a community affairs officer and onto the bus, knocking the of-ficer to the ground. In the end, the man had to be pulled off the bus. In the resulting scene, guards armed with shotguns and—even more terrifyingly—guard dogs (they felt to me like attack dogs) formed an uneasy perimeter around him and the bus to make sure things did not escalate into an all-out riot on the part of the unrepresented.

Still, the rules for attendance were flexible. Mine negotiators didn't want to upset current nonentities who might end up one day living on top of a bit of land that the mine might need. Moreover, the inclusion of different factions tended to split the landowner community internally and thus weaken the LNC's support back in the village, while implicitly challenging its legitimacy as the spokesman for all Ipili. Often, for instance, the mine allowed represen-tatives of the Porgera Women's Association to attend out of a general liberal feeling that women ought to be included in an otherwise all-male process, while powerful and sympathetic Porgerans were often included whether they were technically supposed to be there or not. Finally, there was always a small group of people who managed to charm their way into the meetings without a clear mandate to be there—a group that included me.

In general, the mine structured the monthly meetings with the LNC as a continuation of an established system of consultation: the mine would spread the word that a meeting would occur; it would meet with the LNC and provide it with a proposal; and the LNC's members would consult with grass-roots landowners regarding the proposal and then bring feedback to the next meeting. In practice, the negotiations were much more raucous—any-one who has watched the ferocity with which landowners threw themselves onto the light lunch table, stuffing finger sandwiches and chicken wings into their mouths while competing to shove cans of soda pop into their pockets, shirtsleeves, and pants for redistribution back in the village will realize that I am not exaggerating when I say that anyone in Porgera with aspirations to power, easy money, or just a free lunch sought to attend the meetings.

The Initial Attempt to Sue: April to November

When I arrived in Porgera to begin my fieldwork at the end of 1999, however, this process had been put on hold. Instead, I was told, twenty of the twenty-three members of the LNC had decided to abandon negotiations and pursue litigation against the mine—a move inspired by landowner litigation against the Ok Tedi copper mine a few years earlier (Banks and Ballard 1997). Several members of the LNC flew to Australia to meet with the Australian law firm that had litigated on behalf of the Ok Tedi landowners. According to all accounts, the firm refused to take the case, and the landowners returned to Porgera empty-handed.

The mine felt that the landowners' strategy had inadvertently demonstrated the legitimacy of Placer's approach. In an early meeting, the head of community affairs told me that the LNC's members were elite Ipili who sought to increase their own wealth and power by selectively feeding information to the local community and turning it against the mine. Had there been a lawsuit, he believed, it would have led to a shake-up in the valley's leadership, with the LNC's internal coalitions collapsing in discord and younger leaders coming to the fore. The question he now faced, he said, was whether to work to hold the LNC together or to encourage new and more legitimate (and, presumably, more "reasonable") leadership to arise: to embrace, as it were, the devil he knew or the devil he didn't.

Although mine employees seemed to believe that emerging leaders in the valley were less corrupt and more reasonable than older members of the LNC, in fact it was a junior faction within the LNC that had instigated the lawsuit and whose members would increasingly assert themselves throughout the negotiations. This faction was composed of Nathan Palepa (a member of the Angalaini clan) and three Tiyinis, Palama Peyalu and the brothers Benjamin and Kenneth Lawane. Although the mine referred to this group as the "Tiyini" faction, its main source of power was the Porgera Landowners Association, a pressure group of which Nathan was president and Palama secretary. The Porgera Landowners Association derived its strength and legitimacy from its role in the late 1980s when, under different leadership, it had been one of the main groups that pushed for Ipili benefits during the mine's creation. The Porgera Landowners Association was a particularly feasible leviathan because, since 1995, it had a generous annual budget funded by mine revenues that its executives could (and did) use freely. The result was one of the typical ironies of life in Porgera: the mine funded an institution that was established to oppose it.

The mine countered the LNC by making an end run around it. The community affairs officers had worked to get their message to "the Ipili" directly through a newsletter, a video that could be shown in local trade stores, and meetings with the Porgera Women's Association to discuss the design for the Yakatabari relocation houses on the assumption that they would be the ones actually living in and maintaining them.

In the end, however, the mine's most effective means of unscrewing the LNC's big leviathan was Yakatabari itself: if the plan went through, some clans would be relocated and some would not. The majority of the Pulumaini, Mamai, and Angalaini in the special mining lease territory would be moved, while most of the Tuanda and Waiwa would remain. The powerful Tiyini would be split—some Tiyini subclans would be relocated while others would remain. As a result, the interests of the clans were fundamentally divergent, and it was this divergence, rather than the mine's attempt to reach out to what it called the uncorrupted grassroots that would prove to be truly crucial to the course of negotiations.

When meetings began again in late November, the landowners tried a new tack: to convince the mine to maximize its environmental impact, while the mine sought to minimize disruption to landowner communities. An example of how these dynamics played out at the beginning stages of the negotiations can be found in the LNC meeting held on 23 November 1999.

THE NOVEMBER MEETING

On 23 November 1999 the LNC met with the mine for the twelfth time, the first time since the lawsuit had fallen apart. Forty-six people attended, including a representative from the government. The meeting began shortly after 10:00 AM and continued for roughly two hours. This was the first meeting I attended during my fieldwork. Because it was the first meeting after the attempted legal action by the landowners, it was particularly important—a fact indicated by the mine manager's presence.

The meeting began with a long speech in which the mine manager outlined the "big picture" of what was going on with Yakatabari: the new dump would lower the mine's operating costs and extend its life, and the relocation would offer the opportunity to solve long-standing issues of land shortages and overpopulation. However, there was a problem: under its current plan, the mine would have to buy a new truck every three months in order to keep operating. The longer the negotiations took, the less money would be available for compensation, and if negotiations dragged on too long, the mine would be forced to invest in so many trucks that the window of opportunity for Yakatabari would close. Throughout the mine manager spoke in the idiom of a "win-win" situation. "If you are asking us outrageous things," he said, "that is also no use, because if we have no profits it doesn't make sense for us to do it. There must be gain for you and gain for the company, or else it won't happen." The mine manager was not coy about the mine's intentions: it was a self-interested business designed to make money, and it assumed the landowners sought to benefit as well.

Geraint then ran briefly over how the relocations would work, including the order in which residents would be moved—Pulumaini first, then Mamai and Angalaini. The central issue of the negotiations was then broached: the Tiyini at Yarik and its sister settlement Timorope would not be moved, although the Tiyini at Yunarilama would be. As a result, several of the most important landowners present would not receive new houses. However, Geraint was quick to suggest that this was negotiable: "What we're saying, we're not closing off forever talks on this issue . . . we're not saying 'piss off' . . . we're saying 'let's talk more about this.'"

He emphasized that this relocation would be more generous than the previous one. In the case of a young couple who were just starting a household—"I don't mean sleeping around, people—*marrit tru* [really married], paid their bride-price"—it might be possible to establish a trust fund to buy them materials to build their own house when they were ready. Thus he emphasized that benefits from the mine (specifically, a house) would be given out based on distinctly indigenous criteria (legitimate marriage defined by the payment of a bride-price), an issue that would become a recurrent theme in the negotiations.

Finally there was the house itself. Geraint said he had taken women over to the government station, and that they liked the house designated L40—a standard design for civil servants. It was high off the ground, and had solar-powered hot water and a thousand-gallon water tank with an underground pipe to tanks on the roof that supplied the house directly. The total cost would be K70,000 per house. As murmurs at the figure spread around the room, Geraint said that he mentioned the cost because some people had expressed interest in taking the cash instead of a building and using the money to buy a house in Port Moresby, or putting it to other use. This was something that the mine would entertain, Geraint said. He ended with a plea for real dialogue and honest representation of community interests. "I think that's the basic story. I think we've had a solid earful from the mine manager, some straight talk. We acknowledge there is [*sic*] some difficulties for some of the clans, and we acknowledge we don't have the solutions. If it's possible for you to really, truly talk to your people and come back with . . . not some racist [antiwhite and antimine] talk, but some real information which I can relay to the mine manager," then, he concluded, they could work together.

Before the meeting broke off for lunch, "Chief" Ambi Kipu, the elderly agent for the Tuanda (who would not be relocated) and formerly one of the most important people in the valley, asked ominously whether the Yakatabari dump was part of the original mine plan. The mine manager equivocated, saying that "it is part of the development of the mine. The agreements are part of the development of the mine. And this is still happening." Next Lyndon Koeka spoke in Ipili. As the agent for the Uape subclan of Tiyini, Lyndon would not be relocated, while others of his clan would. This was a particularly thorny point in the negotiations. On the one hand, Lyndon's father had been one of the most powerful men in the valley before his execution by decapitation at the hands of his fellow clansmen in the 1970s, and people at the negotiations remembered this fact. This meant that there were deep personal histories at work amongst the Tiyini that did not unify them. On the other hand, Lyndon was the chair of the board of directors of the Porgera Development Authority, and not someone that anyone could afford to alienate. He had chosen his unusual English name, Lyndon, during Lyndon Johnson's term as president of the United States and demonstrated his namesake's desire for power. He had come to the meeting late and had missed two-thirds of it. Nevertheless, he rose and spoke in Ipili, which was translated as: "Lyndon is saying: on behalf of the landowners we are hearing your plan and your ideas. We want to take it back to our clansmen. We'll bring [the] landowners' response and go through the agenda [the issues] one by one." Lyndon added in mixed Tok Pisin and English: "*Finalisim* [we'll finalize it in] in two, three weeks and sign agreement." With that, the meeting ended on an up note.

These meetings demonstrated several important features that came to mark both sides of the debate during the remaining negotiations. First was the issue of house size: the Ipili universally condemned the relocation houses they had received in the late 1980s as inadequate, "matchbox" houses. They wanted larger houses and knew of several preexisting plans that could be used to build them. These meetings also demonstrated an Ipili tactic that would be used throughout the negotiations: the constant and repeated assurance that they were just around the corner from an agreement, a move used to lull the mine and others into a false sense of security, take up time, and then force negotiators to make last-minute concessions. Finally, the meeting demonstrated to all the landowners present that the mine and the mine manager spoke in a language of self-interest that they could understand. The landowners considered the manager to personate "the mine" unproblematically in a way that, as we shall see, the community affairs staff did not.

manager
personates
the mine

THE DECEMBER MEETING

Many, if not most, Ipili were hoping that Yakatabari would result in their being moved to a large urban area where they would be provided with a large house and a generous monthly pension that the mine would pay them in perpetuity. However, the justification that the Ipili used to gain these concessions had to be couched in terms that the mine would consider indigenous: that clans ought to be moved together, that land is the life of the people, and that subsistence agriculture was an essential part of Ipili life. As a result there was a disjuncture between what the Ipili wanted from the mine and the acceptable reasons they could give for why they ought to get it. This was the major dynamic of the meeting on 9 December 1999.

paradox

At this meeting the main mine negotiators were Geraint and a former kiap named Burt. The main Ipili representatives were Napia Kongoialo, the Tiyini agent for the Akira subclan, and Sianga Yake—a man aspiring to prominence who may or may not have been Pulumaini, depending on whose genealogy you believed, but who had in any event joined forces with Napia on the basis of a matrilineal connection to Tiyini Akira, Napia's subclan. Sianga set the stage for the meeting by presenting a response to the mine's offer of an L40 house: a worn and dirty blueprint for an H90 house that was more than twice the size of the L40 and, at K180,000, much more expensive to build.

After this presentation Lyndon made a speech in which he complained that he and other landowners had no land to move to because they lacked kinship ties to areas outside of Porgera. Geraint replied that his concern was not finding land (that could be managed) but finding land for Lyndon (or, more accurately, his eight wives) that was suitable for the subsistence agriculture to which Geraint assumed Lyndon sought to return. Was that, Geraint asked Lyndon, the problem Lyndon was referring to? Lyndon was nonplussed, since in fact his statement was intended to indicate that he wanted to be settled in an urban area where there would be no subsistence agriculture at all. Faced with Geraint's statement, he finally stated baldly that he wanted the mine to purchase land that he himself had selected.

Still talking past him, Geraint agreed, saying that it was just this sort of feedback that he wanted and asking that landowners come to the PJV office to let him know their preferences, since the last time a PJV employee had visited Yarik he had been stoned. "Ol i ting ting yu wokim old style house [They attacked him because they thought you were planning to build us the old-style house]," said Lyndon reassuringly. Geraint glanced meaningfully at me for a moment, then Lyndon, and then observed sourly: "They didn't ask questions, did they?" Unable to get his point through to Geraint obliquely, Lyndon finally stated explicitly that he wanted a house in the urban township at Paiyam, which Geraint agreed to if the land at Paiyam could be legally acquired.

Ambi took the floor next, asking whether all landowners would be moved, or only those affected by the dump—a relevant question for him since he would not be relocated, although his community would be surrounded by waste dumps on three sides if Yakatabari went through. Geraint replied: "I can't give you much hope. In reply, the mine manager hasn't closed the door. The mine in the agreements [of 1988] does claim to sympathetically look . . . it's not a promise. We're keeping the door open." This was the first mention of the 1988 Relocation Agreement's "sympathetic examination" clause, which stated that "the PJV agrees to examine sympathetically and where appropriate make special provision for any Re-located Landowner whose situation is affected in a special or unusual manner" (Placer Dome 1988, 6). This clause would loom large in what was to follow, since it implied that in certain circumstances (which ones, of course, would be hotly disputed) the mine had obligated itself to relocate landowners.

Ambi, aware of how little leverage this actually gave him, responded with a loud, angry tirade, only to be shouted down by Benjamin Lawane (the secretary of the Porgera Landowners Association) and another prominent Tiyini agent, who told Ambi to shut up. Benjamin also insisted that Ambi's outburst not be recorded in the minutes. Benjamin then delivered a very long and increasingly heated speech in Tok Pisin. He said that Geraint's goal was to get an agreement for the company, and that he didn't care about what happened to Porgerans, while Ipili negotiators were genuinely worried about their future. He then compared Geraint to a bulldozer that destroys everything in its path without even noticing it was there and accused him of trying to trick the older, less sophisticated members of the LNC. He then gave the example of homeless people visible in the large town of Mt. Hagen who run around naked in public and have to dig in trash cans for food when they are hungry. "You," concluded Benjamin, breaking into English, "want to do the same thing to us."

He then presented his demands: "We must have proper planning. Government services, road, power supply. Schools [both elementary and high school]. Power—it has to be free. If you want a power bill, put us on the payroll [give us free monthly paychecks] and we'll pay. This is an example of all the bits and pieces that must be in place." He also insisted that if any of "the Tiyini" were moved, all Tiyini must be moved (as everyone in the room well knew, this was the only way that Benjamin would get a house out of the deal, since he did not live in the affected area). This was because "Pasin blo PNG, clan ties—noken brekim [in Papua New Guinea clan ties cannot be broken]." He insisted that he must have this "in black and white . . . 'door is open' em sampela tok blo yu, em tainim kamap bullshit [this 'door is open' talk of yours is bullshit that won't happen]." He insisted: "Majority of PNG, agriculture is laif blong mipela. Yupela noken bugurupim laif-graun, graun blong mi [Agriculture is our lives. You can't damage the land that we live off of, our land]." He concluded by telling Geraint: "Yu olsem snek lo bush, em no save [You are like a snake in the bush, you don't] go from point A to point B, you beat around the bush!"

There were murmurs of assent and discussion in Ipili about this, and Napia (who would be relocated) told Geraint that he wanted all Tiyini subclans moved, not just his own. At this point Benjamin got the floor again and began a new line of attack. He said: "Yesterday I was at a meeting [of the Fly-In-Fly-Out management committee] with the Porgera Mining Coordinator, Harry Ulin. During this meeting I heard that you are preparing a tunnel to drain water from the mine, and that you have already started drilling. You've hired twenty-seven experts to work the tunnel from the open cut and then out two kilometers and that you've already started drilling. Who gave you permission to do that?"

This touched a nerve, and Burt, the mine negotiator, jumped out of his chair exclaiming: "Mi laik interuptim [I want to interrupt]—these are separate issues!" Benjamin continued to talk, and Geraint began saying very, very forcefully indeed: "Mi no bihainim dispela toktok, mi no raitim lo minutes. Mi finisim tok. Yu laik brukim meetin now. Yu tok win i no istap lo paper [I won't listen to this, and I'm not writing it in the minutes. I've said what I wanted. You want to disrupt this meeting. Your rumors will not be written down]." As he said this, Benjamin was yelling at him: "Pasim maut sindaun! Pasim maut sindaun! Pasim maut sindaun! Pasim maut sindaun! Pasim maut sindaun! Pasim maut sindaun! Pasim maut sindaun! [Shut up and sit down!]" Geraint recovered and noted calmly that he already was sitting and that he wasn't going to be derailed. Burt had blown his top, however, and stalked angrily out the door, and Geraint had no choice but to get up and follow him. As they passed Benjamin, he turned to face them and screamed at them as they left: "You are a thief! It is illegal for you to make that tunnel! I heard rumors of it yesterday. If you do make it, where will your outlet be? If you put an outlet in, you are looking for trouble, my friend!" At this all hell broke loose in the room, with people arguing among themselves (some had wanted the mine negotiators to stay so that they could meet with them). The meeting then dissolved in confusion.

A few minutes later, Geraint, Burt, and another former kiap named Lawrence emerged from the nearby mine mess hall and made for their car. I joined them and in a quick interview asked them how they thought the meeting went. Geraint remarked, incredibly: "I think we made good progress, we had a very reasonable chat with . . . Lyndon." I wasn't sure whether he was trying to put a good face on it for my sake or was truly deluded—Benjamin's ability to control the mine negotiators emotionally would demoralize them and give the landowners excellent ammunition in the future meetings, when they could argue that it was mine employees, rather than them, who had stonewalled and walked out of negotiations.

Benjamin's final speech vividly exemplifies the way that personal and institutional agendas collided in the negotiations: at some level the Yakatabari negotiations were a referendum on the agreements of the late 1980s and, at an even deeper level, Papua New Guinea's colonial history and the worth of the mine negotiators as men. Burt's and Geraint's lives were caught up in the country and they felt a deep commitment to it. Independence—which they considered to have been premature—and the antiwhite feelings it had generated made them feel that their commitment to the country was unappreciated. Papua New Guinea's fiscal and governmental breakdown in the late 1980s and 1990s gave them a certain grim satisfaction in proving that they had been needed after all. Taking careers as community affairs officers was the best they could do, given the state of corruption in Papua New Guinea's government, to continue to help local people as they were accustomed to doing.

For Geraint and Burt, people like Benjamin Lawane were particularly despicable. Not only was he ungrateful for their service, but he did not understand that their current job was still essentially benevolent paternalism in the corporate mode—they considered themselves advocates within the mine for the local people's needs and wishes. Perhaps most distressing to them was Benjamin's ignorance. Despite his veneer of education, they felt, he was still little more than a rural Papua New Guinean with delusions of competence whose excursions into legal and economic policy were so ignorant that he would require extensive education just to understand why they believed him to be confused.

As might be expected, the Porgera Landowners Association faction's view of the mine negotiators was equally complimentary. They did not consider themselves helpless, grateful recipients of Geraint's and Burt's aid. Gold had been discovered in Porgera in the first exploratory patrol into the area in 1938, and Ipili people had experienced a steady increase in wealth and income over the course of their experience with whites. While old men like Ambi might be swayed by these kiaps, Palama and Benjamin saw themselves as members of a newer, more sophisticated, generation who were not willing to be talked down to. These old kiaps, as Palama told me once, ought to be disagreed with on principle—by definition their offers were always untrustworthy and contesting them was, as it were, an act of postcolonial resistance.

As far as the Porgera Landowners Association faction was concerned, the negotiation was an antagonistic process in which they were competing with the mine to maximize their own profits. The negotiations were, in other words, business—not a reincarnation of colonial paternalism. The members of this faction distrusted community affairs officers who worked against the best interests of their employer, the mine. They also worried that senior mine managers did not trust their own negotiators enough to be frank with them about the mine's financial situation. In sum, the faction considered their long colonial tutorial to be over. They considered it to be an insult to have met with these aging, washed-up colonial officers.

The Deadline and the Tunnel: December to February

The tunnel at "Yunarilama" mentioned at the end of the 9 December meeting quickly moved to the center of negotiations. The mine had encountered an engineering problem: the open cut was now deep enough that it was a pit, and it required drainage to remain feasible. The mine thus wanted to build a tunnel from the base of the open cut that would run underneath landowners' areas and empty out into the Kaiyia River. The mine needed this tunnel to be built very quickly or else the alternate plan—to install pumps to drain the pit—would be so expensive that it would shorten the mine's life considerably.

Unfortunately for the PJV, the portal for the tunnel—where it would surface—was on land for which Kenneth Lawane was the agent, and although Kenneth's legal right to prevent the tunnel was ambiguous, he certainly had de facto control of the territory. The landowners could thus use the tunnel as leverage in their negotiations: no relocation, no tunnel.

The location of the drainage tunnel had mythological significance as well. The tunnel emptied out just upstream of the place where the events of the Tiyini origin story involving the python Kupiane occurred. Sianga Yake, who had also provided the alternate house design, had even gone so far as to build a model of the house that features in the Kupiane myth—a sort of shrine—on the site. Given its mythically and cosmically relevant location, landowners considered the idea that the tunnel was merely for waste water to be a ludicrous lie. It was obviously, as far as they were concerned, a mine trick to extract not just gold, but high-quality diamonds—which they understood to be more valuable than gold—from the mountain without paying landowners for the privilege. From this point of view, the tunnel was part of the mine's ongoing attempt to track and capture Kupiane, and its presence confirmed the equivalence between sacred locations and precious mineral wealth.

THE TYINI LETTER

On 20 December, eleven days after Burt stormed out of the *haus win* at Suyan, the most prominent members of the Tiyini clan wrote a letter to the mine manager titled "Principal Landowner Demands on Timorope/Yunalima [*sic*] Proposed Tunnel and Yakatabari Dump by PJV." The letter, signed by nine people from four of the Tiyini subclans, presented four pages of demands that would have to be met if "the Tiyini" were to approve of the dump. In poor English, the letter suggested that other issues—such as the relocation of affected people—could be put aside indefinitely if these demands were met. Sent privately to the mine manager and not intended for public distribution, there was a strong possibility that the letter was intended to broker a deal that would essentially cut off grassroots landowners from receiving any benefits from Yakatabari whatsoever in exchange for direct concessions to members of the LNC. The split between the grassroots landowners and the elite that the head of community affairs had predicted had finally come to pass, but with a twist: now it was the "unreasonable" people who attempted to align themselves with the mine—for the right price.

The demands of the letter were, to put it mildly, extravagant. They included K16,000,000 as a "community facilities grant" to Tiyini subclans, "Bonus Compensation" of an additional K500,000 to the subclans, K10,000,000 for compensation for the tunnel, K2,500,000 for "Kupiane's Sacred Side [*sic*] Compensation . . . for causing destruction and inconvenience to Kupiane's house in mountain Wuangima as a result of the underground tunnel" (compensation for this site had already been paid nearly a decade earlier), as well as "alluvial, terrace gold and environment compensation." Most spectacular, however, was the demand for the "PJV to agree to produce one gold bar each at twenty (25 Kilogram) [*sic*] for the following principal landowners of the gold rich mountain every quarter of each year until the mine life ends." A list of individual names followed.

Mine managers generally assumed that the letter was an act of extortion that combined extreme ignorance of the actual financial capabilities of the mine with a deeply misguided sense of competency. To a certain extent the mine had brought this on itself: for over a decade, its employees had simplified explanations of royalties, equities, and dividends using metaphors of gold bars rather than by tediously explaining the concept of percentages. For example, rather than explain that each of the joint venture partners owned a 14 percent stake in the mine, they explained that the mine produced seven gold bars every quarter and that each of the partners received one. To this extent, then, the letter was merely an attempt to cut out the middleman and get gold directly into the hands of the landowners.

"The Ipili" were now beginning to come undone, as the knot of people gathered under that name unraveled into three roughly distinct groups: first, "the Tiyini" or "the Porgera Landowners Association," who sought to deal secretly with the mine; second, "the Ipili" in the form of the LNC, whose members continued to negotiate with Geraint (and which included some members of the first faction); and third, "the Ipili" in the sense of the generic "local and uncorrupt community" from which the mine hoped newer and more reasonable leaders might emerge.

JANUARY: THE DEADLINE APPROACHES

The mine had originally intended to have the Yakatabari agreements signed by the first of February, and as the deadline approached the frequency of meetings increased—negotiations were held once a week rather than once a month, and there was also a series of private meetings with those members of the LNC who still refused to sign any agreement. However, it was not until a meeting on 9 January that the mine gave a draft of the agreement to the landowners. Several of them were infuriated that they received this formal offer a mere month before the deadline and were now being railroaded into signing it without seeking legal advice. The document was identical in wording to the 1988 Relocation Agreement, with the amounts of money increased and a few clauses added to reflect changes in house size—the mine had made a counteroffer to the H90 model proposed by the landowners and suggested instead that an H75 model might be built. However, what was not included was an appendix listing exactly who would be moved. Landowners, in other words, were being asked to sign a document that did not address the central issue of the negotiation: who would be relocated?

Why didn't the mine put something on paper earlier? Fear of litigation may have been part of the mine's—or at least Geraint's—decision to introduce a written document to the negotiations at this late date. However, the Porgera Landowners Association faction was correct in thinking that Geraint felt it would be easier and less confusing for them if he discussed what they wanted orally and then produced a final written version for them at the end. This was, after all, how Geraint had handled negotiations during his earlier career in Papua New Guinea, and it reflected his sense of the limited sophistication of the landowners—exactly what the Porgera Landowners Association faction was complaining about. Geraint saw meetings as a means of generating trust and understanding, while for landowners they were antagonistic exchanges of proposals and counterproposals. This emphasis on trust and informality was also a reason why there was no appendix attached to the agreement—Geraint felt that everyone knew very well who would be moved and who would not, and that this was a matter that could be implemented in good faith after the construction of Yakatabari got under way. Landowners, on the other hand, felt that they were equals negotiating with the mine, and that if the mine was expecting them to give up their homes and lands, then it should also be willing to present them with a thorough and professionally drafted proposal stating exactly what its intentions were.

THE JANUARY MEETING

It was at this point that the Yakatabari negotiations began slowly spilling out of the valley and into other areas of the country. The week after the mine made its written offer, Harry Ulin, the Porgera Mining Coordinator for the Department of Mining, flew into Porgera from Port Moresby to meet with the landowners and get the process moving.

Ulin's presence marked both a broadening of the conflict outside the valley as well as its continuing personalization. A turbulent national political

47

scene, combined with Porgera's remoteness, meant that elected politicians were often transient players in the valley's politics. It was civil servants like Ulin, who lived through several administrations and visited the valley in the course of implementing and monitoring the agreements of the 1980s, who came to personate "the government" for most Porgerans.

The Department of Mining is the most important part of the Papua New Guinean government that deals with Porgera, and within that department Ulin described himself as a "one-stop shop" for matters pertaining to Porgera. It was his job to liaise with the company and other branches of government on all things Porgeran. This job of personating the government was aided by his long personal history with Porgera: Ulin first came to Papua New Guinea in the early 1970s as an officer with the Australian administration. In 1984 he served as interim provincial administrator after the Engan provincial government was suspended for gross financial mismanagement and the provincial premier was jailed for corruption and removed from office. In February 1990 he was released, and in May he was reelected to the position of provincial premier. Ulin then was made the first assistant secretary of the province's Western Zone, which included Porgera, and was intimately connected with the creation of the mine. Ulin served in this position for several years. Then, after stints as Porgera Mining Coordinator (residing in Porgera) and, later, head of the Porgera Development Authority, he was recalled to Wabag, where the provincial government had been suspended again. He returned as interim provincial administrator, a position that he held until he took up his current position in the Department of Mining. It was this personal history, rather than his position as a bureaucratic officeholder, that gave him traction in Porgera.

Ulin's goal in visiting Porgera was to assess for himself who was responsible for what in Yakatabari and what he could do to straighten out the situation. The mine hoped that his history and experience with the landowners would give him their ear. Ulin opened the 20 January meeting with a long speech explaining the issues as he saw them. He explained that the PJV had submitted a detailed plan, the Porgera Vision Plan, that outlined Yakatabari, and that the Department of Mining had found it acceptable. He said that it was vitally important that the mine continue operations, and he urged those present to sign the agreement.

In response members of the Porgera Landowners Association faction made several arguments. First, they pointed out that they had submitted a letter to the Department of Mining expressing their dissatisfaction with the PJV and had not yet received a reply. Second, they insisted that they had not seen the

Porgera Vision Plan for themselves and wanted an account of what the mine was going to do before they would sign. Third, they were disgusted when Ulin told them that mine employees had assured him they were very close to an agreement—the Ipili pointed out, rightly, that they had only recently received the paper copy of the agreement the week before, and they said they were not happy with it. They neglected to point out, however, that they had spent the last couple of months telling the mine that an agreement "was right around the corner." Finally, Benjamin Lawane and Palama Peyalu, among others, pointed out repeatedly that they were not the same people who had signed the agreement in 1988—they were more experienced and cosmopolitan now. Thus they insisted on negotiating an agreement that was not literally cut and pasted from the 1988 agreement and on receiving proper paper copies of reports. Finally, they insisted to Ulin that he and the negotiators for the mine were from the old kiap times, and that his speech was essentially an attempt to scare (*praitim*, in Tok Pisin) and intimidate the Ipili into compliance, and that there was no way that such tactics were going to work.

After more discussion, the meeting closed with some good will between the mine and landowners restored, but with no substantive change in their positions. Whether the mine liked it or not, Yakatabari was now officially on the government's radar.

THE FEBRUARY DEADLINE AND AFTER

As the deadline grew closer and closer, the mine's options began to run out. On 2 February I interviewed a community affairs officer named Lawrence who told me that the mine was not willing to budge on the issue of house size, although it was willing to offer lucrative business contracts to Lyndon Koeka and Kenneth Lawane if they dropped their opposition to the plan. I suggested that if someone didn't understand that properly, they might mistake it for bribery. "Properly called, it is bribery," replied Lawrence, with a certain frankness that I am sure his employer wished he did not always exercise. I suggested that Lyndon and Kenneth would not take the offer because they had serious, principled, and reasonable disagreements with the mine. Lawrence disagreed. Did he really think the landowners were totally self-interested, I asked? Yes, he replied. Altruism and thought of others "was lacking in Ipili culture," as proof of which he said that Ipili had no word for "thank you."

It turned out that I was correct. The landowners did not take the bait, and on 9 February the mine manager released a public letter to the Porgera

Landowners Association faction categorically rejecting the demands made in their letter of 20 December. Community affairs officers began handing out copies of the mine manager's response along with the original letter to select members of the community (including me) in an attempt to discredit the faction by publicizing its members' attempt to cut a deal. The next day, 10 February, the mine manager attended a special LNC meeting whose only agenda item was to convince Ipili to sign the agreement. This important meeting ultimately failed to produce a consensus. As a result, the mine now officially had a full-fledged crisis on its hands: it was at the point at which it had to begin investing in additional trucks to build its fleet capacity to be able to accommodate a Yakatabari-less future. The window of opportunity was still open, but it had begun to close, and the space for negotiation became increasingly narrow.

THE DISTRICT ADMINISTRATOR'S LETTER

With the situation in Porgera coming more and more conspicuous to the people in Port Moresby and the official deadline for signing a document now passed, the district administrator, or DA began intervening in affairs. On 16 February, he wrote a three-page letter to the mining warden (the official responsible for adjudicating disputes between landowners and mining companies) and sent copies to the provincial administrator, the mine manager, the chairman of the LNC, and the secretary of the Department of Mining. The letter thus became the most official, on-the-record statement of the situation in Porgera yet to come from the civil service.

Its true power, of course, came not from the title at the top of the letterhead but from the signature at the bottom: the DA had a complex history in Porgera, and his biography indicates how complex ethnicity and Porgeran identity can be. He was born in Tari (Southern Highlands Province) to ethnically Huli parents. His uncle was one of the first Huli people to accompany an Australian patrol out of the valley during World War II. After the war, his uncle moved to Porgera and served as a translator, foreman, and general middleman for expatriate alluvial miners. The DA was raised by his uncle and was in the first class to go through the first school in Porgera, paying his school fees by working as a domestic servant—literally a tea boy—to the kiap at the time. Ironically that kiap was working in Porgera as a community affairs officer during Yakatabari, but he was not of a sufficiently august position that he attended the meetings in which the DA's words would play such a great role. After high school the DA returned to Porgera, first as a kiap and later as an employee of Placer during the period when Porgera was still being explored as a mine site. He then served as an advocate for Ipili landowners during the negotiations to create the mine in the late 1980s. Thus by the time of his ascent to the district administratorship, he had represented the mine, the government, and landowners—sometimes simultaneously. At once an immigrant and one of the most important representatives of the Ipili during one of the most crucial times in the valley's history, the DA exemplified the personalistic nature of ties in the Porgera community and the way influential individuals could represent a variety of institutions rather than merely a single one.

represent multiple roles

Having previously remained neutral in the discussion, he now threw his hat into the ring in a move that both raised the stakes and provided the possibility that a crisis might be averted through his intervention. Broadly sympathetic to the Porgera Landowners Association faction, his intervention worked on their behalf—in fact, his letter was the most articulate and reasoned criticism of the mine to date.

Ironically, the letter began by justifying his intervention in the debate with a reference to a clause in the Land Act designating the DA as "the protector of landowners and their rights in any dealings with the owners in relation to their customary land"—the paternalistic clause dating from the colonial period that so incensed the Porgera Landowners Association faction. He then moved on to use the mine's own documentation against it, quoting at length from the mine's 1996 social monitoring report that found that "Special Mining Lease communities face a severe crisis in land" and that "a relocation of these communities will be essential at some time over the current mine life of 13 years regardless of whether or not further reserves are found." The DA argued that the Special Mining Lease was in such a state in 1996 that the PJV was bound by the original "sympathetic examination" clause of the 1988 Relocation Agreement to relocate all landowners and that now, in 2000, the situation was even worse.

The letter's particular genius lay in its justification for relocating all, not just some, of the Tiyini subclans: since all Tiyini had "primary gardening land" in the affected area, they qualified for relocation whether they lived there or not. Subsistence, rather than residence, was the key criterion for relocation. In effect, the DA provided the Porgera Landowners Association faction with a reasoned, eloquent, and official argument to justify relocation.

On 21 and 22 February there were long, intense meetings between the main players in the negotiations. The meetings were held in the boardroom of the main administration building—the swankiest and most official space that the mine possessed. They were meant to be the final, definitive signing event after the previous planned signing had gone awry. Although central to the mine's timetable, the meetings were hamstrung by the fact that Henry (the head of community affairs) and the mine manager were on leave, and their replacements had to step in at a critical time. The meeting on 21 February lasted four and a half hours, but the agreement was not signed.

"The Ipili" and the LNC: March to June

By 1 March the negotiations had ground to a halt. Mine negotiators had tried for five days to arrange some sort of group meeting for yet another attempted signing, but it was not going to happen. As a result they switched tactics and began asking individual agents to come to community affairs headquarters in Yokelama to sign the agreement privately. They hoped that if a majority of the committee signed they could claim that, in effect, landowners had signed an agreement—something their lawyers had told them would probably stand up in court.

It might stand up in the valley as well, provided that the consensus thus formed could be used to force the nonsigners to capitulate. But in pursuing this course of action, the mine gave up on a full and public LNC signing, one of the few stable sources of legitimacy in the valley. The agreement might be signed, but it would not be well-signed. The mine was entering unknown territory, gambling that a novel form of concession from someone who might be "the Ipili" would render Yakatabari feasible. To many in the valley, this strategy appeared to be simply one of intimidation in which community affairs officers drove agents into their offices and pressured them to sign behind closed doors.

The scope of the agreement was shifting as well—on 1 March Lawrence told me that the word "Yakatabari" was misleading, since the document that landowners were signing was meant to apply to all future activity inside all of the Special Mining Lease territory. Thus the people who signed the document would be entitled to increased levels of compensation if they were relocated in the future for any reason, while those who did not sign would be stuck with the terms of the 1989 agreement. I was surprised to hear this because such an understanding of the agreement had never been mentioned or discussed at any meeting I attended or had heard about. The mine, it seemed, was sweetening the pot for collaborators.

That evening in Apalaka, where I lived, I saw the agent for my adopted clan, the Waiwa. He brandished his still-blackened index finger and told me that he had signed. (In practice, "signing" often meant that illiterate members of the LNC had put their fingerprint on a document.) He began chewing out a friend who was with me (who lived in Yarik and hence was "Tiyini" despite being related to Tuanda, agnatically Angalaini, and married to Waiwa) and insisted that he, an old man, simply wanted to get rich before his death and that my friend should leave him alone. This theme was repeated with vehemence by one of the more prominent Apalakans, and a crowd of about twenty people gathered and began excoriating my friend in particular and the Tiyini more generally. The general sense of the crowd was that their compensation money was being held up by "the Tiyini." Such a view overlooked the facts that many Tiyini agents supported the agreement and that the Tuanda would not be moved as a result of Yakatabari.

On 15 March I went to visit Geraint in his office in Yokelama. By this point he had grown less involved with events in Porgera, and several of our recent meetings had focused mainly on his past time in the valley. Visibly moved, he told me that he had been sidelined, and that the company was more or less done with him. His time would now be best spent, he decided, assuming that the deal would go through, doing land work identifying new house sites for relocated landowners. This nonconfrontational work, designed to help rural and largely uneducated Papua New Guineans, was reminiscent of his original work as an agricultural extension officer in the 1970s. It was familiar and comforting to him.

THE TUNNEL AND THE SECRETARY: MARCH TO MAY

As these events occurred, the issue of the Yunarilama tunnel became increasingly pressing. With the tunnel completed, opening the portal was all that remained to complete the project—a task crucial to the mine's continued operation and one that Kenneth Lawane, the agent for the Lakima subclan where the portal was located, would not allow without concessions from the mine.

But Kenneth was not the only landowner involved. Although he was the legal agent for his subclan, the actual resident of the portal site was an elderly man named Busane, who had lived there for decades as the patriarch of an extended family. Busane was not himself Lakima, Tiyini, or even Ipili—he was born in Tari and was ethnically Huli. He moved to Porgera in the early 1950s and had worked as a foreman overseeing the Porgerans who worked with white alluvial miners, married a Tiyini woman, and settled there. Thus his proximity to the portal entrance was not mere chance—the same flat land that was suitable for alluvial workings in the 1950s proved to be the best spot for the mine to open the portal five decades later.

The mine argued that the portal was inside the special mining lease territory and that it was legally obligated only to pay Busane compensation for his land and relocate him in accordance with the agreements of the 1980s, regardless of Kenneth's pretensions to control the area. Busane was keenly aware of the delicacy of his position: he hated the idea that Kenneth could prevent him from receiving large amounts of money and a free house, but he knew that threatening to form an alliance with Kenneth strengthened his position vis-à-vis the company. After a period of very intense and very private negotiation with the Busane family, the mine agreed to relocate them under the terms of the as-yet-unsigned Yakatabari agreement, complete with lucrative compensation rates and a large new house. The mine painted this turn of events as the victory of a grassroots Porgeran over the valley's corrupt elite, and it heralded its generous settlement as a demonstration of Placer Dome's sense of social responsibility and stewardship of the valley.

THE MEETING WITH THE SECRETARY

Although local politics had been addressed by Busane's deal with the mine, national actors were now increasingly drawn into the Yakatabari negotiations. Throughout the month of March, members of the Porgera Landowners Association faction had been in Port Moresby, attempting to broaden the conflict by enrolling new allies in the Department of Mining. As a result, the secretary for the Department of Mining, top civil servant in the department, flew into Porgera on 24 March to meet with both the mine's representatives and landowners.

The secretary spent the early morning meeting with senior managers of the mine. News of his presence had spread among members of Porgera's elite and aspiring elite, so the crowd that gathered at the Suyan haus win for the 10:00 AM meeting with him numbered about forty people. As it turned out, the secretary's meeting at the mine site took longer than planned, and it was not until 12:05 that the secretary, one of the mining engineers from his office, the DA, Harry Ulin (also up from the coast), a variety of community affairs officers, and the mine manager arrived.

Lawrence, the community affairs officer whose frank comments to me appear above, began by giving his apologies in Tok Pisin and explaining that the group had come to meet in order to "pinisim dispela toktok blo Yakitibari [finish this talk about Yakatabari]." The meeting began. After the usual lengthy greeting to everyone and every notable person present, Lawrence turned the discussion over to the secretary, a small man of obvious refinement. He spoke mainly in Tok Pisin for the benefit of the landowners, with occasional interjections in English—indeed, as a highly educated man from a Papuan (or coastal) ethnic group, he appeared to be more comfortable with English than Tok Pisin. His words were then translated into Ipili. "The company is important and must go ahead as soon as possible," he said:

> Lo taim kampani wokim dispela project, ol i tok we [When the company undertook this project, they agreed that if] anyone is affected or impacted, they must be provided for . . . We believe about ten have signed out of twenty-three. From the delegation i bin kam lo Moresby, mipela bin autim two problems. Namba wan em haus design kampani wokim, ol i tok haus i liklik because yupela gat bikpela family, na blo facilitatim family ol i mas expandim haus [the delegation from Moresby talked about two issues. First is the company's design for the house. They said it was small given the large size of your families, and wanted the size of the house expanded]. Can the company do this? Second main problem ol i autim em i gaden land [the second problem was gardening land]. Taim ol i wokim [when they will create the] tunnel, their ground will be taken away. So can the company find land? Land em olsem tradestore blo mipela [the land is your trade store]. Your lives are connected to the land. So can the company find more land? Lain i kam tok lo mi, sapos graun i long we [the group who saw me asked whether, if the replacement land was far away], can the house be built there?

He concluded by saying that "purpose blo kam lo hia [my purpose in coming here] is to find out is this the only problem that's keeping you from signing? Can we not find a way? Do the three people who came to see me share your views?"

Lyndon took the floor next and made a speech that grew increasingly heated. "Mipela stap lo banis," he said, "o mi nap tok, lo bel blo pik [We are fenced in, I could even say that we are in the belly of a pig]!" He went on to state that the lives of people in the Special Mining Lease territory had been overwhelmingly affected by mining. The Ipili, he reiterated, simply wanted to be relocated—all of them—off the mining lease land, and after that the mine could do anything it wanted without interference. However, the mine wanted to move only four groups and refused to be reasonable and negotiate. As his temper grew more and more out of control, his sense of betrayal became almost palpable: he castigated the secretary for failing to protect

Ipili—citizens of Papua New Guinea—from the mine and claimed that in fact thirteen people had not signed the Yakatabari agreement. He said: "We'll get lawyers or legal advice. You are supposed to advise us, but you stap lo [stay in] Waigani and Konedobu [government centers distant from rural Papua New Guineans] . . . So second question: what is the government's plan lo muvim ol manmeri baggarup lo en? Yu lukim plan blo kampani [to move the people who are affected? You've seen the company's plan], so where is the plan?"

The secretary responded: "Dispela design kampani salim i kam [the design [the tunnel] the company sent us], em [it's a] minor alteration. Em includim lo MDC [It's included in the MDC]. It's already in the approval. That's why it's considered to be a minor alteration . . . Depatment i no approvim Yakatabari dump as yet. It's separate. That's why we want to focus on the tunnel, because it's important to the company."

In this exchange Lyndon purposefully conflated the waste dump and the tunnel, arguing that the simplest thing to do (which also happened to be in his own best interest) was to relocate everyone from the special mining lease territory and thus remove all future obstacles to the mine's development. He also thought of the secretary as someone whose job it was to protect him, a grassroots citizen of Papua New Guinea, from an international mining company. The secretary, on the other hand, separated the issues of the dump and the tunnel and focused on the tunnel, which he considered to be unproblematic. Unfortunately his emphasis on the tunnel merely made him look as if he was siding with the company rather than the Ipili. The fact that he was obviously antagonized by the landowners' aggressive behavior did not help: being shouted at for minutes on end is not a pleasant experience, particularly when you are an important person to whom this does not normally happen. He was losing patience with the landowners. Lyndon then stood up and moved to the center of the room:

> Mr. Secretary, thank you. Em no olsem Ok Tedi, Misima, Lihir, Tokuluma. Em no stap lo big thick jungle. Taim i laik mine, ol i laik rousim olgeta i go outside Special Mining Lease [This isn't Ok Tedi, Misima, Lihir, or Tokuluma. Porgera isn't in the middle of a big thick jungle. When they want to mine, they move everyone outside of the Special Mining Lease]. They don't mine in the same place people are living because life is important.

At this point Lyndon began to lose his temper again: "You think the safety of the people is safe?! Em lo dispela as mispela sendim delegation lo yu [This is the reason we sent that delegation to you]. Em [This is an] international company! They are here today and gone tomorrow, we are baggarup [screwed]! What is your plan? Yu no tok tok. Mi no satisfy [You have not spoken and I am not satisfied]."

The secretary remained calm and reiterated his position: "The purpose of me coming here is to listen to whether what the company says is satisfactory. Position blo mi [My position] is to see if the company has fulfilled its agreement [that is, its requirement to consult with landowners]. It's supposed to negotiate with you. That, we believe, is what the company is doing."

At this point Lyndon attempted to speak again but was drowned out by four or five other people who wanted to say something. Eventually Kenneth Lawane got the floor and asked: "Yu tok tunnel i stap lo original plan. Ating yu mas sowim [You say the tunnel is in the original plan. You must show us where]." The secretary deferred to the engineer he had brought down from Port Moresby, who confirmed that the plans in the Mineral Development Contract allowed for a tunnel. Lyndon then began another tirade, which grew in force and intensity until he was livid:

> Yu tok mine life bai go siot, kost lo usim pump i antap, who wokim decision na wokim license. Tasol you no wokin study o investigatim mine i baggarap life blo as ples.Yu no gat plan blo helpim mipela. Gavman yu laik kissim tax, pjv laik wokim profit, na yu laik mipela i baggarap! [You talk about a shortened mine life, the cost of using pumps, and who makes decisions and who issues leases. But you haven't done a study of how the mine has destroyed the lives of local peoples. You have no plan to help us. The government wants taxes, the pjv wants profits, and you want us to suffer!] . . . They are foreigners. They work twenty-four hours [that is, the mine is unnatural and mechanistic]. Then want quick money!!

At this the mine manager actually got to his feet and attempted to intervene, but Lyndon was still shouting: "What they are doing, Mr. Secretary, is going door to door getting people to sign! It's illegal! This is an independent country. The government must witness!"

Finally the mine manager was able to speak and attempted to calm everyone down:

> We bought you a proposal. Do we want to talk about that or not? We wanted to make money for the mine and the landowners. I'm sorry if that was misunderstood. If it was misunderstood, then a lot of people have been wasting their time here. If we are now saying there is no plan, there is only profit for the company, then we can't talk anymore. If we want to

talk about the tunnel, then we can talk about opening the portal to the tunnel. If not, we can forget about the dump altogether, because without that portal we will be even more earlier out of business.

At this point Kenneth Lawane attempted to take the floor but was headed off by the secretary: "Yu tok tok tumas [You talk too much]. We have to leave at two o'clock. You sent a delegation down and talked about two problems. We need to focus. We're going off topic. I want to focus on those two. I've been corrected. There are sixteen signatories out of the twenty-three. So maybe seven of you are not happy about houses and gardens. That's what I want to talk about. So Kenneth, if you have something to say, please make sure it's to do with gardens or houses."

Kenneth now began a long speech in which he claimed that these two points had not in fact been what he had met with the secretary about, and he insisted that the secretary must instruct the company to start a brand-new negotiation with the landowners. He even said that as far as he was concerned, the people who signed the Yakatabari agreement could move and he would stay on his land—a way to present himself as respectful of other Ipilis' rights while also continuing to prevent the portal being opened.

The secretary then attempted to hear from some of the landowners present, but Kenneth attempted to interrupt again. "We've given you a chance, so please . . ." began the secretary.

"Sapos i no laik negotiate gen, yumi sanap lo cot box [If you don't want to negotiate again, we will see you in court]!" replied Kenneth in a stern, angry tone.

The secretary attempted to signal someone else to speak but was shouted down by Kenneth, who demanded to know what the secretary's response to his question was. The secretary broke down and replied heatedly, although his temper was still under control: "Mi harim tok tok blo yu [I've heard what you said]. After these discussions [in Port Moresby], we discussed three points: gardens, housing, and the contract. You agreed the agreement needed fine-tuning, so what you said now [about me misunderstanding you or forgetting what you said] is not correct."

This was remarkably effective at silencing Kenneth, since in fact these were the arguments he had made in Port Moresby and the secretary had inadvertently pulled off the typical Ipili rhetorical tactic of publicly revealing information from a private meeting in order to call someone's bluff. After this the secretary finally managed to allow Samuel Talepa to speak.

As the foremost, youngest, and most Christian member of the Pulumaini clan, Samuel represented the most legitimate and heartfelt opposition to the old, "corrupt" landowners. It was clear to me that Samuel got along well with the mine because their interests were identical, a fact that the mine's representatives tended to interpret as "uncorrupt" since, they reasoned, what was good for the mine was good for the valley. In the past Lyndon and others had managed to intimidate Samuel into silence in these public meetings, but now he stood up to them and finally had his day in court, despite the attempts of members of the Porgera Landowners Association faction to shout him down. Samuel proceeded to tell the secretary that the faction did not represent his interests, but only their own: "Ol landowner no tok tok lo pipol. Ol i tok tok lo bel blo en, ol i no tok tok lo pipol. [The landowners do not speak on behalf of the people. They speak on behalf of their own bellies, not on behalf of the people]." Samuel continued, now addressing the Porgera Landowners Association faction:

Mi signim dispela agriment. Yu tok tok bel blo yu, yu go lo cot sapos yu laik kisim double stori haus. Mi signim lo eye blo district administrator na papa blo graun. Lo pinisim tok tok, sapos yu laik cot, ok. Insait lo four mun, start relocation. Mipela dai. Wanem hap mipela laik wokim gaden, kampani bai bihanim. Em tok tok lo mi lo Pulumaini Ambo. Mi no stap aninit wanpela man o ol Tiyin line—Travelodge kamap olsem haus man blo ol [I signed this agreement. You speak on your behalf—if you want a two-story house go ahead and sue them. I've signed in front of the district administrator and the land owners. In conclusion, if you want to sue, ok. But within four months, our relocation must start. We are dying. The company will buy land where we want to plant gardens. This is talk of the Pulumaini Ambo. I don't answer to the Tiyini or anyone else— the Travelodge [the finest hotel in Papua New Guinea] has become their men's house].

After Samuel finished speaking, the secretary attempted to hear from another Pulumaini agent, but the struggle to respond to Samuel became overwhelming. "Please!" implored the secretary over the chaos in the meeting room. "We should and must respect people!"

"You are not chairman," said Lyndon to the secretary. "Keep your mouth shut and keep quiet."

Two more Pulumaini agents then spoke, emphasizing that time was running out and that the mine had already agreed to several of their demands.

In the aftermath of Samuel's speech, the furor over who would speak next was intense, and the translator attempted roughly to sketch out clan divisions for the secretary, suggesting perhaps that one representative from every clan should speak their mind in closing. This idea was replaced by a shouting match between Lyndon and the agent for the Mamai, who was able to get the floor long enough to indicate that he too was happy with the agreement as it stood.

At this point it was 1:45 and the secretary was scheduled to depart in fifteen minutes. In an attempt to finish the meeting, he designated four more people whose points of view he would like to hear. However, Lyndon once more interrupted him and, in an attempt to adhere to the secretary's request for comments, he began addressing the issues that the secretary had outlined at the beginning of the meeting: "Namba wan haus lo Lihir na arapela gold main is H90 [the good house model found in Lihir and other gold mine areas] . . . This is a world-class gold mine. Whether they like it or not they have to give us H90." He told the secretary: "Mi laik yu directim decision lo dispela [I want you to formally direct their decision in this regard]" and reported that—the mine manager's shocked face notwithstanding—"mine manager no rejectim, em tok em reasonable, tasol ol tea boi blo en twistim—olgeta lain grisim em because lo colonial times they are kiaps and didiman [the mine manager didn't reject this. He said it was reasonable, but his tea boys have twisted his words—they want to fool him because they were kiaps and agricultural extension officers during the colonial period]."

This elicited laughter from the community affairs officers, who felt that Lyndon's comments demonstrated that if anyone was stuck in a colonial mentality, it was Lyndon himself, who was acting like a paranoid Ipili *bush kanaka* (rural bumpkin). Nevertheless, Lyndon had spoken clearly what was in the minds of several landowners in the room.

The secretary thanked Lyndon and concluded that there was some "fine tuning" needed in regard to the choice of house model—a pretty blatant whitewash of the considerable differences that had been enunciated in the meeting. Nathan Palepa replied by noting that the PJV had not yet agreed to purchase land for relocated landowners, and that this was a major issue. The secretary then held up a memo that, he announced, said the mine would undertake to purchase this land. Nathan Palepa and Kenneth—outraged at what he saw as a PJV trick—replied that that language was not in the agreement and they had not seen that memo before.

At this point Waipa (a Tiyini agent) asked if the government was telling them to negotiate with the company on just these two issues or on the entirety of the agreement. The secretary claimed that he had summarized the content of the agreement, and that these two issues were the only ones that were still outstanding.

"Yu gavman," replied Kenneth, "yu lukautim interests blo papa blo graun. Company em foreigner. Position blo yu, yu mas klarim gut lo position blo yu . . . yu mas tok olsem yu mas go lo round table na negotiate gen. Klarim mipela na go [The government safeguards the interests of the landowners. The company is run by a bunch of foreigners. You must clarify your position . . . you must tell us that we must negotiate from scratch. Say that clearly, and then we'll go]." In other words, Kenneth wanted the government to order the mine to undertake a completely new negotiation regarding land in the Special Mining Lease territory.

The secretary then gave the mine manager the floor. "The clear message was that the Yakatabari negotiations are close," the mine manager said. "That is still slightly the case. What I am prepared to do is to have you work together with [the] community affairs [staff] on the house and the gardens. By the time I come back [from a regularly-scheduled break], not this week but next week, we can meet again. What I want to know, particularly from the Tiyini, is if, under these circumstances, the tunnel can go ahead."

When one of the community affairs officers demanded that this be translated, the resulting argument grew so heated that it became impossible for the conversation to continue. "Please, please," implored the secretary with no effect, "I have to catch a plane."

"We're not going to negotiate with Geraint!" screamed Lyndon. "We're going to negotiate with the mine manager!" More furor ensued, but eventually it was calmed down. The DA gave a final speech urging unity, and the meeting broke up. But Kenneth Lawane departed with the ominous words: "Mr. Secretary, my brata, tunnel nogat until we finalize this agreement."

THE INJUNCTION

A week later, the mine received a fax from the secretary on official Department of Mining stationery. Written on 31 March, it stated that he was "satisfied that the actual landowners have given their consent for compensation to be paid" and agreed that "the tunnel portal must be commenced immediately so that the orderly flow in the development of the approved stages of the Porgera Mine are completed." Mine managers photocopied this document, and community affairs officers began disseminating it to select people in Porgera, including me.

The Lawanes remained intransigent, however. This was partially due to the fact that Benjamin Lawane was impossible to track down. His house in Paiyam was across the street from the local high school, and earlier that month one of his two wives had asked a young girl (to whom she was enatically related) from the school to come over to Benjamin's house, where she was invited to have dinner and spend the night. Apparently Benjamin had sex with the girl that night—possibly without her consent—and she was not allowed to leave the house for the next week. When she was let out, she had agreed to marry him, and he sought to arrange for the payment of a bride-price.

The girl in question was a Kuala and the member of an old and distinguished Porgera family with branches in Hagen, Wabag, and Port Moresby; her parents expected their daughter to become educated and actively involved in business. They believed that she had been raped and brainwashed by a man twice her age who was not the kind of affine with whom they wanted to forge an alliance. Benjamin was jailed, bailed out, and jailed again before he finally won his freedom. At this point the girl's family began making death threats, and Benjamin was forced to go underground. Since the Kuala clan's land included the location of the government station, it was impossible for Benjamin to attend meetings at government offices or, for that matter, anywhere else.

Factions within the landowners began to shift. Lyndon and Takipe began to distance themselves from the Lawanes, whose recent activities and failed attempts to get the government to oppose the mine had damaged their credibility. As a result the Porgera Landowners Association faction was now clearly separated from whatever Tiyini support it had previously had. The association's next step was to hire a lawyer to seek an injunction against the PJV to prevent them from working on the tunnel. The case was heard in Mt. Hagen, and the injunction was affirmed in the absence of PJV lawyers, who were informed of the ex parte order after the fact. The mine was furious—not only had its lawyers not been informed of the case, but it felt the mining warden, rather than a civil court, should have heard the case since it had to do with a mining lease. The mine appealed the injunction, and it was overturned. The Porgera Landowners Association promptly appealed the appeal, which bumped the case up to the National Court, the highest level of the judiciary short of the Supreme Court.

The case was heard on 18 April in Port Moresby. I flew down to observe the case, as did Nathan Palepa and a few other Porgerans. At the hearing, the judge stated that injunctions were applicable only in situations where any damage done was irreparable, and since all concerned had agreed in principle that the mine could construct the tunnel and that what was being argued about was merely the price that would be paid, an injunction was not in order. Indeed, the families on whose land the portal would be located had agreed to its creation.

The injunction was thus set aside, providing that the mine give one week's notice that it intended to carry out the work. The mine did so, and fifteen days later, on 25 April, PJV workers under police escort entered the portal area in order to do some basic survey work. There was no opposition, because the people who actually lived in that area had agreed to the sale of the land and because the Lawanes were not expecting the workers. But when PJV workers returned two days later, they were met by Benjamin Lawane and a crowd of curious onlookers, including me. After a tense, angry confrontation, the community affairs officer who accompanied the workers decided the situation was hopeless: Benjamin was willing to use force, and the mine was not yet ready to risk a violent incident.

On 29 April the DA weighed in with yet another letter in his official capacity. The letter—which circulated in Port Moresby as well as the valley—once again articulated a legal argument regarding the state of affairs in the valley, albeit in a way that was more obviously biased in favor of the landowners and less logically coherent than his first letter.

The DA granted that the mine had the legal right to construct the portal. However, he argued, before this could happen the mine needed approval from "traditional owners." He argued that Busane's family "were not legally authorized by members of the clans owning the land, thereby rendering any agreement executed by them illegal." Note that he did not claim that Busane was a non-Ipili and hence not a true landowner—which speaks volumes about the strength of claims of residence over claims of descent in Porgera that will be explored in future chapters. Instead he claimed that "the Agents [in this case, Kenneth Lawane] claim that all members of the clan owning the land in question have vested authority to deal with the land in the Agents and other members of the clan cannot deal in the land, thus rendering any dealings made by unauthorized persons illegal." In other words, the DA argued that the agents created in the late 1980s were not merely representatives of a community but had greater powers to make deals about the land than the people who actually lived on it, and that those people had to request the permission of their agent to effect any sort of land transaction at all.

Claims of residence vs. claims of descent [handwritten marginal note]

63

Thus, as part of a larger attempt to support the Ipili against an outside force, the DA argued that agents represented a leviathan called the "clan" rather than a particular aggregate of people. This seemed to undercut individual Porgerans' autonomy and to emphasize the power of the agents.

On 8 May the LNC convened to hear about the outcome of the court case. Prior to the meeting, the mine had discreetly disseminated the court's decision throughout the valley, and community affairs officers made photocopies of the one-page ruling and distributed them to the members of the LNC. In its entirety, the decision read:

The court orders that:
1. The Porgera Landowners Association (Inc.) by its officers and members and the 13 other Plaintiffs by their agents be restrained from interfering with or obstructing the construction of a tunnel or portal and related activities by the Defendant or its agents at Yunarilama and that the Porgera Landowners Association (Inc.) by its officers and members and the 13 other Plaintiffs by their agents be restrained from interfering with or obstructing the relocation of the Lokopa family and the Busane Family from Yunarilama [sic].
2. Liberty to apply on 3 days' notice to the other party.
3. The time for entry of this Order be abridged to the time of settlement by the Registrar which shall take place forthwith.

However tangible the copies of the decision were, the legal language was beyond most people in the valley. Amazingly, Benjamin Lawane—who had not been present in Port Moresby because of his attempts to avoid revenge for his alleged rape—picked up a copy of the decision and told the assembled members of the LNC that the mine was lying. He argued that the paper indicated that the Porgera Landowners Association had won the court case and that the mine was under a restraining order that prevented it from constructing a tunnel. He further claimed that he knew this because he had been present at the hearing.

The result was a simmering sense of confusion in the valley regarding what had actually happened—Benjamin's claim diverged so sharply from reality that it seemed impossible to the members of the community affairs office that he could be taken seriously, while the audacity of his deception was so great that many landowners could not imagine that it would be possible for him to lie so boldly.

At this point I became entangled in the negotiations against my will. Copies of the decision began circulating freely in the valley, and I was asked my opinion by several people from Apalaka, my home community, who knew that I had attended the hearing. In the past I had respected the confidentiality of my informants and had not discussed the negotiations with people who had not been present. However, I felt unable to avoid responding to a direct question about material they had independently obtained regarding a public trial. As a result I told people, when pressed, that I thought the words "the court orders that the Porgera Landowners Association . . . be restrained from interfering with or obstructing the construction of a tunnel" meant that the Porgera Landowners Association was not allowed to interfere with the construction of the tunnel.

As a result of my comments, Benjamin Lawane confronted me in front of a crowd of roughly seventy-five people and instructed me to tell people that the Porgera Landowners Association had won the court case. I replied that I had not spoken to people about the court case, but that when pressed I had had no choice but to answer their questions honestly. He then accused me of lying, and I reminded him that I had been present at the hearing while he had not—my field notes included not just a list of participants but a sketch of the courtroom that was so detailed it showed everything from where people had sat to the location of the window-mounted air conditioners. Outraged, Benjamin called me a liar and insisted that he had been present.

After some further argument, our discussion ended inconclusively. The next day, rumors began spreading around Apalaka that I was a spy sent from the mine to write secret reports about the Ipili in order to keep them from receiving benefits from the mine. This resulted in a brief struggle over my legitimacy inside my field site. Luckily, I had a long track record of taking friends and members of my adopted family to the hospital and the bank, purchasing antibiotics for them, and attending church services regularly. The Lawanes, on the other hand, were seen as greedy members of the elite whose extravagant demands for money had prevented the Tuanda (the clan of my place in Apalaka) from receiving the benefits of the Yakatabari agreements. After a few very uncomfortable public meetings, rumors of my duplicity faded away.

At any rate, I was scheduled for a break in my fieldwork. I spent most of June in the United States, touring the country with a Porgeran friend. When I returned to the valley on 1 July, I found the portal completed—the Porgera Landowners Association faction had been unwilling to risk physical violence and had allowed construction of the portal to go ahead.

Ministerial Involvement and Internal Politics: July to September

With the tunnel under construction, the immediate future of the mine was no longer in jeopardy, even if the Yakatabari agreement still was. In the final stage of the negotiations, both landowners and the mine took the conflict to the highest level of the Papua New Guinea government. As negotiations played out more and more in offices in Port Moresby and less and less in the valley itself, following their course became more difficult. Nevertheless, I believe I can sketch the main shape of what happened based on statements made by the people involved, which have been corroborated by other participants.

The raising of the stakes in Yakatabari was symbolized nicely by a visit someone had made to Porgera during my absence: Sir Michael Somare had visited the valley in order to see the mine's operation for himself. People in Apalaka eagerly described his visit to me and remembered that he had expressed unhappiness with how landowners' lives had been affected by mining, although there was some disagreement about whether he had done this from within his car or murmured these sentiments as he stood at the edge of the village and gazed at the massive expanse of the Anjolek waste dump, which covered the location of their original village. Regardless, Somare's visit was truly memorable. He was not merely the minister of mining, he was also the father of the nation—the central figure in Papua New Guinea's movement to independence and the country's first prime minister. His face graced the fifty-*kina* note—the only human to appear on the country's paper currency. His presence reaffirmed for local people Porgera's centrality to Papua New Guinea.

However, it proved to be the other minister on the trip—Herowa Agiwa, the minister for environment and conservation—who would play a larger role in the events of Yakatabari. The Department of Environment and Conservation (DEC) was in charge of overseeing the water permits that the mine was required to obtain in order to discharge tailings into the river system, to use running water for the mining camp, and so forth. One of the DEC's routine functions was to oversee the renewal of these water permits. DEC personnel made annual trips to the mine site to make sure that the mine was in compliance with the terms of these permits. On 7 July DEC officers visited Porgera and held community meetings with people in the Special Mining Lease territory as part of the standard procedure in the renewal of permits. Typically, I was told, unless the mine has done something extraordinary, the

renewal of water permits is yet another one of the complex ongoing processes that are routinely carried out as part of keeping the mine open.

This time, however, landowners quickly moved to pressure DEC employees not to renew the permits. The DEC representatives were resistant, since
they considered the mine to be in compliance and did not feel they could
refuse to renew permits because of other, unrelated inequities. Additionally,
they were not particularly sympathetic with landowners. Many remembered
a community meeting in the mid-1990s when they had also not been able
to support landowner demands. The DEC representatives told me that the
meeting had degenerated into a riot and that they had had to clamber onto
the roof of a building and be evacuated by helicopter.

The landowners now urged Herowa Agiwa to ignore the decision of his
executive council—which is normally binding—and refuse to renew the
permits anyway. They also encouraged him to make use of his authority to
argue in public that by the standards of the DEC, the people in the Special
Mining Lease territory were affected by mining and that under the "sympathetic evaluation" clause, they ought to be moved out of the territory. On
22 July I heard from senior community affairs staff members that the minister had accepted both of these requests. He had instituted a plan whereby
the relocation would be paid for partially by the mine and partially with tax
money the government received from the mine.

At the same time, who counted as "landowners" and "the Porgera Landowners Association" was changing. Within landowner communities, there
was a strong sense that the twenty-three members of the LNC had let a golden
opportunity for compensation slip through their fingers because of their
own overreaching avarice. As a result an alliance of influential but out-of-
power Ipili coalesced and made a legal challenge against the Porgera Landowners Association. The two most important players were Victor Alene and
Andrew Konema.

Victor was famous for a spectacular raid in the mid-1980s on what was
then Placer's prospecting camp, which resulted in the theft of tens of thousands of *kina* and the passports of all the foreign workers in the mine. Andrew was the head of the Porgera Landowners Association and a key negotiator of the Porgera Agreements in the 1980s. He had fallen from a position
of enormous influence after his part in a clan fight that devastated his home
village. Victor and Andrew organized a meeting, claimed that it was a legitimate meeting of the board of the Porgera Landowners Association, and had
themselves elected as the association's new executives.

Technically the Porgera Landowners Association received its budget from a portion of the royalties that the mine paid quarterly to the Porgera Development Authority. I was told by senior staff members of the Porgera Development Authority that they had deposited K5,500,000 into the Porgera Landowners Association account in the previous six years, and that currently there was only K300,000 in the account. There appeared to be no clear record of how the balance of the money had been spent—although, to be fair, this was not an unusual state of affairs for projects funded by the Porgera Development Authority. In the past, it was in the interest of many parties that accounting not be too specific. Now, with legal action in the offing, the head of the Porgera Development Authority (an accountant originally hailing from Ghana) invited PricewaterhouseCoopers to audit the Porgera Landowners Association's books in Porgera in an attempt to provide some impartial bookkeeping and to deflect any criticism that might come his way.

By late July opponents to the Porgera Landowners Association faction had hired a lawyer from Mt. Hagen and obtained an injunction against the association that froze its funds. The opponents claimed that, if they were to replace the current leaders, the Porgera Landowners Association budget (minus, most likely, their own salaries) would not be used to fund lawyers and stay in fancy hotels but would instead be directly distributed to Ipili as a cash payment. This effectively meant the dismantling of what had been—regardless of how justly it had been used—the most effective political tool landowners had in the Yakatabari negotiations. The popularity of this proposal demonstrates the Ipili interest in both egalitarianism and direct cash payments.

At roughly the same time I heard from a lawyer working for the provincial government in Wabag that the mine was shifting its position and attempting to classify Yakatabari as a "minor change" to the original mine plan and thus on the same scale as the tunnel. This was verified for me in Port Moresby on 1 September by DEC officials. They also told me they considered Placer's submissions to be unusually uninformative about what the mine was planning. Even Ok Tedi, the notorious polluter, submitted plans and then just carried them out—unlike Placer, it didn't attempt to revise or reframe its submissions.

On 15 August I was told by Andrew there was to be a hearing in Mt. Hagen on 4 September to freeze the funds in the Porgera Landowners Association's account. That same day the DA told me that negotiations were still stalled, but that he thought some "pressure at the top," including an upcoming meeting of ministers in Port Moresby about the problem, would help resolve the remaining issues. Apparently he felt that the mine's tax and royalty payments could be massaged to get the mine the money it needed to meet landowners' demands.

The next day I asked a senior (and Papua New Guinean) member of the community affairs staff about Yakatabari. He laughed ruefully and said, "It's dying a slow death." There had been no official feedback from the minister for mining about the plan for the government to take some of its tax money and plow it back into a resettlement scheme. I was also told that the minister for environment and conservation was "overstepping his power" and that granting water permits related to the Special Mining Lease is the mining minister's decision, because the DEC could regulate only water that flowed off the territory governed by the lease. Ironically, the community affairs officer noted that the mine would soon start relocating the owners of the land on which the portal had been built—and giving them the H75 houses that the Yakatabari group missed out on. He also sourly noted that in the newspaper a few days earlier there had been word of moving the long-anticipated natural gas pipeline to Australia from Papua New Guinea to East Timor. What kind of world were we living in, he mused, if East Timor was seen to be a more stable investment environment than Papua New Guinea? He used this as an example of the long-term consequences of politicized ministerial intervention on major resource development projects.

On 21 August I had a short conversation with Geraint, who had not been actively involved in the negotiations for months. He was extremely negative about the whole situation, but at least he could take comfort in the fact that the worse Yakatabari got, the less his lack of progress looked like a personal failure and the more it seemed to be inevitable. The situation also clearly demonstrated to him just how right he had been in his opinions of the shortcomings of landowners. He told me that it was increasingly looking as if nothing would be done at all: there would be no dump, and "the so-called zero option is beginning to look like a possibility." He said that there would be no more negotiations (this is something all of us closely involved in the situation had recognized long ago) and that the mine now just had a single, nonnegotiable offer to make—"and it's not going to be an H75, let me tell you." He said that the people who were lucky were the owners of the portal's site, who had signed an agreement and were going to get H75s. If other landowners were moved, they would get the old relocation house model.

Still, Geraint understood what had happened to his negotiations not in terms of the paradoxes at the heart of personating "the Ipili" as a larger actor. Rather, he considered the pathologies of their personators to be at fault.

He said that it was unfortunate that some people in the government were getting on the whole "social and environment impact" bandwagon that "the DA and his boys" were pushing. He said he was sorry that he had wasted eighteen months of his life attending "all those fucking meetings." "To have negotiated for so long," he said bitterly, "and then to turn it down at that last moment is stupid, just stupid."

I said that I was glad I was distanced from the process and that it just ate people up. He said yes, it was too bad, as he enjoyed doing implementation. He said he was happy to do work in the village now that the political part of the job was over, and happy to be actually working with local Porgerans who wanted to help—not people like the landowner representatives, whom he called "rapist embezzlers." He much preferred to sit down with the people, most of whom were just trying to get along and raise their children. He said people loved to talk about their gardens, the great frost of 1973, and so on. It was just "the scum on the surface" that was the problem, "some prick putting a layer on it" and separating the mine from authentic and decent Porgerans. Ultimately what Geraint was unhappy about was not what was being mediated at the negotiation table, but who was doing the mediating.

THE ANAWE SPILL

With all of these issues still up in the air, the mine had the perverse good luck to be subject to a serious environmental incident. The tailings discharged by the mine's mill had overflowed the banks of the waste dump leased for them and had flowed onto land outside the Special Mining Lease territory. This was clearly, and very seriously, illegal. However, the mine responded quickly by announcing that it would "buy the land" (that is, apply for a lease to the land for mining purposes) and indemnify its owners. In fact, the mine's first move was to indemnify the owners by paying them large amounts of cash in anticipation of a lease being granted. In theory, such an action was perfectly legal—the mine was paying for land that it had not yet (but would) acquire, an expedient tactic that had been used several times before, when the engineering schedule of the mine ran ahead of the cumbersome government mechanisms for acquiring leases. When both lessor and lessee were agreed in principle, use of the land and payment for it could occur before the final lease was approved. In this case, such payments also secured landowners' satisfaction, before (perhaps) they realized that litigation could be a more lucrative route for them.

This spill—in the Anawe area—also quickly proved to be a solution to the Yakatabari impasse. Engineering reports indicated that Anawe could be the future site of a smaller waste dump that could serve as an alternative to Yakatabari. The site was less optimal technically but infinitely more attainable socially, and the damage to it had already been done. The mine began discussions with Anawe landowners that eventually were a success.

The logic of the mine's offer was simple. First, by inadvertently ruining their land, the mine had presented the landowners with a fait accompli—now that the land was already despoiled, why not gain as many benefits from it as possible? Second, Anawe landowners had never received much money from the Porgera gold mine compared to Special Mining Lease landowners—although many of them had benefited from earlier mining booms in the valley's history. Over time, they had watched themselves be eclipsed by the Special Mining Lease landowners, and their sense of jealousy was almost palpable. Living well, they decided, would be the best form of revenge. Finally, the Anawe landowners had lower expectations (and no baggage) because they had never received Special Mining Lease money. As a result they were easier to please and—despite attempts to disrupt the negotiations by agents of the Special Mining Lease landowners—they were in fact finally pleased. Negotiations for Anawe stretched on for another dozen months, and it was not until my departure from the field halfway through 2001 that the Anawe agreement was signed. I attended the negotiations for it as well, but that story is beyond the scope of this book.

With negotiations for the Anawe dump well under way, the mine officially withdrew its offer for Yakatabari on 21 September 2000. The story of Yakatabari circulated in many places and was told and retold by its participants. One of the people who pondered it the most was Guy Mascord, the British consultant the mine hired to produce the *Porgera Mine Sustainability Report: 2000* (Placer Dome Asia Pacific 2001). His long experience in Porgera gave him several ideas about how best to portray what had happened. The night before I left Porgera to return to the United States, Guy let me stay in his apartment in Suyan so that I could catch a lift to the helicopter pad the next morning. He showed me his draft of the report and asked me if I had anything to add, since by this point I was well known in the valley as the expert on the now-moot negotiations. I couldn't think of anything to add. Stripped of authorship and written in the formal third person, his narrative became the official version of the story that I quoted at the beginning of this chapter (fig. 1.1). In 2004 I flew to Australia and met some Placer executives, who told me they remembered Yakatabari as a distant and unpleasant memory that they had "moved on from." The anthropologist involved was not so lucky, however—it would take me five years of musing over the events recorded in my field notes before I could find my own way of telling the story of Yakatabari.

Conclusion

The Yakatabari negotiations allow us to see in action several of the themes that I mentioned in the introduction. First, the personal backgrounds of the negotiators on both sides of the table affected the way they personated their respective leviathans. Secondly, which leviathans existed and who represented them was often up in the air. Third, the mine's critical reliance on infrastructure like the tunnel demonstrates its vulnerability to Ipili control of even small amounts of territory. And finally, the case of Yakatabari indicates how a negotiation in Porgera can spill over to the highest levels of the Papua New Guinea government in Port Moresby. In these other spaces, actors such as "the landowners" or "the state" are portrayed as unproblematically as actors who speak with a single voice and have a clear objective in acting. As I hope to have shown in this chapter, however, is that inside the valley these leviathans are complex entities composed of multiple actors with diverse interests. Such is the nature of the dizzying realm of mine politics "on the ground."

At the same time, this chapter raises questions as well. Who are the individuals in this enormous cast of agents, civil servants, and clans? Why is it that idioms of subsistence agriculture and clan unity were the acceptable method of argument in Porgera, when they so poorly described the landowners' actual aspirations? What is the nature of Ipili kinship that led to the landowners splitting into so many factions? How did the white negotiators get to Papua New Guinea in the first place? Why do Ipili feel so cheated of revenue from the mine? We have seen that there are people jockeying for power other than the elite that I have discussed—who are they, and what other arenas exist in the valley for the pursuit of power and influence? We have seen that Port Moresby is also an arena for action that bears on the mine—what, then, occurs at the national level?

Each of the following chapters will deal with the issues raised in the course of this discussion of the Yakatabari negotiations, discussing in greater detail topics that have only been introduced here. The next chapter seeks to answer some of these questions by turning to the valley's past: What, exactly, was the nature of the shared colonial past of the negotiators involved with Yaka-tabari? How were the agreements of the late 1980s—the keystone of so much of life in the valley—established? What is the history of mining in Porgera? How did institutions like the state and the global financial market come to know the valley?

2 The Birth of Leviathans

Hobbes was driven to myth, because Leviathan has this at least in common with the immortal gods: that we know little or nothing of his childhood. That is not strange; for no god is quite immune to ridicule . . . A god must feel secure in his divinity to let himself be laughed at, and Leviathan is not sufficiently at home in heaven to allow it.
—John S. Furnivall, *The Fashioning of Leviathan*

John Furnivall, like Bruno Latour, believed leviathans gain power only by concealing the associations of which they are composed. While Latour describes, rather than endorses, the ontological claims of the leviathans he describes, Furnivall's history of British rule in Burma unmasked one leviathan's pretensions by writing a history of its origins. As Danilyn Rutherford (2012) has demonstrated, Furnivall operates in the comic mode, yoking a keen appreciation of the potency of colonial power to a deflating critique of the tenuousness of imperialism at the moment of its birth. Following Furnivall and Rutherford, this chapter takes up the analysis of Porgera's leviathans by tracing their historical origins, from "first contact" between Ipili and Australian exploratory patrols in the 1930s to the signing of the Porgera Agreements in the 1980s.

On the surface, Porgera seems ripe for a narrative lifted from the work of James Scott (1998), in which the Ipili are made increasingly legible and governable by leviathans called "the state" and "the mine." In 1938 Porgera was literally a blank space on the colonial map, but by the time of my fieldwork in 2000, it was one of the most studied places in Papua New Guinea. Mining had led to an unparalleled level of geological knowledge about the valley—a knowledge simplified by its disinterment. Anthropologists and linguists had produced accounts of Porgera's culture and language. Government and mine employees took regular censuses of the population. The mine stored land records in a computer database, cross-referenced to a digital orthophoto of the valley's topography on which every property boundary from the household to the clan level had been recorded.

Accompanying this knowledge was a variety of forms of governmentality that produced the Ipili as subjects (Foucault 2000; Pels 1997). Missionaries have spread practices such as confession and baptism that institutionalized a pastoral mode of power. The government pacified the Ipili and replaced warfare with a system of courts. Ipili working for the mine accustomed themselves to twelve-hour shifts as they became complicit in the temporal rhythms of industrial power. Ipili relocated by the mine had been given houses made of metal and wood and undergone training courses in which they were taught how to care for durable goods such as textiles and houses— how to sweep, how to cook with stoves, how to wear clothes, and how to wash their feet before they came inside. The Ipili were quite literally being domesticated. One could find misrecognition here, as the state and its capitalist partners reified Ipili customs whose complex reality escaped their high modernist gaze. One could even find resistance in Porgera: theft, corruption, and other "weapons of the weak," as well as the more straightforward strikes and industrial actions that Ipili and other Papua New Guinean mine workers have undertaken.

But such a story could be told only if one failed to enquire too closely about the actual efficacy of individuals "on the ground" and if one took seriously their pretensions to personate leviathans. As Furnivall's account of the beginning of British rule in Burma reminds us, leviathans such as the colonial government do not emerge beautiful and fully formed like Aphrodite from the sea foam. And—Morton Fried (1975) might add—neither do "tribes," which are often the result of, rather than the precursor to, the extrusion of complex polities into their peripheries. Thus in this chapter I do not tell the story of the arrival of a powerful leviathan in Porgera Valley. Instead, I describe the birth of leviathans, the way "the Ipili" and "the mine" slowly became assembled out of the personal networks of the early explorers and entrepreneurs who lived and worked in the valley. In addition I will focus on a third, less successful, leviathan: "the government," which very early on failed to establish itself authoritatively in the valley. This story of leviathans in the making is the backstory of the Yakatabari negotiations.

A key feature of these developments was the creation of what Latour calls the "paper world" (1987, 65) of documents and other artifacts that claimed to represent the truth regarding the state of affairs in the valley. These documents were a central way in which knowledge of the Ipili and Porgera's gold resources circulated outside the valley. These archival sources are thus key to understanding how "the Ipili" as a leviathan were put into a black box, and how the bureaucratic systems that standardized them as an ethnic group continue to shape perceptions of them today.

1938–49: Taylor and Black

For all intents and purposes Porgera's first contact with the outside world came on 12 September 1938 (Gammage 1998, 248), when the Australian government—personated by the Australian *kiap* James Taylor and his second in command, John Black—entered the valley during the Hagen-Sepik exploratory patrol (Gammage 1998; Golub 2001, 138–39; Jacka 2002). The patrol's purpose was to fill in the last blank spaces on the map of Papua New Guinea, and as a result it was nothing if not well documented. The work generated by the patrol includes maps, photographs, landscape paintings, anthropometric measurements, film, geologic samples, artifacts, and the pièce de résistance, Taylor's 501-page official report—the first of many texts that outsiders could read to learn about the valley without going there or meeting someone who had. But it was Black who literally put Porgera on the map, for it was he that produced a map of the patrol's route. Five feet long and two feet high, it was the first relatively accurate survey of the area between the Fly River and the Wahgi Valley (Gammage 1998, 214). Although later kiaps would make sketch maps of the area, a more definitive mapping of the valley would not occur until the 1960s.

The knowledge Taylor and Black brought back to the metropole was more a translation of local knowledge than any discovery of their own. The local guides they recruited led them over well-known routes used for long-distance trade (Mangi 1988), and their guides' influence can be seen in the ethnic and topographic names used in Taylor's report. His "ethnographic appendix" was the first writing to indicate that the Ipili were a distinct ethnic group, but he refers to them as "Hoiyamo," a generic term for "outside" or "other" people that Taylor's translator applied to the Ipili. "Ipili" would not become the name of an ethnic group until the 1950s. Taylor used it, correctly, as the name of the valley (1939, appendix 8, 7). The name "Porgera" is a neologism based on Black's mishearing of "Pongema," the name of the river that flows through the valley. Black later noted his mistake in his patrol diaries, where he wrote "PORGERA = PONGOMA" (National Library of Australia, MS 8346 Diary #11 [series 3] 29 March). Nonetheless, the name (albeit with the variation "Pogera," since the Ipili language is unused to consonant clusters) stuck and continues to stick to this day. The history of misunderstandings of valley life on the part of outsiders is just as long as the history of the valley's contact with the wider world.

Of course, some of Taylor and Black's discoveries were genuinely novel, chief among them being the discovery of gold in the valley. In the course of their patrol the two men split up, and Taylor passed quickly through the lower portion of the valley in September 1938 without discovering gold (Gammage 1998, 131–32). It was only when Black traveled through Porgera six months later, on 25 March 1939, that he discovered what Taylor had missed. Black's patrol routinely prospected for gold, and many of its members came from areas on the coast where gold had been worked in the past. One of them, Porti, first found gold in the Pongema River where Black had set up camp. Excited, Black prolonged his stay in the valley for a few extra days to prospect (Gammage 1998: 188–89). When he and Taylor returned to the valley at the end of their patrol, they traced the gold much closer to its source, at Kakai Creek, quite near the Yunarilama portal area. For all intents and purposes, the history of Porgera's entanglement with the world was from the very beginning a history of gold. Taylor's official report noting the presence of gold at Porgera indicated that the field was not "feasible"— despite the presence of gold nuggets the size of pebbles, its distance from urban centers made working Porgera more trouble than it was worth.

Knowledge about Porgera did not circulate only in the form of a paper world of representations preserved in texts. Alongside these official reports was the informal circle of expatriates known as "territorians." White society in New Guinea was a very small world, and Black and Taylor were at the center of it. Knowledge about Porgera thus had a double life, circulating through the territorian grapevine as well as the paper world of government reports. As it happened, it was the former kind of knowledge that would continue to influence the valley's history. Black and Taylor's report was suppressed when World War II broke out, for fear that it could provide the Japanese with information about the interior of the island, and coastal knowledge of Porgera was largely restricted to word of mouth and the internal bureaucracy of the territory.

As a result, invitations to Porgera's global coming-out party were distributed by word of mouth. The territorian grapevine was one informal network of people who knew about Taylor and Black's patrol, but there was another: the indigenous guides and translators who had accompanied the patrol. Taylor and Black were not just the people who repackaged indigenous knowledge into colonial texts; their patronage also created a personalistic society of middlemen that allowed ambitious highlanders to parlay their knowledge and expertise with whites into prosperity for themselves and their families. Beneath the paper world of patrol documentation, the Taylor-Black patrol helped crystallize a small but influential network of people, both black and white, who specialized in Porgera. Even as late as the 1950s kiaps on patrol into Porgera chose guides who had been there with Taylor and Black.

The centrality of Porgera's small world can be seen if we return to Taylor's ethnographic appendix: his correct use of the word "Ipili" as the name of a place rather than an ethnic group comes from "vocabulary obtained from GWARA of Ibiri" (1939, appendix 8, 7). "GWARA" was Kuala Laipia, a young man who joined Taylor's patrol in Porgera and returned with it to Hagen. From his start as a terrified teenage boy in 1938, Kuala would go on to leverage his knowledge of the outside world for all it was worth, becoming a businessman, gold dealer, and polygynist. Fifty years later his son would become a powerful figure in Papua New Guinea's trade union movement, at one point dining with Fidel Castro in Havana, and his granddaughter would allegedly be raped by Benjamin Lawane at a critical stage of the Yakatabari negotiations.

The Strickland Syndicate

World War II slowed the development of connections between indigenous and expatriate networks, and the valley was patrolled only once between 1938 and 1948. In 1945 the improbably named Captain Neptune Beresford Newcomb Blood (National Archives of Australia B883 PX169) led an exploratory patrol into the valley—ostensibly to find and rescue downed Allied airmen, although it is likely that Blood, an amateur ornithologist, organized the patrol chiefly because he yearned to conduct a grand exploratory patrol in the style of Taylor and Black to collect undiscovered bird of paradise species. Accompanying him on the patrol was William MacGregor, an experienced prospector who had heard of Porgera's gold through the territorian grapevine and wanted to have a look himself. Records of Blood's patrol were largely lost during the war, and it was again the territorian grapevine—personated in this case by MacGregor—that kept the explorers' work alive and efficacious. Unlike Taylor and Black, MacGregor considered Porgera a rich prospect—so rich, in fact, that he abandoned Blood's patrol after testing Porgera's waters and headed back to plan his own trip into the valley.

By the spring of 1949 MacGregor was ready to lead a large-scale prospecting patrol into Porgera, sponsored by Bulolo Gold Dredging. Before the war Bulolo had been a major gold producer central to the economy of what was then the trust territory of New Guinea (Healy 1967). Its facilities had been destroyed by retreating Australian forces in order to deny them to the Japanese, and the Porgera patrol was sold to the territorial administration as an opportunity to help rebuild the company and New Guinea's postwar economy. At the time Bulolo Gold Dredging was owned by Placer Gold— the company that would eventually operate the Porgera gold mine.

The Bulolo Gold Dredging expedition was slow to get started due to its size and complexity, and news of its plans spread. A group of expatriates— including the brothers Michael and Dan Leahy, the group's main instigators; Neptune Blood and John Black, who had both been to Porgera; Joseph Searson, a kiap who had legal training and had worked with Dan Leahy during the war; and Doug Elphinstone, a pilot who could provide air support—formed a business group called the Strickland Syndicate and decided to organize a preemptive strike into Porgera to stake claims before MacGregor's patrol could reach the valley. The syndicate needed special permits to enter what was then known as "uncontrolled" territory, and it got them from Jim Taylor, who was both the officer in charge of the area and a close friend of every member of the syndicate. Blood and Searson, still officially kiaps, submitted identical, one-line resignation letters a day before the patrol set off (these letters and other documents about the syndicate discussed in this section can be found in National Library of Australia, MS 8346 Series 7, Folder 1). Appropriately certified, the syndicate's members sped off to the edge of controlled territory to await the date the administration had set for when prospecting in Porgera would become legal—1 April 1949.

The punctilious acting director of the Department of District Services and Native Affairs, Ivan Champion, was furious when he heard that two of his men had resigned to pursue a frolic of their own. He also felt that their permits had been issued illegally—although on what basis is not clear (National Archives of Papua New Guinea 458 LF 555). The fact that Champion was part of the Papuan civil service and Taylor was part of the rival New Guinea service probably did not help. As a result, the nearest patrol post was radioed, and a cadet patrol officer was instructed to march out to the syndicate's camp at the edge of uncontrolled territory and order the men to return.

When the patrol officer arrived at the camp on 31 March 1949, he found himself face to face with some of the most experienced patrol officers in New Guinea, the very people whose travel writings and popular accounts of their journeys had influenced young men such as himself to sign up with the New Guinea service in the first place. Faced with such opposition, his attempt to personate the government failed. Searson, the group's legal expert, pointed out that the syndicate had met all legal formalities and suggested that the scrap of paper with pencil notes from a wireless transmission that the patrol officer claimed were from Champion—items without a seal or signature—hardly constituted an official signal from the acting director of the Department of District Services and Native Affairs. Michael Leahy suggested that the entire incident was an elaborate April Fool's joke. The patrol officer, the group decided, was not personating the government, but impersonating it. They marched on to Porgera.

By the time Champion flew to Wabag, the nearest airstrip, to deal with matters himself, the syndicate was already on its way back to Porgera, hat in hand. Sure enough, the results were as Taylor and Black had predicted: both the syndicate and the Bulolo patrol—when it eventually got there—decided that the valley was not feasible. Searson decided to stay on and try his luck in Porgera, the Leahys returned to their businesses, Black went south to start a farm, and Blood became the head of an experimental sheep farm funded by an Australian refrigerator magnate (Baglin 1988; Blood 1949).

As brief as this incident was, it was a structural conjuncture (Sahlins 1985) that was to have profound repercussions in the history of the valley. This first, failed attempt to govern gold mining in the valley both inaugurated and epitomized a long history of tenuous relations between law, personation, and power in Porgera. From then on, a distant metropole would claim for itself an authority and force to structure life in the valley that it never quite had in actuality. Yet it is not as if the members of the syndicate denied the power or legitimacy of the state. They followed the letter of the law and hoped to fend off a large multinational mining company by establishing a prior legal claim to the land. The state's power was not ignored by the syndicate— indeed, it hoped to use that power for its own purposes. Rather, what counted as order and who counted as the state was up for negotiation. It was not the last time that access to Porgera's gold would hinge on such a dynamic.

Porgera as an "Uncontrolled" Area

From 1948 to 1962 Porgera was officially a "restricted" area. The idea was an old one, although the term was new. Former colonial regimes had long labeled interior areas of the island "uncontrolled," making them off-limits for all whites except government employees and those who successfully applied for special permits. The newer, face-saving term "restricted" was used to accomplish the same goals as the old term: to maintain the safety of whites (who were vulnerable to indigenous violence), to protect blacks (who were vulnerable to illnesses introduced by whites), and to protect the administration (which lacked the capacity to exert any real control over these territories).

Uncontrolled areas were meant to be slowly pacified by repeated patrolling. Kiaps based at government stations in controlled areas led semiannual patrols into restricted areas and attempted to stop violence, heal sick people, take censuses, and distribute steel tools. Eventually patrols would find a suitable location for a new government station and airstrip, the area around it would be derestricted, and the process would be repeated. By 1952 administrative responsibility for Porgera had moved west from Goroka to Hagen, Hagen to Wabag, and finally from Wabag to Laiagam. As a result, between 1948 and 1962 the government's presence in Porgera was restricted to a small number of patrols. Although the kiaps on these patrols were not particularly knowledgeable about life in the valley, it was their understandings of who "the Ipili" were and what they were like that were recorded and disseminated in the paper world.

The government was not particularly successful at census taking, mapping, pacification, and its other duties. On the whole, Porgerans viewed state representatives as powerful but easily fooled individuals who could be manipulated to serve local ends—a lesson they would not forget about a circumstance that would not change. The early Ipili attitude to the government is best summarized by J. R. Hicks in his remarks about patrolling into Paiela in the early 1960s: "Concerning the ethos of the Pai'ela [sic] people I gradually came to the conclusion that he regards himself as a superior being to the European, in fact as being superior to any other race of people. The superior material possessions and powers of Europeans are nonchalantly passed away as being essential to the white man for him to survive, whereas he, the Pai'ela, needs only a garden of sweet potato, his axe and a bow to exist" (PR Porgera 1 of 1965/65, J. R. Hicks). Throughout this period Ipili attempted to co-opt government patrols for their own internal political ends while satisfying government demands for pacification through simple dissembling. In 1952 B. Corrigan wrote: "The Ivi [Ipili] are now happily at peace. Not so very many years ago the Ivi were from time to time devastated by the hordes from the upper and lower reaches of the Porgera . . . the last raid of any consequence took place some years ago ... unless there is a conspiracy to conceal crime, and this I very much doubt, everyone seems to be living in harmony and are [*sic*] at peace" (PR Laiagam 5 of 1951/52, B. R. Corrigan). In fact, it appears that exactly such a conspiracy of concealment was in place and had succeeded. Two years after Corrigan's patrol, Denys Faithful recorded that "the natives still live dangerously. They are continually having intertribal fights. During a court sitting made on the Patrol we heard that the habit of these natives is as follows. When Europeans are in the area they discard their arms. When Europeans leave the area they all carry them again" (PR Laiagam 1 of 1954/55, D. E. Faithful). "Law and order" could be turned into a tactic in vendettas. In 1960 Graeme Hogg noted that "it has apparently been the usual practice for murderers to give themselves up in order to escape the local consequence of their actions—pay-back killings. Not only does Perari's [a murderer's] evasion of the patrol introduce new tactics to the locally accepted norm in such cases, he also exhibits the ease with which malefactors may escape the long arm of the law in such areas such as this" (PR Laiagam 4 of 1956/60, G. J. Hogg).

This period of patrols also resulted in the first anthropological knowledge about the valley. In February 1957 Mervyn Meggitt accompanied a government patrol into Porgera as part of his larger project of mapping the ethnic groups of Enga Province. The ethnographic report he attached to the patrol report was published in *Oceania* (1957), and this piece, the first published scholarship on the valley, had a defining effect. The ethnic identity of Porgerans and place names in the valley were hazy before Meggitt's trip. After it, official reports adopted "Ipili" as the name of an ethnic group and "Porgera" as the name of the valley itself. Only native police continued to refer to the Ipili as the "Ipi."

If the government was noticeable largely by its absence, the same could not be said for miners. The fact that white men—and, soon, black men— would come to Porgera to work gold meant that the valley's history would differ from that of the rest of the province. Despite the attempts of distant government whites to control and regulate Porgera, it would be the miners on the ground who would come to know Porgera and its people. Throughout the 1950s, a small group of expatriates emerged who worked Porgera's gold and relied on their own personal ties to keep their operations feasible. These small-world connections continue to have ramifications today: James Taylor was the kiap who accompanied Michael and Dan Leahy during their initial exploration of the Mt. Hagen area. Later Dan married two sisters from Hagen while Taylor settled down in Goroka with his own Papua New Guin-

govt absence
miners' presence

ean wife. Joseph Searson had served with Dan Leahy during World War II and sent his own interracial son to live with Dan and his children in Hagen. Searson worked leases in Porgera that were later transferred to Taylor, and Dan's nephews were the main gold buyers in Porgera when I lived there. Meg Taylor, James's daughter and a former ambassador to the United States, visited Porgera as a child; in Goroka, she played polo with George Brugh, whose Australian father oversaw Searson's leases and whose mother was Porgeran. George Brugh's wife's brother was also his overseer, and he and his sons were close friends of mine in Porgera.

It was these networks of kinship and consociation—intensely personal and often incestuously small—that were responsible for so much of the action that occurred in the highlands. Oftentimes, the government officers who officially made the valley "legible" were on the edge of these networks. This was to become one of the enduring traits of Porgeran history: personal ties, sometimes dressed up as official ones, were central to the valley's entanglement with wider networks of power and knowledge. The kiaps generated the texts about Porgera that would circulate at the urban center, but it was the middlemen who made facts "on the ground."

It all began when Searson, a member of the Strickland Syndicate, decided to try his hand working gold in Porgera, becoming the first person to stake a claim and the only white man to live in highland New Guinea between Wabag and Telefomin. Searson took up two leases, one at the junction of the Kaiyia and the Pongema Rivers (where Black had first discovered gold) and another on the Kakai (where Taylor and Black had set up a sluice when they returned to the valley). Soon Jim Brugh, George's father, began working the Kakai claim on Searson's behalf while he lived and worked on the Pongema.

On paper, the laws governing Searson's leases were straightforward: any expatriate with a mining license, which was easily obtained, could stake claims on land after submitting a simple one-page form and a sketch map of the area in question. Miners also lodged a cash deposit with the local kiap, who could distribute it to "natives" (a legal term) as compensation for any damage done to their land by the miners. There were no cadastral records— land was under customary ownership and was inalienable—and leases were issued based on the kiap's judgment, rather than the landowner's consent.

Legal details would shift over time, but these changes had little effect on the realities of gold mining in the valley: teams of workers, each typically containing about two dozen men, worked alluvial deposits in gangs, forcing water through sluices and breaking up larger rocks with crowbars and hammers. The ore that resulted was put into empty coffee cans. When a coffee can was filled—which typically took two months or so—it would be taken to a white man who would pay the workers for it in textiles, axes, machetes, and (in the early period) shells. These work groups were overseen by a group of Papua New Guinean men who could communicate with whites using Tok Pisin. Although these men were sometimes Porgeran, many were not. In addition to the Gorokans whom Searson and Brugh left in charge of their camps when they left the valley to get more supplies, there was also a group of Enga and Huli men who used their ability as translators and guides to establish a local power base in Porgera.

Kinship and business relations were interconnected in other ways. Between 1948 and 1951 Searson lived in Porgera with an Engan woman, and Brugh was soon—without his Australian wife's knowledge—to take up residence with a Porgeran woman, the sister of one of his foremen. The steel axes, machetes, and shells that Brugh and Searson used to pay their workers were turned into bride-price, although it is not clear if these white interlopers were aware that helping a young man amass bride-price was customarily the role of an older brother or uncle. What is clear is that Ipili immediately understood the confluence of kinship and business and worked hard to supply women to the powerful white outsiders who came to live with them. The personalistic network in Porgera was thickening.

Searson left Porgera in order to make a go of farming when the first agricultural leases in Goroka were issued in 1951 (Downs 1980, 179). He was tired of the incredible work it was necessary to put into mining gold in Porgera, and of the minimal returns that resulted. His leases on the Kaiyia were transferred to Taylor, now a private citizen and Goroka coffee farmer. In 1957 Brugh—who had lost his hand while trying to save his dog from a stick of lit dynamite it had unwisely chosen to fetch—slipped and fell during the course of one of the fearsome walks he periodically took from Porgera to Laiagam to buy supplies. Thrusting his stump into the ground, he swore that the small round hole it left was the last Porgera would ever see of him (George Brugh, personal communication). He left to pursue coffee farming in Goroka as well and took his two children with him. By 1957, then, the valley was empty of whites, and although Taylor remains a figure of myth and might for Porgerans, he was largely an absentee landlord.

Papua New Guineans who had previously been translators and guides quickly filled the void, and now it was they who mediated between the Ipili, whose labor was necessary to wrest gold from Porgera's rivers, and the distant whites, who purchased the gold they worked. These new, indigenous middlemen were responsible for keeping Porgera's alluvial gold mining feasible: they kept the peace, kept the workers working, and made sure that the gold got to market. They conceived of themselves as middlemen who bridged a gap between two different cultures even as they became the creators of a third. The origins of these men varied. Some, like Kuala, had left Porgera with Black and Taylor. Others had come over from Paiela. But the group's core consisted of Huli whom Dan Leahy had taken out of Tari in 1945, when he was an officer in New Guinea's military administration. These Huli included men like Ipape Papume, whose son served as District Administrator during the Yakatabari negotiations; Busane, who settled on land that would eventually become the mouth of the Yunitilama portal; and, especially, Tongope, who oversaw Taylor's operations. Tongope quickly became one of the most important men in the valley, setting standards still emulated today for wearing clothes, eating canned fish, and using his power and wealth to marry multiple wives. As Huli, these men came from a dominant ethnic group whose language Porgerans could speak, and they were also familiar with Tok Pisin. Often they did not learn Ipili. Tongope's Ipili, for instance, never became very good.

These new middlemen also began working gold for themselves. In May 1958 Puluku Poke became the first Papua New Guinean to deal in Porgera's gold when he traveled to Laiagam and sold 14.4 ounces of fine gold to the kiap there, who weighed it out on a postage scale (National Archives of Papua New Guinea Lands Department, Accession 52, Box 3025, MF 57/7/1). Puluku was raised in Paiela and had traveled to Goroka with Searson, whose domestic servant he had been. After watching indigenous small-scale mining in the eastern highlands, he returned to Porgera and began mining in the lower part of the valley. Another miner, Pawe Lembopa, was soon to follow. He was an Engan who had been taken from his family as a child and trained by whites as a medical orderly. After traveling around, he too saw gold being worked by indigenous people, and when he settled down in Porgera he began working gold as well. By 1962, when the valley was derestricted, over twenty men had licenses to work gold and sell it to the government.

Indigenous people had been working gold in Papua New Guinea since the late 1890s (Nelson 1976, 41), and by the 1950s the government's official policy was to encourage small-scale mining. It introduced Papua New Guineans to the cash economy, accustomed them to a work ethic that was considered civilizing, and facilitated the exploitation of marginal prospects that were unprofitable for whites. In 1957 the Department of Mining estimated that there were 5,000 "native" miners in Papua New Guinea, centered mostly on fields in Sepik, Morobe, and Bougainville. Apart from a different method of registration, the regulations that governed native miners were more or less identical to those governing white miners. Natives could apply for the same sorts of leases as whites, could sell gold in the same way as whites, and were bound by the same forms of adjudication under the mining warden.

In 1959 Puluku brought another parcel of gold to Laiagam for sale. This one was worth £547 (National Archives of Papua New Guinea 52 3025). This was too large an amount to be ignored, and the kiap suspected that Puluku was illegally working gold on one of the leases held by Taylor. Puluku was flown to Mt. Hagen—a remarkable experience for someone who had grown up in Porgera in the 1930s and 1940s—where his case was heard by a judge. Puluku explained that he was working an area below Taylor's. He was acquitted, and a patrol was designated to visit Porgera to stake the limits of his claim (NAPNG 52 3025). Unfortunately, the trip into the valley was so grueling that by the time the mining warden reached Porgera he had become "a medical casualty through badly blistered feet, and was unable to assist in the field work" (National Archives of Papua New Guinea Lands Department, Accession 52, Box 3025, MF 57/7/1). Once again, the government's exercise of power was defeated by the fallibility of its personators.

After Puluku's success others imitated him, and there was increasing competition between indigenous gold miners. By May 1960 the situation had become so convoluted that a *kiap* noted that it had "degenerated into a seething mass of intrigue" (PR Laiagam 4 of 1956/60 G.J.H.). When he arrived in Porgera, he was besieged with requests for exclusive permission to work gold in various parts of the valley. He ducked the issue, arguing that these claims had to be adjudicated by a mining warden. This happened two months later, with the arrival of another patrol that included the chief of the Department of Mining and N. C. Robinson, the native field assistant for mining.

The court case at issue boiled down to a rivalry between Puluku and Kuala, Taylor and Black's interpreter in 1939. Both Puluku and Kuala said they had legitimate claims to the same area of the Pongema. However, neither was a native "landowner"—Kuala was an Engan who had lived briefly with distant relatives elsewhere in Porgera before joining Taylor and Black, and although Puluku had distant consanguinal ties to the land in question, he was originally from Paiela.

Under the law, indigenous rights to mining leases were based on being the first to stake a claim to a particular area, not on being the indigenous owners of that claim. Thus Puluku and other miners couched their claim to work gold in the same colonial framework that whites used to expropriate land from Papua New Guineans—yet another example of the repurposing of the law in order to shape it to local ends. The result of the case was a decision that was extremely appropriate to Porgera's rapidly emerging history of rule by compromise. After a period of negotiation, it was decided that Puluku would divide his claim into several smaller areas and give other miners the right to work them in exchange for a one-time payment of £30 per claim. A report on the case noted:

> The apparent "sale" of portions of Puruk's [Puluku's] claim is not in accordance with the Mining or other Ordinances relating to transfer of land, but it does conform to local indigenous conceptions of compensation. To have redistributed the claim without requiring compensation would have implied official sanction to the illegal pressures applied by the applicant miners. Reports of all previous patrols to the Porgera, and the report of an anthropological study agree in reference to killing and violence as the common method of adjusting disputes. In view of this it was felt that the duty of this patrol lay in the resolution of tension rather than in the illustration of a system of law foreign to the concepts of such primitive people. The actions taken to resolve the tension were frankly expedient measures, to be interpreted within the existing local concepts of justice rather than in relation to existing statutory legislation. (National Archives of Papua New Guinea 52 3025)

This was not only expedient, but also precedent. The case taught Porgerans that the law of the government was something that could be negotiated with and not merely submitted to, and it taught the government to couch novel and expedient legal arrangements in terms of "local indigenous conceptions." As would happen again and again in the history of the valley, an arrangement would be made that would keep mining in the valley feasible, and a narrative would be created afterward that would tell a story of law, legality, and the state to distant whites. The intervention of the mining warden marked the introduction of a new layer of administration to the valley, but not necessarily another layer of control. By the time the Porgera mine had to be negotiated into existence, Ipili had been litigating against each other and outsiders for three decades. The Ipili experience with government, then, taught them to see the personator, not the leviathan.

Derestriction

The Porgera airstrip was completed on 15 May 1961, and the Porgera government station was officially upgraded from an outpost to a permanent patrol post on 1 July 1962 (PR Laiagam 4 of 1960/61 KGO O'Brien). This meant that Porgera was no longer a restricted area—a kiap would be stationed there at all times, and whites could come and go from the valley without applying for a special permit. The result was a growth in preaching and prospecting, as Christianity and intensive gold mining took hold in the valley. Both of these trends marked an increasing regimentation of knowledge about the valley, although the personalistic dimension of feasibility did not fade away.

In the 1960s gold mining had expanded in scope. Taylor's leases were still functioning under Tongope's direction. The number of small-scale miners also grew, as did their regulation by the administration. Robinson, the native field assistant for mining, visited the valley bimonthly, and a permanent native mining warden was also stationed there. This man was Ludwig "Ludi" Schmidt Jr., whose father was the infamous Austrian prospector Ludwig Schmidt, the only white man ever to be hanged in Papua New Guinea (Mennis 1979). On paper, the younger Schmidt was the representative of a leviathan. In practice, he was a middleman whose power in the valley hinged on his ability to interface with both distant whites and players in the local power scene. He soon became part of the growing Porgeran high society of middlemen—as shown by the fact that he moved in with Searson, who had given up on coffee in Goroka and returned to Porgera to pursue large-scale mining. Now that Porgera was derestricted, Searson could take out exploration leases and court large companies interested in working his claims. Like many before him, Ludi Schmidt would develop relationships with Porgeran women, and his son by one of them worked for the mine during my time in the valley. The mining warden was not only the official face of the law, but his romantic liaisons with local women also made him an affine in the minds of many prominent Porgerans.

Theoretically, increased government control also meant increased government knowledge. In fact, official state projects often had little or no effect on life in Porgera, and knowledge of the valley continued to be relatively circumscribed. It was in the 1960s, for instance, that the first definitive mapping of the valley took place (probably in 1962), when the Division of National Mapping of the Department of National Development of Australia surveyed the highlands as part of a project to make a complete set of 1:100,000 topographical maps of Papua New Guinea (Sinclair 2001, 291–92). These maps continue to be used today throughout Papua New Guinea and are readily available from the country's National Mapping Bureau.

A classic form of colonial control (Anderson 1991, chapter 10), mapping proved to be relatively unimportant to life in the valley, and informal knowledge continued to be central to life on Porgera. For instance, aviation in New Guinea relied on the skilled pilots rather than maps. Pilots who flew from Laiagam to Porgera Station or the Kolombi strip in Paiela followed routes that were obvious and dictated by the extreme geography of the area. Typically, aviators would circle Laiagam as they gained altitude and then enter Porgera through a well-known pass. In cases of inclement weather (which was not uncommon), there was a southern route known as the "bad weather" route (Barnard 1969, 88–89). Ground travel was also relatively unaffected by mapping. The traditional trade route used by Ipili to travel from the western edge of the valley to the salt springs at Pipiraka had been used by Taylor and Black and continued to be used by people traveling in and out of the valley. It was well known and relatively well traversed, but various attempts to turn the rough bush track into a road were essentially unsuccessful—the terrain was simply too rugged. There were some well-developed roads within the valley, but even after the first official "road" was constructed going into the valley, the first car in Porgera had to be carried in on peoples' shoulders. Flying, rather than walking, became the main method of entering and leaving the valley. Thus, despite the panoptic potentialities of a new regime of mapping, informality continued to reign in Porgera.

The prospecting that began in the 1960s expanded in the 1970s. Mt. Isa Mines took up rights to drill on Searson's leases and began a medium-scale alluvial operation intended to offset exploration costs. As would often be the case in Porgera's history, the individual person on the ground, rather than a leviathan, was the one who had a large impact on the valley. Rudi Jezernik, a Czech national, became Mt. Isa's man on the spot, and he lived in the valley for the next fifteen years. Jezernik became a member of Porgera's high society and constituted one of the main links in the social networks that flowed through Porgera. Local people who brought gold to him to be weighed and assayed were technically operating on a tributary basis. But as far as they were concerned, Jezernik was merely another gold buyer like Searson and Brugh before him. Porgerans did not connect his personation of Mt. Isa Mines to his role as owner and operator of the alluvial workings where they also occasionally worked. Nor were they particularly aware of the fact that he was the representative of a foreign business, which seemed to them mostly to be a foreign name with no strong influence in the valley.

Between Jezernik, Schmidt, the local kiap, and the Catholic missionary in the area, the valley became more and more tightly engaged with institutions that existed beyond its borders. The Catholic priest also administered first aid, making him similar to the government medical orderlies from whom

Porgerans received medical treatment. In addition he opened—at their request—one of the first stores in the valley.

By the 1970s, then, there was a small but significant expatriate elite in Porgera. Their presence indicated the success of distant leviathans in gaining traction in the valley, but that power was based on the fact that their representatives were part of a tight-knit, face-to-face community. This community's solidarity was evinced in its commensality: a small private club was built on the crest of the Warokari summit and christened the Porgera Heights Country Club. In the end this institution showed the limits of community and intimacy, however. Originally members could simply take beers from the refrigerator, put a mark by their name on a list, and settle their account later, but soon people were putting marks by other people's names, and Jezernik was forced to actively tend bar. In sum, outside forces such as companies and governments still relied on the distinct character and personality of their representatives in order to get things done in the valley.

Wealth from gold contributed to the valley's social stratification. Throughout the 1960s the Melanesian middlemen who had grown to prominence a decade earlier attempted to cement their position as elites. Puluku was the de facto ruler of the lower valley; Tongope controlled the area around Taylor's leases; and a coalition of three or four translators took power in the upper valley, around the old Kakai workings. The 1970s marked the end of this incipient elite, whose members had grown so powerful in Porgera, because more and more people were working gold, more and more of them spoke Tok Pisin, and more and more the deep-seated egalitarianism of Ipili culture began to work against the consolidated power of Porgera's middlemen. In 1971 or 1972 this was made particularly clear during the public and fantastically graphic decapitation slaying of Koeka, the father of Lyndon, the future Yakatabari negotiator.

Koeka was from Tari, but he had left that area early in his life to work gold in Porgera, where he affiliated himself with the Tiyini clan on the basis of shared residence and a tenuous genealogical tie—his father's mother's brother's wife's mother was Tiyini. Koeka rose to power on the basis of his forceful personality and his ability to speak Tok Pisin—a rarity at the time. He soon had his fingers in all of Porgera's pies: he was appointed *luluai* (headman) by the government and was one of the first seventeen local miners to receive a lease from Robinson in 1960. In addition, Koeka used polygamy to thicken his social networks: marrying into Paiela, establishing ties with Tongope by marrying his wife's sister, and giving wives to both Schmidt and Searson (Searson actually married two of them), who lived on Tiyini land.

Koeka's extensive personal network also included "Chief" Ambi Kipu (the future Yakatabari negotiator), who occupied a similar role as leader of the Tuanda at Apalaka. Together Koeka and "Chief" Ambi exerted enormous power over the people of the upper valley.

In the end, Koeka became too successful, and some Tiyini hatched a plot to equalize power in the region. During pandanus season, someone stole some of Koeka's pandanus nuts from trees growing in the upper rain forest—an egregious act in Porgera, where pandanus was highly valued. Koeka was outraged. A group of young men from the area were framed for the act, and Koeka scheduled a public hearing to deal with them. He began the proceedings in full form, laying out his claim to the trees from which the nuts had been stolen. According to Ambi, when Koeka claimed that the land where the trees were located was his own, a young man named Kakale, a cousin of Koeka, stood up and pretended to be outraged. He claimed the land was his, not Koeka's. Without further ado, he took his axe and struck Koeka on the neck. To the surprise of all present, Koeka remained standing and, although partially decapitated and bleeding heavily, said to Kakale: "Do you think I am a woman? Come here and fight me!" Then he walked over to Ambi, put his hand on Ambi's shoulder and asked for his help, and fell dead.

Ipili are not the most level-headed people at the best of times, and this shocking turn of events galvanized the entire area. Even Searson and Schmidt are reported to have rushed to get their guns to avenge Koeka's death. However, as people say today, Kakale had "merely swung the axe"—the real killers of Koeka were the Tiyini who had planned his death. Knowing that they could not kill Koeka and let Ambi live, the conspirators spread the rumor that Ambi had planned Koeka's death and had held Koeka down while Kakale cut him. They leaked this news to the Pulumaini, Koeka's affines. Ambi was surprised, then, when a Pulumaini, supposedly one of his allies, gave him a full-on blow to the head with his machete. Ambi's head was split open—by all accounts his brain was visible—and he would have died if Les Barnard, a Seventh-Day Adventist missionary and amateur pilot, had not been visiting the station with his Cessna. Ambi was carried to the airstrip and became the first Porgeran ever to be medevaced out of the valley. The large scar above his eyebrow from the blow was visible when he spoke at the Yakatabari negotiations.

The death of Koeka is a dramatic story, but it is also important in understanding the history of the valley. It made Koeka's sons landowners—most notably Lyndon, who seized Kakale's land after he fled to Paiela to avoid revenge—a move that would pave the way for their rise to prominence during the late 1980s and 1990s. Even more important, the death of Koeka was a visible sign that middlemen had failed to institutionalize inequality in the valley. As accommodating as Ipili were, deeply held agnatic claims worked to keep life in the valley egalitarian. Throughout the 1970s, power shifted from a few key middlemen to an amorphous web of local notables whose fortunes were often in flux. During the next twenty years Porgera would have a pool of possible leaders from which it could draw, rather than an elite with which it would have to deal.

Placer and Exploration

In 1980 Placer Gold (as it was known before its merger with Dome Mines) joined a business group exploring Porgera and became its principal partner. This altered the course of the valley's history. Placer could bring to bear resources—both human and financial—that would ultimately result in the creation of the mine and mark the start of a new era for the valley. The situation the company faced was not good: a consultancy report suggested that a large-scale mine in Porgera was not feasible because the valley was too distant for its ore to be processed elsewhere, and on-site refining processes created too much pollution (Jackson and Banks 2002, 111–14). In order to make the mine feasible, the exploration team would need to become socially feasible: more prospecting meant more drilling, more compensation, and more entanglement in the valley's local affairs. Additional expertise would have to be brought to bear.

It was rough in the beginning. In the early 1980s Placer hired Ian Smalley, a former kiap turned consultant, to conduct a census. Even by the standards of previous census work in the valley, Smalley's work was particularly inaccurate. Smalley took genealogies of one clan at a time, then added up the results. Since clan membership is not exclusive in Porgera, most people in the census were counted multiple times. The result was that Smalley estimated the population of the valley to be 30,000 people when it was widely acknowledged that the true population could not be more than 10,000. One of the earliest critics of Smalley's work was Philip Gibbs, a Catholic missionary in the valley who had a postgraduate degree in anthropology (1975) and who became, in essence, the first anthropologist to conduct extended fieldwork in Porgera. Gibbs approached the company and asked to help create a more accurate record. The genealogies that resulted proved to be highly accurate and formed the basis for the mine's—but not the government's—records of who "the landowners" were in Porgera.

Here again we see a situation in which a local person is able to transform knowledge gained through informal mechanisms into a text artifact that could be used in distant circles for official purposes. Gibbs's methodology was simple and relied as much on his anthropological training as it did on his engagement with the local community: he asked the dozen or so men who were acknowledged leaders and expert genealogists to come to his house in Mungalep. There, over the course of fifteen hours—with breaks for food, cigarettes, and the bathroom—they enumerated their entire "clans," starting with an apical ancestor and ending with the current generation of children. Gibbs did one clan a day. The entire process took a week and a half.

Social feasibility required more than just a census. Placer needed someone to organize its greatly enlarged exploration camp and to mediate between the exploration crews and local Ipili—someone, in short, to personate it in Porgera, thus undertaking in a transformed and expanded role the same task originally performed by Tongope and other early middlemen. This logistically complex task was turned over to Mick Searson, the son of Joe Searson and a woman from Sirunki. She had run away from Searson while she was pregnant, and Mick had been raised in the village. He had been one of the first students at the University of Papua New Guinea but, like his father, he grew restless and dropped out, roaming over Papua New Guinea and working in construction, aviation, and coffee farming. Between 1974 and 1976 he worked with Jezernik in Porgera, and he was brought back to work as the camp manager for Placer in 1980.

Mick's ties were multiple. Half white and half black, Mick was technically an Engan but was—and continues to be during my fieldwork—considered by everyone in Porgera to be Ipili, and particularly a Tiyini. When members of the Porgera Landowners Association faction went to Port Moresby to attend the association's court case about the Yakatabari tunnel, it was Mick who picked them up at the airport and gave them a ride to court. Although non-Porgeran Papua New Guineans had often worked as middlemen before, Mick was different: as a "mixed blood," educated Papua New Guinean, he was emblematic of the way that whites' knowledge of the Ipili and Ipili knowledge of whites were blending together. His ability to move fluidly between both cultural worlds essentially collapsed the space between them. He became a role model for future Porgerans who would serve as the interface between the Ipili and the mine (and vice versa), such as the District Administrator from Yakatabari and especially Jonathan Paraia, discussed below. By combining a multitude of different skills, Mick became a vital part of the reality management pool working in the valley during the 1980s, making sure that work could go forward by making sure that the story of "what was going on" was shared by both Ipili and outsiders.

Throughout the early 1980s, then, knowledge of the Ipili and their valley solidified but was still spotty—a fact both caused and symbolized by the method of exploration used: clearing small spots of land on which portable diamond drills would take rock samples. Placer's knowledge of Porgerans— who owned a particular piece of land, what sort of compensation they had received, where their land was located, and what their clan affiliation was— closely paralleled its knowledge of the gold resource: every sample spot on the prospecting map corresponded to a compensation claim and land-holding record. And just as prospectors attempted to deduce the geological makeup of the mountain through a few small samples, each one of these compensation claims build up a set of haphazard precedents and expectations about Ipili social life, landholding patterns, and identities.

The future of the valley changed in 1986 with the discovery of a high-grade zone of gold in Porgera. This discovery catapulted the mine into financial feasibility while also demonstrating the challenges to social feasibility that a large-scale mine would face: the Porgerans hired to dig the exploration trench where the vein was discovered smeared mud on the walls of the trench to keep it secret from their supervisor so that they could take the ore out themselves, and it took some time for managers to discover their deception. It was now clear that a large-scale mine in Porgera would be technically feasible, and the question then became its social and legal feasibility. When paying individuals under an exploration license, the company dealt with individuals. Now that the company sought a special mining lease, it would have to deal with a corporate group, the leviathan known as "traditional landowners."

The informal network of middlemen, their sons, present and former kiaps, and mine employees now had to be supplemented with a series of paper accounts of landownership that could circulate in both Vancouver and Port Moresby. Although previously miners and local powerbrokers had relied on face-to-face communication and personal knowledge of the individuals involved with mining, the people in the distant metropoles responsible for creating the mine needed a slew of text artifacts that described what the Ipili were like, and indicated that life in the valley was structured in ways that external forces considered legal and ethical. When Placer started feasibility studies for the Porgera gold mine in 1987, the number and kind of stories circulating about the Ipili increased in both quantity and quality.

Perhaps the two most important documents written during the late 1980s were the social and economic impact assessment (SEIS) and the land study. The SEIS was a two-volume study conducted by Pacific Agribusiness (1987) based on six weeks of research. Despite its purpose as the authoritative document on which future knowledge about the valley would be based, it is not regarded as one of the most thorough accounts of the valley. There was no anthropologist or sociologist on the team of consultants that created the document, and the section on Ipili culture and social organization consisted of a summary of Aletta Biersack's dissertation (1980). One member of the team told me: "Bob Mckillop [the head of the team] did it [the section of the report on social organization]. The origin of his knowledge was Aletta's unpublished Ph.D. Yeah, we had a special bloke to read it—I'm not kidding, it was so dense, and he said 'Ah!' You'd hear him at eleven o'clock at night: 'Ah! That's what she bloody well means!'" As John Burton has written, "asking a neophyte to stray into the ethnography of a previously unresearched society is a reckless practice" (1999, 286). His evaluation of the SEIS is quite damning: "It is very unlikely that a social impact study team, without an anthropologist, would properly characterize Ipili society in a matter of weeks. To be frank, the SEIS authors should have owned up to this, but instead presented 'data' of a quality that is embarrassing to mention, such as a land tenure survey based on a questionnaire administered to Grade 6 school children. When, in the report's findings, it is claimed that 'Ipili society and land tenure were studied in detail,' the writer or writers are having us on" (Burton 1999: 285). The SEIS, in other words, continued the tradition of texts that appeared to be authoritative but that in fact had little connection with Porgera's lived world. Theoretically an objective and scientific document making the Ipili legible, the lack of vision in the SEIS was not the result of a leviathan's myopia. The document certainly contained simplifications, but they were motivated by and explicable through the sociotechnical network that produced them.

The land study, the first step in the process of winning a special mining lease, was produced by a different set of people. The study was undertaken to determine which of the Ipili were "landowners." As everyone knew, its findings would set a precedent of enormous consequence: being deemed a "landowner" made one a point of articulation between the valley and Port Moresby, and decades of experience with middlemen made everyone aware of how lucrative that could be.

In a country where "accurate" land registration had become a major problem, the land study had proved to be remarkably durable and influential in valley life. Unlike the SEIS, which was written by expatriates, the study was conducted by Jeffrey Puge, a kiap originally from the Mt. Ialibu area of Southern Highlands Province who had worked in Porgera and Paiela for years prior to the creation of the mine. He directed a team of people, including many Porgerans, whose task was not to delineate which clans owned the land the mine would be built on—after two decades of compensation payments and local politicking, it was clear that there were "seven clans" in the future special mining lease territory—but rather which individuals were members of these particular leviathans: who, in other words, got to be "the Tiyini" or "the Tuanda."

Puge's guide to this task was a thin, photocopied booklet written by a senior civil servant in the Department of Mining that stated that all land studies were undertaken by recording the names of the adult men as "landowners," each of whom could belong to only one "clan." The government, in other words, expected the Ipili to be organized into lineages with definite leaders ("elders") who could make decisions for the whole group. Clans were divided into subclans, and beneath the subclans were the individual households or extended families, each of which had a head of household.

The reality of Ipili kinship, as we shall see, was quite different. Ipili were resistant to this method. As Frank Faulkner, then the provincial government's mining liaison officer at Porgera, noted to his superiors in the Department of Mining in a memo attached to the land study:

> The main purpose of my letter to you is to re-emphasize the very difficult task that field officers had in preparing this report. The Porgera landowners are not only a particularly volatile people, they are possessed of an intricate customary land tenure and inheritance system which is probably unique both to and within Papua New Guinea. It is an extended cognatic descent system in which all individuals have multiple clan affiliations and recognized rights to parcels of land in several clan territories, and they exercise these rights simultaneously . . . The result of this has been the absolute insistence of landowning family heads to include all of those who have rights (including all children) into the Schedule of Owners.

The result was a compromise between Ipili notions of relatedness and the segmentary, unilinear government model. The final report included the names of every man, woman, and child (even infants) who were members of a clan, and individuals could be listed as members of more than one clan. As a result, well-connected Porgerans (including the ones doing the fieldwork on which the reports were written) would be listed two or three—even seven—times in the study. (I examine this study in more detail in the next chapter.)

The decision by the land study team to allow people to be listed in more than one clan register had several feasibility-enhancing results. Government officers avoided creating enemies by casting a very large net. At the same time, the team created a list of "landowners" but did not explicitly articulate the principles—either imposed or indigenous—by which they had decided who to include or exclude. By relying on the expertise of educated Porgerans and the sensibilities of Papua New Guinean government staff, the land study finessed definitional difficulties in the present but failed to produce guidelines that might be used in the future. The result was the precedential creation of a bounded arena for contests of identity without the creation of strongly ascriptive rules that could define the outcomes of those contests. Finally, it definitively extinguished the claims of some people to ownership of the land in the special mining lease territory. Accompanying the land study was a document signed (that is, thumbprinted) by local leaders outside the territory in which they explicitly rejected any claim to an interest in the land in question in return for smaller spin-off projects in their areas such as an airstrip or township. Their noninclusion disambiguated the edges of landowner identity, even as the rules for inclusion kept the situation within landowning clans quite fluid.

As we shall see, the segmentary lineage system assumed by the land study got the sociology of Porgera wrong in principle, while the document itself exemplified the valley's coping style—which is probably why Porgerans liked it so much. Legally a document meant to describe and fix right to land, it in fact became the raw material for a creative semiotics of landownership that enabled a wide variety of claims to be made.

Compensation and Relocation Agreements

As we saw in chapter 1, the land study resulted in a distillation of agency that eventuated in the appointment of the twenty-three members of the Landowner Negotiating Committee (LNC). With a set of official representatives in place, the government and the mining company finally had a feasible corporate interlocutor—"the Ipili" had finally been created as a leviathan, which was ready to come to the table. Although the LNC had yet to be finalized on paper in the land study, its existence dated back to Mick Searson's development of an informal group of people with whom he could discuss the relationship between the mine and the community. As we shall see in chapter 3, it was not so much that twenty-three subclans had representatives as that twenty-three already important people had "solidified"—or, as Thomas

Ernst (1999) would put it, "entified"—twenty-three subclans that they could represent (Golub 2007a).

By this point the Ipili had developed millennial aspirations regarding mining and a strong sense of progressive enlightenment about the value of goods from "outside." In the 1950s it took three or four months of hard, physical labor with pickaxe and shovel, while standing in freezing water, for Ipili to receive a piece of shell, a handful of salt, and—if they were lucky—a steel axe. In the 1960s they learned to work for themselves and began being paid in cash. By 1979 alluvial miners were selling K100,000 worth of gold in Porgera by alluvial miners (Jackson and Banks 2002, 39). The Ipilis' wealth seemed to be increasing exponentially every decade, and with the construction of a large-scale gold mine, their expectations of further wealth would most likely be met. When it came time to negotiate, the Ipili were highly motivated.

Mick Searson did not play a role in the compensation agreement. He had already left the valley when negotiations for the agreement got under way. Placer had found its gold, and there was going to be a gold mine. Mick felt that he had done his part, and that it was best for him to leave the next stage of the valley's history to younger, less weary men. His job was split into three separate positions: business development, lands, and community affairs. Graeme Hogg, a former kiap who had been on patrols into Porgera in the late 1950s, was brought back to serve in business development and to help manage Ipili Porgera Investments, the business arm of the Porgera landowners that sold shares to individual Ipili families, a concept designed by Mick. David Moorehouse, another former kiap, oversaw lands work. Community affairs was headed up by Kundapen Talyaga, one of the first Engans to graduate from the University of Papua New Guinea. Kundapen's assistant was Jonathan Paraia, Mick's protégé. It was Jonathan who was to do most of the translating at the LNC meetings, just as he would a decade later at Yakatabari.

The most prominent person on the Ipili side of the table was Andrew Konema. One of the first Ipili to get a formal education, he had left his position as a policeman in Lae in the 1980s when he was elected as Porgera's representative in the Enga provincial assembly. He was a key part of the creation of Ipili Porgera Investments, the business arm of the landowners described above. Although his English was limited, Andrew could make forceful, coherent arguments in Tok Pisin with a logic that whites could follow, and he was an even more powerful orator in Ipili.

In June 1987 negotiations got under way on the compensation agreement.

A similar agreement at Placer's Misima mine had been signed a month before, and it formed the basis for the Porgera negotiations, although landowners in Porgera were also given information about compensation at Bougainville and Ok Tedi to use in their negotiations. Meetings were held every Friday, and Ipili immediately showed their toughness as negotiators. After four meetings Faulkner noted that "proceedings are, as expected, proceeding very slowly with the representatives using every argument both rational and irrational to press for as much compensation as possible . . . initially of course nothing quoted is 'acceptable' to the landowners. The statutory occupation fee is not acceptable, the 5% royalty payment is not acceptable, and so it goes" (PPCU Report 6 July). In August the Porgera Joint Venture (PJV) gave the landowners a draft agreement to review. The landowners were unhappy with the compensation rates for sweet potato and pandanus—plants marginal in Misima but central to life in Porgera. More broadly, the LNC feared locking itself out of additional benefits and was unwilling to commit itself to a settlement without knowing what Placer's plans were for the mine. The company, of course, argued that it would not know its plans until other pieces of the puzzle—including the compensation agreement—were in place.

Finally, on 31 January 1988, the compensation agreement was signed. Altogether, occupation fees were K20 higher per hectare than the agreements at Misima and Ok Tedi. Although the Misimans had only a short list of plants such as yams and coconuts that were highly valued, the Ipili applied their tendency to take distributive justice to its extreme: each and every kind of plant conceivably used had to be valued so that everyone would get exactly what he or she was entitled to, even if that plant was worth a very small amount. Nearly all of the fifty-eight trees and plants on the Ipilis' list were valued at more than the rates set by the Valuer General, the government's authority for statutory evaluations. Sweet potato was priced at K6 per mature mound—three times the value set by the Valuer General in 1985—and a mature pandanus tree was valued at K12, four times higher than the Valuer General's recommendation. By all accounts, the negotiations were a success.

As soon as the compensation agreement was signed, the LNC began negotiations for the relocation agreement, which specified who the mine would displace in the course of its operations and what sort of compensation and replacement dwelling the displaced people would receive for their destroyed houses.

Placer had hoped to avoid dislocating anyone in building the mine because of the difficulties it would cause. The only precedent for what was to be done at Porgera was Bougainville, where the mine had moved 200 house-holds at a cost of AU$1.64 million. However, as Douglas Oliver pointed out, "its cost to the relocated people, in terms of physical and psychological hardship, cannot be expressed in figures. Their sufferings stand out as a grim reminder of the human costs of operating an open-cut mine" (1991, 138). Discontent over relocations at Bougainville and the armed insurgency there was a precedent that no one wanted to repeat.

Nevertheless, it soon became clear that relocation was inevitable. The proposed site of the future processing plant was occupied, and people were moving onto other future sites of the mine and building houses at a furious pace in order to receive the maximum compensation possible from the mine when it destroyed their (newly built and planted) property. It became clear that the relocation at Porgera was to be larger than that at Bougainville: Bougainville had moved 200 households in twenty years, while the PJV was seeking to move around 230 in the course of the first twelve to eighteen months it would take to build the mine.

Although the PJV was right to be mindful of the negative social consequences of relocation, the situation in Porgera was fundamentally different from that in Bougainville. The people relocated in Bougainville were fundamentally opposed to the presence of the mine and to their relocation. But the local people in Porgera had decided to have a mine in their valley. Richard Jackson wrote,

> It cannot be said too often or too forcefully that for Papua New Guineans the focus of life is land. In the Porgera setting, it might be very easy to begin to doubt exactly how sacred and inalienable land is; at first sight, Porgerans seem to fall over each other in trying to offer their land for use by the PJV. For example, during my short stay there individuals during group discussions wanted to offer their land for township development, and the Paiyam people jointly wrote to the Site Manager offering their land for the same purpose. (1986, 28)

Porgerans saw relocation as a fundamental transformation of their lives for the better. Specifically, relocation was combined with expectations for a mining township in Paiyam, where Ipili would live with white people. This desire for increased material well-being was tinged by and inseparable from the millenarian prophecies, which viewed relocation as the arrival of a long-deferred time when wealth and plenty could be had without work. Porgerans did not want to be relocated in houses that were "traditional" or to protect their communities from the corrosive effects of culture contact. Rather, they embraced the relocation project and saw it as the start of their own modernization. Thus, although Ipili claims for compensation developed through a rhetoric of landownership and ecological purity, skepticism about the authenticity of this idiom of articulation of demands was born alongside them. As we have seen in the last chapter, this disconnect between what Porgerans want and what they have to claim in order to get it continues today.

The minutes of the relocation meetings make it clear that the landowners expected to be relocated in a compound essentially similar to the workers' camps that were later built at Suyan and Alipis. Their vision was of a special mining lease territory fenced off from the surrounding area, with paved internal roads and a boom gate at the entrance to control traffic. Furnished housing with free electricity and water would be provided. Children in the territory would be taken to school and back in a PJV school bus at no charge. The Ipili would live white lifestyles (insofar as they understood those lifestyles) in white houses. One Ipili man told Jackson in 1986:

> We expect the Company to provide free permanent houses; when the Company wants to start a mine, all our houses will be replaced with permanent buildings. This includes our haus kuk (kitchens), toilets, piggeries, chicken house and our residence and stores with exactly the same dimensions we have on our own land. We will live like the white men. These houses will be used by our sons and daughters when we die. There will be deep freezers, entertainment facilities, furniture and such other accessories in houses. We expect the Company to build our houses with wire fences around it [sic] and these houses will have security gates, etc. (quoted in Robinson 1988, 13)

No wonder, then, that house size was a sticking point in the Yakatabari negotiations—landowners were reiterating in the late 1990s the demands they had made a decade earlier to the same mine representative.

The design of the relocation house was the biggest issue in the negotiations. Landowners rejected a PJV design because its timber frame and large windows meant that it could be burned down and that people could see into it—drawbacks for the Ipili, who valued privacy and feared that their houses might be burned down in fighting. An alternative design with metal walls and small, barred windows was eventually drawn up based on a sketch done by Peakope Auwikini, a Pulumaini leader, although the final version did not include a veranda that landowners wanted but that the PJV thought was too expensive.

In the future, Ipili would compare their relocation houses unfavorably to matchboxes and view many of the other subsidiary benefits guaranteed in the Relocation Agreement as useless and unacceptable. Although many of these criticisms would be valid, the houses the Ipili received were made to their own design, and it was inevitable that the PJV would not be able to fulfill the expectations of the landowners involved, informed as they were by quasi-religious expectations of a total transformation of Ipili life.

The Porgera Agreements

The PJV had fulfilled its legal obligation to consult with landowners by signing the Compensation and Relocation Agreements, and the Ipili had made history by the size and scope of the relocation project that they had signed on for. However, on 15 May 1989 Porgerans broke decisively with the past by signing the Porgera Agreements, another unprecedented set of agreements that resulted from a development forum attended by landowners and representatives of both the Enga provincial government and the national government. These were the agreements that demonstrated the full range of Ipili ambition—they created the town of Paiyam, the Kairik airstrip, and the Porgera Development Authority. They would prove to be precedent setting—every future mining and hydrocarbon development project in Papua New Guinea would include a development agreement based on the Porgera Agreements.

Several intersecting orders of determination created an opportunity that a few Ipili negotiators seized in order to make the forum a reality. The most important factor was the Bougainville crisis. On 21 August 1987 a group of Bougainvilleans repudiated their leaders—calling them yes-men installed by Bougainville Copper Ltd.—and created a "new executive" that threatened "massive demonstrations" if it was not recognized by the company as the legitimate landowners' group. Joseph Kabui, the premier of the province, backed the new group, and the first roadblocks at Bougainville were set up in the same month that the Porgera feasibility study was submitted to the government.

At roughly the same time, the government of Prime Minister Paias Wingti received a vote of no confidence, and Sir Rabbie Namaliu became prime minister. When he was in the opposition, Namaliu had endorsed justice for local people and a revamping of mining laws. The financial crisis created by the sudden loss of revenues from Bougainville made negotiating with the Ipili a smart thing to do. Namaliu's moral commitment to justice for grassroots Papua New Guineans convinced him it was also the right thing to do. He told me:

We didn't want what had happened in Bougainville to happen in Porgera or anywhere else in this country, and we wanted to create a situation where as much as possible issues and grievances were sorted out before an agreement was reached and before a project was developed. From our perspective, it's extremely difficult for the state to impose its will on the people without expecting some reaction and in some cases some very strong reactions from some quarters. We have many different cultural-linguistic groupings in this country and we must respect them, and the way to do that while at the same time strengthening the nation-state is to bring them into your confidence. Because if they feel they are involved and they have a meaningful role to play in something like that, then in the broader context that's also contributing toward building up the state as a nation.

Of course, a moral sense was not the only thing that brought the national government to the table. Bougainville did not have a monopoly on disorder, and events in Porgera made it clear that the government could not force a mine on local people. In 1987, for instance, the PJV's prospecting authority came up for review. Renewal of its permits should have been a routine matter, but in this case a group of Porgerans headed up by Victor Alene (who would later attempt to usurp control of the Porgera Landowners Association in the course of the Yakatabari negotiations) demanded that Placer stop operations and return to Canada until Porgerans were satisfied that Placer, rather than another company, should develop the Porgera gold mine. This did not happen, and soon thereafter Nelson Akiko and Victor Alene (who were related because of a shared connection to the Waiwa clan) launched a daring, night-time guerrilla raid against Coya Construction, the contractor that was drilling a test adit (horizontal passage) into the newly discovered high-grade ore zone that had catapulted the mine into feasibility. The raiders located the camp's safe and somehow, despite its enormous size and weight, managed to escape with it into the Warokari Mountains. On their own land, an area of formidable terrain and no vehicular roads, the raiders were safe. Many people in Apalaka and Yarik today can excitedly describe the sight of Victor stripped to the waist, covered in mud for camouflage, brandishing an automatic weapon "just like Rambo" on the summit of Mt. Warokari defiantly screaming the Ipili equivalent of "come and get me, you bastards!" as PJV helicopters buzzed above him.

According to Victor, the safe contained K69,000 and, more important, the passports of every expatriate worker in the exploration camp. In a single stroke "the Ipili" (here, Victor and Nelson) demonstrated that they had the power to cause real harm to expatriate mine workers. In retaliation—perhaps spurred on by the mine—the police sacked the community of Alipis (despite the fact that Victor and Nelson had escaped to Paiela) and engaged in a spree of looting and pillaging. Houses were burned to the ground, leaving many innocent bystanders without shelter, and some inhabitants claimed that gold was also stolen. This would be the first of many illegal mass house burnings conducted by the police in Porgera, allegedly to maintain law and order—another example of the disjunction between the role of the state as macro actor and the idiosyncratic behavior of its representatives.

In the resulting furor negotiations for the Compensation Agreement were stalled. Tensions ran high, and many people in Alipis argued for retaliation against the police. Eventually the situation was resolved, when Victor turned himself in and was sent to Baisu Prison for two years. Most of the money and all of the passports were recovered. Nelson was not jailed or even charged with a crime. He disappeared for a couple of months, eventually resurfacing in April. As Faulkner noted at the time, "the leader of the gang responsible for the Coya holdup and robbery Nelson Akiko who has been 'on the run' for some months has re-appeared and strangely enough has been employed by the PJV (they are aware of his identity). I suspect for perverse reasons out of curiosity to see whether or not the Police actually attempt to arrest him" (PPCU Report 11 April 1988). In fact, Nelson had become a contractor who provided janitorial services to the PJV after a white mine employee, following the precedent established by Searson and Brugh, married one of Nelson's sisters. The position of contractor would make Nelson one of the valley's richest inhabitants. Ten years after the raid, a reporter for the Papua New Guinea *National*, ignorant of Nelson's personal history, would write: "It is still universal that honest sweat always pays off eventually. Nelson Akiko is another one of those numerous people who sail the crest of success and attest to this phenomena" (Paupa 2001). The police had demonstrated that they could make the Ipili as a collectivity suffer, but that they could not contain the threat posed by individuals, who could hamstring the delicate logistics of the mine. The raid on Coya Construction demonstrated that it was not just Bougainville that could experience a meltdown.

Finally, the Ipili needed allies to lend their cause legitimacy. The main ally came in the form of the Enga provincial government. Until this time the government had suffered from crippling corruption. The PJV's social and economic impact study was quite critical of it:

It is widely accepted that there has been a significant decline in the operating performance of PNG public sector institutions since Independence. Services to villages no longer patrol to outlying villages and are unable to maintain effective supervision of existing projects; basic procedures are subject to excessive delays; cost recovery and financial control are plagued by mismanagement; and the breakdown in law and order is attributed to ineffective performance by responsible agencies . . . [T]he outlook for the Porgera people in the short to medium term is that they will have to muddle through with government services of limited effectiveness. (Pacific Agribusiness 1987, 1:79)

By 1988, however, the government had stabilized under its new premier, Ned Laina, and a staff that included some of the first Engans to graduate from the University of Papua New Guinea, such as Luke Kembol, Philip Kikala, and Kundapen Talyaga, as well as expatriates such as Harry Ulin, the future mining coordinator introduced in the previous chapter; and the new provincial lawyer Harry Derkley, a Tasmanian with a history of working with the Tasmanian aboriginal community. This group was determined to demonstrate its competence and to make sure that the entire province, not just Porgera District, benefited from the gold mine.

As a sign of its commitment to increased control over mining operations within the province, the Enga provincial government launched a set of proposals at a press conference and reception at the Islander Hotel in Port Moresby on 5 June 1988, demanding that the province receive increased compensation, including equity, and that the provincial government, like the national government, should be a signatory to the Mineral Development Contract. Throughout the following year the Enga provincial government worked through the Premiers' Council (a forum for provincial leaders and national politicians) to build a coalition with the government of the Southern Highlands Province, where there was also resource development, to advocate for reform of the 1977 Mining Act, then under review. The council created a Mining and Petroleum Working Committee composed of the premiers whose provinces contained resource developments, which then endorsed the Enga provincial government's proposals for development and produced a series of recommendations for the new mining act.

In other words, by 1988 the national government was ready to hold a forum with representatives from the Enga provincial government and the landowners in order to create a novel and precedent-setting series of concessions. Set in Port Moresby and composed of so-called apex institutions, the forum process was the purest form of leviathan politics. And yet behind even these negotiations, personal networks still played a very large part.

On the landowners' side, the key players were to be Andrew Konema, Jonathan Paraia, and Langaiya Ipate, who would later be the district administrator during the Yakatabari negotiations. By this time, Andrew had grown even more prominent—not only was he the unofficial leader of the LNC and a minister in the provincial government, but he had also made a fortune at the Mt. Kare gold rush and become president of the Porgera Landowners Association. Although a powerful presence, Andrew was not exactly a policy wonk. Jonathan and Langaiya, therefore, took up the task of briefing Andrew regularly and doing the nitty-gritty work of the negotiations. By this time, Langaiya had replaced Faulkner as the provincial mining liaison officer, and Jonathan was president of the Porgera local government— Namaliu's invitation to the development forum had been addressed to him.

These men represented the next generation of Porgeran middlemen: Lyndon Koeka and his brothers, the sons of the decapitated former leader, were coming into their own as landowners. Andrew, Langaiya, and Jonathan—all members of the first group of students at the Porgera elementary school— had graduated and returned to the valley. Jonathan was the first Porgeran to earn a bachelor's degree—in political science at the University of Papua New Guinea—and had attended college on a scholarship from the mine. He now quickly put his education to use by pressuring the mine. Langaiya was the first Porgeran to be trained as a kiap. This was a continuation of the middleman politics that had long been central to Porgera. These men had come of age at a time when innovative ideas and excellent role models abounded. Although young—Langaiya was only twenty-six—they felt that the time had come for them to show what they were capable of.

The national government drew on a wide range of people to represent it as well, but the most important figure was probably the secretary of the Department of Mining, Bill Searson. Bill was Joe Searson's son and Mick's half-brother. As a child, Bill had been raised by his mother in Porgera until Searson had kidnapped him and shipped him off to be raised in Hagen with the Leahys. Bill became the first Papua New Guinean geologist and was appointed to several prominent positions in the civil service under the National Party, a highlands-based political party that needed educated men who could understand and deal with often unschooled highlands politicians. Although Mick had inherited Joe's restlessness, Bill had his cultivation and tact. Bill was a naturally quiet man, like his father, but without Joe's penchant for solitude. Bill's personal network was large—it is hard to dislike him—and he had connections in a variety of places. He quickly became the éminence grise of the Porgera project.

The starting point of negotiations for the provincial government was an eighteen-page development proposal that was a compact version of the proposals for development released at the Islander Hotel earlier that year.

The landowners were prepared as well. Jonathan Paraia told me:

[We] gathered all the clan leaders and even councilors and we developed a development proposal, and in the proposal we told them we want a high school, we want an international school, we want the hospital, we want the long-term economic development plan, and provide us with the economist. We want a road, road development; we want the Tari road surveyed; we want the airstrip to be built; we want a town to be built—you know, all that. All the services that were not available here, we put it to the national government: if you agree to this, we will sign on the dotted line, and you will have a mine. Otherwise—forget it! [laughs] Yeah! We gave it to them at the forum. And whatever was missing we talked to them and said this is what we want, and on the cover of the proposal we put a man with a bow and arrow, and said, "If you don't give it, we'll fight!" [laughs] Yeah.

After this first meeting, the forum process continued for months. The size, structure, and location of the meetings depended on what was being discussed. Sometimes individuals would meet, sometimes large groups. Despite the often heated nature of the debates, all those involved realized that it was in everyone's interest to work together—something that would not be true with the Yakatabari negotiations. Given the current events at Bougainville, everyone realized that it was quite possible that there would be no mine in Porgera, and that was an outcome everyone wanted to avoid.

In all of these meetings, the interests of the landowners and the Enga provincial government were closely connected. The provincial government by itself lacked the power and legitimacy to ensure the national government that the mine would go ahead—no one could guarantee that but the landowners. The landowners, in turn, found a powerful ally in the provincial government, and the two cooperated most of the time in order to gain concessions from the national government.

The tenacity with which the landowners negotiated was impressive. The reputation they had earned as negotiators of the two earlier agreements proved to be well deserved. A single example, the negotiations for an airstrip at Kairik, serves to illustrate this point as well as to show how particular issues were worked out over the course of the forum. Both the landowners and the provincial government originally requested that the planned airstrip at Kairik be upgraded to be able to handle Dash Seven aircraft. A group of senior ministers met at Waigani to consider these points on 3 February 1989 and were informed by the Department of Civil Aviation (DCA) that Dash Sevens could not land at Porgera due to a variety of factors, including the altitude. To an outsider, this seems like an open-and-shut case—if the plane was not physically capable of landing at the new airstrip, then it was not physically capable of landing at the new airstrip. But when Langaiya faxed back his response to the decisions made at the meeting a few days later, he replied:

> We intend to challenge DCA's story that Dash 7s cannot land in Porgera due to high altitude. We insist that the Kairik airstrip be built to take larger aircraft than the Twin Otter only. So a clause in the agreement to be signed between the landowners and NG [national government] should read: "that the Kairik airstrip will be built to take in larger aircraft than the Twin Otter and should the landowners prove to the national govt. that Dash 7s can land in Porgera, the NG will undertake to ensure that Dash 7s will extend services to Porgera."

The truth—what was physically possible and what was not—was not something that the landowners were going to concede to the government without a fight. They insisted, as Latour would say, on going "upstream" and challenging the truth claims of their opponents (1987, 220). Although the clause was not ultimately changed (because it is impossible to effectively run Dash Sevens into Porgera), the example illustrates the way that landowners were willing to test and challenge every assumption to get the best deal possible for themselves and their community.

The result of the development forum was a tripartite set of agreements. These consisted of an agreement between the Enga provincial government and the national government, an agreement between the Enga provincial government and the Porgera landowners, and an agreement between the Porgera landowners and the national government. Placer was not a party to the agreements but was made to adhere to the agreements' provisions, which were written into the mining development contract Placer signed with the national government.

Each of these agreements described the same state of affairs, but they varied in their specifications of the roles of all parties involved. This sounds complicated, but it made sense in practice. Again, the Kairik airstrip provides a good example. Everyone wanted the same thing: that the PJV would build an airstrip at Kairik and hand it over to the Enga provincial government (although the landowners would have the option of taking over the maintenance of the airstrip if the provincial government was lax in its duties), and the national government would then organize regular flights into the valley. The way that this was spelled out in the agreements was as follows: In the national government–landowner agreement, the government promised the landowners that it would make the PJV build the airstrip. In the landowner–Enga provincial government agreement, the provincial government agreed to take responsibility for the airstrip once the PJV had built it but promised the landowners that the newly formed Porgera Development Authority could take over maintenance of the airstrip if it wished. In the provincial government–national government agreement, the national government officially gave its consent to this arrangement. In all of these arrangements, the only thing the landowners had to promise to do was to refrain from interrupting the mine's operations.

The end of the development forum was an arbitrary one. The state of affairs in Bougainville had worsened. The presence of four hundred police officers there had temporarily halted the deterioration of the situation, but in early May attacks by dissidents increased in frequency. The national government was eager to get Porgera up and running. Namaliu remembers:

> We had a situation where Bougainville was closed, we wanted to see a new project going, not just in terms of seeing a new mine developed but in the whole context of macroeconomic development. We wanted to see a project going quickly that would take the place of Bougainville in terms of revenues and also stimulate economic activities within the country. I suppose if it was a situation that was different, we might have had a bit more time to talk through some of these things. We concluded some things maybe a little earlier than we should have, but as a result we got a project going, had a billion dollars coming in at a time when we needed something like that to happen.

The landowners were not so enthusiastic. Jonathan Paraia remembers:

> Actually, we were not quite ready to sign, but the prime minister sent a plane to Porgera and said, "Hey, the aircraft is here. If you want to participate as you have been always complaining to participate, then you jump

on the plane and come to Port Moresby and sign it. If you don't come, we won't wait for you, because no law in the country says we have to sign an agreement with you. There's no requirement for you [to participate]." So we took it as a threat, and we sort of—see, if we don't go, what's going to happen? Maybe whatever we have not secured maybe we can negotiate and discuss later. It's good to protect whatever we've got on our plate already and grab it rather than letting it go, so we developed that kind of attitude and we said okay.

Ultimately, though, the landowners were happy with the agreements. They had received the best deal in the history of mining in the country—so good, in fact, it was in violation of the Mining Act of the day. What most disturbed them was not the content of the agreements so much as the haste with which the final documents were presented. Derkley later noted that he believed that "the final draft was prepared in haste and was executed before a final 'vetting' took place." Jonathan was more blunt in his assessment of the situation: "Mind you, everything that we agreed they had changed in the computer. We said 'shall' and 'will be,' they said—oh, they changed it to 'undertake to consider,' you know? Not 'shall' and 'will'—all that we put in there had been changed, and then we were not shown the final copy before we signed." As it turns out, the agreements were signed just in time—on 15 May 1989. Three days after the signing, Bougainville Copper Ltd. shut the Bougainville copper mine for good. What the development agreements really amounted to was less a legal document than a simple agreement between parties who have all made a commitment to the provisions in the agreements in good faith. They were not settled issues—they were the starting point of discussions that would continue into the future. Thus, although the contents of the agreements would continue to be matters of contention, future disagreements would be settled through negotiation and consultation rather than in court or through violence. By creating arenas within which debate could occur and be controlled, the agreements made Porgera and the Ipili feasible. Derkley has written:

> The agreements are not simply legal arrangement but political ones between powerful political players in the Papua New Guinea context who all felt that when the agreements were made they should combine to accommodate each other's legitimate interest so as to ensure the orderly development of a project in which each have an important stake. Thus it is probably the political, economic, and social consequences for the na-

tion, the province, and the local clans of failure to make them work which is the more effective guarantee of the validity of the agreements and the ultimate sanction of their enforceability.

Ultimately, some of the leviathans involved were happy with the agreements and their implementation. The landowners were not so positive. They felt that they had finally received the promises of development that they longed for—but could what actually happened on the ground in Porgera be considered the fulfillment of those processes? Such was the question that they would face in the following years and that would structure so much of the personal dynamics that drove the Yakatabari negotiations.

Conclusion

In this chapter I have provided a history of how outsiders came to know the Porgera valley's mineral resources and its Ipili inhabitants. I have argued that James Scott's idea of "legibility" has a certain prima facie validity when events are examined at a distance. When one examines the history of Porgera in detail, however, narratives of the state as a single coherent actor and observer grow problematic. As I suggested in the introduction of this book, the interplay of representative and represented institutions is much more complex than Scott's vision of the myopic high modernist state allows. I have attempted to substantiate this claim by examining the history of the Porgera valley.

Despite official attempts to know and control the valley, the group of people most successful in getting things done there were often those involved with mining but removed from official state institutions—first the middlemen of the 1950s and then their children, who composed the Porgeran high society of the 1980s and 1990s. The interaction of local efficacy and distant authority was complex, but it is clear that the history of Porgera has consistently been one where "the state" or "the Ipili" are hardly unproblematic leviathans. Instead, I have attempted to provide a richer and more fulfilling analysis of the way abstract institutions are personated in the course of everyday life. "The state" cannot be assumed simply to "see," as we have seen here and shall see in future chapters. To judge records of Ipili lifeways by reference to their accuracy is to miss the way in which official representation is part of a complex process that creates groups and institutions by the act of eliciting information about them.

Finally, this account has a genealogical angle: partially successful attempts of large, institutional actors to regiment life in the valley created new idioms of landownership and rights that were actively appropriated by a wide variety of actors. These idioms continued to remain relevant to life in the valley and formed an inventory of rhetorical strategies and claims that became the textual patrimony deployed in the Yakatabari negotiations.

3 Being Ipili in Porgera

Every attempt to specify the set of agents to whom an issue of justice pertains will itself, as an act of identification and recognition, be a potential site of injustice . . . because those people for whom justice is a live issue are not done becoming who they are; or, better, who they will turn out to have been.
—Patchen Markell, *Bound by Recognition*

They're cognatic, if by "cognatic" you mean "accommodating."
—Director of community affairs, Porgera Joint Venture.

The *Porgera Social Monitoring Program Annual Report 1996*—an in-house report written for the Porgera Joint Venture (PJV)— noted a variety of alarming trends in valley life: the breakdown of law and order, inequality in the distribution of money, and a shortage of arable land within the special mining lease (SML) territory. One of the most important problems was the state of government administration in Porgera. "The quality of government services in Porgera continued to decline in 1996," noted the report:

> It is hard to imagine how government services could get worse. Not only was there inadequate funding for the designated tasks of the various divisions, but budgeted funds (including salaries) did not get to the district in a timely fashion and sometimes not at all. Senior staff were continuously going to Wabag [the provincial capital] in an attempt to obtain budgeted funds. Transport was also a critical problem. At one point 6 of the 8 district vehicles were off the road and unserviceable. There was a lack of houses for staff for the existing positions and a lack of main-

tenance on houses which did exist. As if this were not enough there were no typewriters, computers, fax machines, telephones . . . even paper and pens. (Banks and Bonnell 1997, 5)

The exact status of Porgera as an administrative unit was itself unclear:

> The interim arrangements for the new Organic Law on Provincial Governments and Local Level Governments . . . have added another element to the confusion. This centers around Porgera's status as a district. According to the OLPG & LLG [the 1995 Organic Law on Provincial and Local-level Governments] Porgera is part of the Porgera Lagaip District. However most, if not all, Porgera public servants believe that Porgera is a separate district. It is possible that this is also the viewpoint of senior Enga District Administration staff. In early 1997 Enga Provincial Administration advertised a long list of positions for both Porgera District and Laiagam District. (Banks and Bonnell 1997, 5)

Although "cynics would argue that since government services are so bad in Porgera it is hardly likely for them to get any worse if administered from Laiagam," the report noted that "Porgera's status as a District in Enga Province needs to be clarified" (Banks and Bonnell 1997, 5). This issue was still up in the air in 1998 at a meeting of the monitoring committee that I attended; only then were the committee members finally and definitively assured that Porgera was in fact a separate district from Laiagam.

This absence of definitive information about even the most basic facts regarding Porgera's status as a unit of government speaks to the central issue of this chapter: the haphazard and tenuous articulation of everyday life in the valley with the bureaucratic regimes governing the mine and the state. This is not for lack of trying: as we have seen, references to "Ipili life" and "how the Ipili live" flitted through the negotiations and policies described in previous chapters, surfacing mostly to ground the claims political actors have made in the name of "custom" or "tradition." What is the status of each of these claims? Is it true that Ipili believe that members of the same clan should always live in close proximity with each other? What sort of connections do the Ipili have to the land? What is the nature of Ipili subclans, such as the Tiyini? The goal of this chapter is to understand how narratives of Ipili sociality and identity help make the Ipili feasible as a governed and surveilled population in the Porgera Valley.

In this chapter I hope to show that there is no coherent account of who "the Ipili" are among government and corporate leviathans—or even the

Ipili themselves. During the Yakatabari negotiations, participants talked about Porgera as if there were a sharp contrast between the paper world of writings about the Ipili and actual "life on the ground" or "how things are in the village." In contrast to this black-and-white story, I will argue that decades of wrangling over land and compensation have engaged Ipili and outsiders in a mutually determining relationship in which what it means to be Ipili is shaped by outside requirements, even as outsiders seek to use Porgeran notions as the basis of their regimes of recognition. The result is an interplay between cosmology and bureaucracy in which bureaucratic leviathans believe themselves to be accurately discerning a population whose existence they elicit in the course of their project of "description."

In recent years anthropology has trended away from James Scott's popularization of Foucault in *Seeing Like a State* (1998) to produce a literature that insists local actors are constituted, rather than misrecognized, by various regimes of governmentality (Moore 2005; Li 2007). I build on this growing body of work, but with a difference: in Porgera, at least, models of pervasive governmentality are inadequate because they overestimate the power of these regimes. It is not just that "the village" and "the paper world" are mutually constitutive, but that the bureaucratic apparatus that attempts to subsume the Ipili lacks any sort of coherent scheme by which to do so. Furthermore, because the concept 'Ipili' is an ethnic category which lacked bright and clear boundaries prior to colonization, Ipili themselves do not have a clear, delineated sense of what it means to be Ipili that would allow them to easily and routinely exclude people from that category. As a result, indigenous identities are as ambiguous as the valley's administrative status. Thus, in contrast to the many cases in which we see "the development of bounded, land-owning groups to fit corporate conceptualizations of patrilineal models in Melanesia" (Gilberthorpe 2007, 103) and elsewhere (see, for example, Fried 1975), the Porgera case is one in which the ambiguity of the local resource frontier has created a discursive space for descent claims without creating a hegemonic account of what those descent groups are or how they operate.

In making this argument, I hope to create a more inclusive account of life in the valley. Moving beyond the to-ing and fro-ing of elite politics, I focus here on the everyday life of grassroots Ipili people who are affected by the negotiations carried out in the name of their future, the people whose sociality creates a backdrop that informs and potentiates the agents in these negotiations. Although Yakatabari dealt with novel, unprecedented issues, this chapter examines how Ipili shopped their identities around to the various institutions in the valley that handed money and resources out to "true landowners" according to rules and policies created by precedent-setting events such as the Yakatabari negotiations. Dealing with Porgera's institutions during the course of their stereotypic reproduction required them to be subsumed under the proper categories in order to be processed in the correct way by the valley's institutions. Quarterly royalty checks, annual occupation fees, preferential hiring, and compensation payments are all available to people who can be incorporated into the administrative machinery of the mine and the government. By moving beyond the high-stakes negotiations that go on behind the barbed wire of Suyan to the more mundane spheres of life in the valley, then, I hope to open the black box of "the Ipili" and show how people create feasible lives out of the bureaucracies that are their inconstant companions.

One thing I do not intend to do, however, is argue that the nebulous nature of Ipili identity means that particular Ipili are not entitled to recognition. Simply because claims to Ipili identity are complicated does not mean that Porgerans ought be disenfranchised. Opening black boxes is not an unmasking, disempowering move. As Patchen Markell (2003) points out, when we assume that we have a finished, fixed identity, we foreclose other possibilities and suppress the recognition of our fundamental existential openness. This openness is something that Ipili have long recognized—their kinship system is accommodating—and the incoherent regimes of recognition in the valley are, in many ways, very culturally Ipili. Their multiple, overlapping standards allow an ambiguity in which political compromises between the mine, landowners, and governments can be worked out. Thus this chapter (and the next) stresses that the inability of the government and mine to establish a single, coherent criterion of identity is a sign of success, not failure, in how the valley is run.

One note on terminology: this chapter focuses on kinship because in Porgera descent is the main criterion for recognition as a landowner. This focus on descent is the result of anthropology's influence on the valley's history and politics. Yet anthropologists no longer endorse the blunt ascriptivist vision of kinship that this regime of recognition is based on. For this reason, much of the chapter undertakes the ticklish task of describing how various conceptualizations of kinship are both separate and related: a paper world of representations of Ipili kinship, practices in the valley that have been elicited by this world and that begin to resemble it, what actually goes on most of the time in the valley, and my own anthropological attempt to describe a phenomenon that looks like a kinship system while demonstrating why the language of kinship cannot be used to describe it. It is for this reason I will speak of "Ipili sociality" in the sense of "symbolic domains that constitute the collective image of human interaction in any society" (Weiner 1988, 3), rather than "social organization" or "kinship," as I attempt to describe why I find the generally used idiom of kinship at play in the valley to be inappropriate, both ethnographically and theoretically, to describe this sociality.

I begin by describing Ipili ethnic identity in its wider regional setting and then move to Ipili sociality within the valley, particularly within the SML territory. I next discuss how official and government representations of Ipili identity affect Ipilis' access to goods and services in the valley—how well, I ask, do the criteria of receiving compensation, royalty payments, and preferential hiring correspond to indigenous notions? In the final section of the chapter I conclude that even these institutions lack any sort of coherent internal logic that might provide a simplifying clarity that Ipili identity itself lacks.

The Ipili as an Ethnic Group

Many maps of Papua New Guinea represent the Ipili and their neighbors in the same way that maps represent nation-states: a border encloses a territory containing several similarly discrete smaller administrative units in the form of subclans. This vision of Ipili identity—the name of an ethnic group in the center of a colored patch on a map—is not how Ipili conceive of themselves. It is telling that the term "Ipili" appears to have first been widely used in colonial times, with its popularity inspired by Mervyn Meggitt's early work in the valley (1957). And it is ironic that the word "Porgera"—which, as we have seen in chapter 3, comes from a mishearing of the "Pongema" River—is unpronounceable to Ipili, whose language eschews consonant clusters. Even today, when elderly Ipili speak among themselves, the names "Ipili" and "Paiela" refer to the two valleys in which "the Ipili" (as we call them today) live. Thus discussions of "Ipili" identity must start by recognizing that there does not appear to be an indigenous term for "the Ipili" at all.

Up to the present time Porgerans have been, as Aletta Biersack puts it, "centered not on themselves as geographical isolates but on culturally diverse fields in which their mythology, trade routes, and marriage practices embedded them" (1995a, 7). As a result, "the region was neither atomized nor centralized but was organized (through its myths, rituals, trade, and intermarriage) as a polycentric system of overlapping yet noncoincident worlds" (Biersack 1995a, 7). This regional embeddedness is tied to kinship at the most general level. Ipili genealogies run deep—typically covering more than ten generations—and terminate with an eponymous apical ancestor. These genealogies frequently trace the migration of ancestors across the region, leaving communities dotted throughout the landscape that are inhabited by peoples who are related to one another. These mythological accounts of ancestral movements seem to correspond, at least in Enga, to actual migrations of clans from one area to another (Wiessner and Tumu 1998, 119–55).

The result is what P. Wohlt refers to as a lineage "diaspora" (1978, 43)—a network of related lines that spread over the Southern Highlands and Enga Provinces and that cut across the ethnic boundaries of what are today considered to be the three distinct ethnic groups of the "Huli," the "Enga," and the "Ipili." Although the fact that both the Huli and the Engans are well known for their strong sense of ethnic particularism would seem to undercut this approach to regional ethnicity, it should be remembered that the term "Enga" is, like "Ipili," a colonial neologism and that the Huli have always conceived of themselves as members (albeit of the most superior sort) of a galaxy of related ethnic groups (Ballard 1995). Thus although the literature today discusses three separate groups—the Huli, the Ipili, and the Enga—most scholars would emphasize that ethnicity in this area is based on continua of cultural difference in a population crisscrossed by flows of people.

These mythic linkages were and are mobilized by Ipili and their neighbors. As Papua New Guinea modernizes through the spread of roads in the highlands and the development of resources in formerly peripheral areas, these regional identities have grown stronger. In the past, shared genealogical connections were used to facilitate long-distance trading (Mangi 1988), to gain concessions at locations such as salt springs controlled by related groups (Wiessner and Tumu 1998), and to request hospitality when ecological hardships such as drought and frost made people temporarily migrate away from their homes (Wohlt 1978). Today Papua New Guineans use these ties to conduct business along the Highlands Highway, to find hosts when they go to areas near mines and hydrocarbon projects, and to travel safely through areas where tribal fighting occurs.

These diasporic relations have a real sociology and use, but it is important not to overstate their coherence. It is tempting, as John Burton puts it, "to uncover as many of them as possible and map them out" (1999, 284) when doing fieldwork in this part of the world, but to do so would not result in some sort of master narrative that was coherent enough to identify landowners entitled to land rights. Even master genealogists cannot state with precision the specific spread of lineages and clan ties beyond the mythical level—and even these are unclear and subject to confusion. It is tempting to consider this to be a sign of the loss of genealogical knowledge as the result of contact with the West. However, it is important to note that Wohlt, who conducted research in the region twenty years before I did, observes that although everyone "knows the gist of the myth," in fact "if one asks a dozen informants over [the] age of forty the particulars of genealogical connection . . . one gets a dozen different versions" (Wohlt 1978, 42). He concludes that "beyond the unity maintained through oral tradition and the ceremonies described above, relationships among tribal members entail little else than hospitality, and that only in need" (54).

So although these lineage diasporas are not literally corporate groups that have lineal, segmentary genealogies, they do link communities through an ideology of ancient consanguinity. This ideology has implications for how one understands ethnicity in this part of the world. Writing of Wohlt's analysis of these diasporas, Burton notes that a recognition of their prominence "throws into question whether the Ipili people even 'exist' in the same way as, say, Motuans or Hageners do . . . They begin to look far more like the local representatives of regionally dispersed 'genealogical groups,' lumped together under one name only because they live in one place as neighbors" (1999, 284). This is not to say that there is no such thing as the Ipili (neither Burton nor I would make that argument) or that there is no sense of a coherent and unique set of culturally specific practices for people in Porgera. But it is to say that belonging in Porgera and to Porgera is much less about being part of an externally bounded group, and much more about living in one of the many culturally distinct centers whose influence on the others fades away as the distance between them increases. Thus the situation we are presented with is a continuum of cultural differences across a landscape through which people have long moved. Ipili identity is not something externally bounded, with clearly visible internal demarcations. There is clearly something culturally distinctive about the people living in Porgera, but they are situated as one of many groups in many valleys, as an ethnic universe connected by vague but felt ties of agnation.

The Problem with "Clans"

Just as there are no clear boundaries between "the Ipili" and "external" peoples, there is no clear distinction between different corporate descent groups "within" Ipili society. As I mentioned in the previous chapter, most external leviathans consider the Ipili to have a cognatic descent system of landowning "clans" composed of one or more "subclans." Thus there are seven landowning clans within the SML territory; they are composed of twenty-three subclans, and one person can be included in several of these groups.

That all sounds very anthropological, yet anthropologists are emphatic that this clan-based model does not fit life in the valley. "In fact," Burton writes, *"there are no corporate groups we can call 'clans' in Porgera"* (1991, 9; italics in original). Biersack, the most senior scholar to address this topic, writes that Ipili sociality is "anomalous yet also brilliant at every turn, and with an unsurpassed openness, and ability to respond organizationally to every contingency" (1995b, 262), which "provides us with an opportunity to transcend dichotomies such as system and agency, structure and history" (1996b, 41). How can we explain the contradiction between the fact that "all landowner agreements, the SEIS [impact study], English speakers locally, and the national media speak of the landowner 'clans' in Porgera" (Burton 1990, 8) and the fact that anthropologists insist that this account is wrong?

It is one of the small ironies of world history that Papua New Guinea's regime for landowner recognition was built around a conflation of descent and residence, since it is Papua New Guinean ethnography that has done the most to demonstrate how flawed that conflation is. Classical British social anthropology imagined humans to suffer from a "problem of order" and to desire "an arrangement which enables persons to live together and co-operate with one another in an orderly social life" that "controls and limits those conflicts that are always possible as the result of divergence of sentiment or interest" (Radcliffe-Brown 1950, 3). The solution to the problem in "stateless" or "acephalous" societies of coordinating the "innumerable social activities that can only be efficiently carried out by means of corporate groups" was "unilineal reckoning," which "makes it possible to create corporate kin groups having continuity in time extending beyond the life of an individual or family . . . [W]here, as in so many non-literate societies, the chief source of social cohesion is the recognition of kinship, corporate kin groups tend to become the most important feature of social structure" (1950, 43). Thus structure functionalism imagined a world in which kin-based corporate groups—including cognatic ones—recruited and socialized members whose actions were regulated by norms, something I've called a "cosmological" form of leviathanness.

The colonial administration of Papua New Guinea was trained largely in this structure functionalist tradition through the Australian School of Pacific Administration (Lawrence 1964; Campbell 1998; Bashkow 1995). It is difficult to gauge whether or not *kiaps* took the book learning of their anthropological mentors seriously. However, it is clear that when models of social organization were called on, these were the ones they used. This training was then passed on to Papua New Guinean civil servants in the period after independence.

At the same time that corporate, lineage–based models colonized the imaginations of Papua New Guinea's colonizers, Papua New Guinea's grassroots people were demonstrating to anthropologists that the "African models" used by A. R. Radcliffe-Brown would not work in the New Guinea highlands (Barnes 1962)—or possibly anywhere else, for that matter. In 1962 Barnes famously argued that African models could not make sense of the ethnography of the highlands region of Papua New Guinea, and a series of papers with detailed field data followed. These early papers revealed that descent and residence were not correlated—Paula Brown (1962), for instance, documented large numbers of nonagnates living on land that was supposedly the home of a particular patriline. It seemed, as Lewis Langness put it, *residence → kinship* "that the sheer act of residence . . . can and does determine kinship. People do not necessarily reside where they do because they are kinsmen; rather, they become kinsmen because they reside there" (1964, 172). There didn't seem to be corporate descent groups in the highlands; descent was not tied to residence; and people seemed to feel free to ignore, bend, and rewrite the rules that Radcliffe-Brown's model predicted would regulate their conduct. "Descent theory in New Guinea has more creases than a secondhand suit, and looks as disheveled," Paul Sillitoe writes, and "each effort to iron out the shortcomings . . . seems to add disconcerting new wrinkles, virtually destroying the integrity of any descent construct" (2010, 45–46).

In fact, "scarcely had the archetype," of Structure Functionalism, "been realized historically than its typological unity began to fragment" (Stocking 1995, 438). Lineage theory was soon foundered on a series of questions: Could kin groups be considered "corporate" in any strict sense (Appell 1983)? Could we speak of ontologically real kinship systems at all (Holy 1979; Schneider 2011)? Were exemplary case studies such as the Nuer (Hutchinson 2000) and the Tiv (Turton 1979) actually lineal or were "even the Nuer . . . not like *The Nuer*" (Kuper 1982, 84)? Can we speak of a difference between ascription and achievement in social life at all (Comaroff and Roberts 1981)? Some anthropologists attempted to untangle these issues by distinguishing between local observed statistical behavior on the one hand, and local ideologies and anthropological models on the other (Keesing 1972). But these approaches imploded, as their conceptual separations of "behavior" from "model" became increasingly untenable.

New trajectories of research emerged out of these approaches. Cultural

anthropology developed phenomenological approaches that redescribed
kinship as part of a broader field of practices of relationality within which
people constructed meaningful lifeworlds, typically through the transaction between words and things (Munn 1986; Stasch 2009; Carsten 2000).
A "pragmatic-poetic" approach (Silverstein 2004, 603), influenced by linguistic anthropology, demonstrated that conduct involves the creation of
intersubjective understandings such that there is no pure behavior that can
be separated from interpretation. According to this view, anthropological
analyses are themselves reentextualizations (or retellings) of local narratives
(Merlan and Rumsey 1991; Lederman 1986). This insight freed anthropologists from attempts to ground their discipline on the distinction between
"our models," "their models," and "reality." Another, more esoteric approach
derived from the work of Marilyn Strathern and Roy Wagner, which was
once called the "New Melanesian Ethnography" but might better be called
"Stragnerian." This approach eschewed the epistemological pretensions of
science and undertook the exegesis of local sociality, which was then used as
an analytic tool in its own right, and as a provocation to rethink ethnography
as a genre (Wagner 1978; Weiner 1988; Strathern 1988; Da Col and Graeber
2011). As a result, anthropology in Papua New Guinea has moved beyond a
focus on lineages as corporate groups and now examines how humans create
and maintain sociality through language and other forms of action.

Yame as Group, Circle, and Set

We can now see the challenge that Porgera poses for a study of kinship. On
the one hand, it requires a nuts-and-bolts approach to social mapping that
articulates well with traditional studies of kinship but is often uninterest-
ing to Stragnerian approaches to sociality. On the other hand, theoretical
sophistication is necessary for the use of conceptual tools from a branch of
anthropological theory that has moved away from circle-and-square genealogical mapping.

Let's begin with terms for groups. What do we mean when we say that
Tuanda and Waiwa are "clans"? The most common term used to describe the
Tuanda in Ipili is that they are a *yame*—Tuanda yame. The term "yame"—
sometimes confusingly translated as "clan"—refers to everyone who shares
a common ancestor: the ancestor Tuanda or Waiwa, for example. Technically we can refer to yame as "cognatic stocks" (Lawrence 1984, 36): each
individual has a "name set" (Biersack 1980, 67) or portfolio of eight yame,

one from each grandparent (the other seven yame in a grandparent's name set are overlooked).

These stocks are recorded in *malu*, or genealogies, which Ipili remember and record. Although malu begin with an apical ancestor, after a few generations comes a level of ancestors after whom "subclans" are named. Shortly thereafter genealogies include people within living memory of the current oldest generation, and the genealogies begin to form something approximating my own census data. The pattern here, in other words, is similar to that used by the Enga, in which there is a sharp break between "historical" events (*atome pi*) and "mythic" ones (*tindi pi*) (Wiessner and Tumu 1998, 25). Although Ipili do not draw this distinction as sharply as Engans appear to, it seems clear to me that it exists for them. "Real" genealogical time seems to start just after the ancestors of the several subclans. The result is a wide swath of collateral space within the lineage that extends up a few generations. When people trace their connections with their relatives, they tend to move horizontally through that space in ways that are often quite elaborate, to locate themselves in relationship to other consanguines, and to shoot directly up through layers of mythical forebears to the apical ancestor. Although the structure of malu suggest some level of segmentation in the orthodox lineage model, they are more properly read as the media through which people establish relationships.

Having—or "taking," as the Ipili say—a name is not the same as being a member of a corporate group; rather, it is "merely the potential for a kinship relationship" (Biersack 1980, 79). Like genealogies reported in nearby Duna, "what is articulated in malu genealogies is a principle not of group recruitment but of individual entitlement" (Stürzenhofecker 1998, 79–80). Name-set affiliations must be potentiated by action—the transaction of goods, simultaneous presence through shared residence, and the other imponderabilia of everyday life—that creates a feeling of amity between people. Biersack refers to this process as the "service economy" (1994, 243; see also Stasch 2009). Ipili conceive of this economy as a transmission of life through exchange and feeding, and it is this transmission that creates a sense of "relatedness" (Carsten 2000). Thus "what is important about the name set . . . is that it makes it possible to define relationships between persons based on the choices each makes" (Biersack 1980, 68). Two people who are Tuanda share this affiliation because they have invested time and energy in that yame—to the detriment, inevitably, of another. In sum, to Ipili, the mean fact of genealogical relatedness does not necessarily produce a relationship.

Consanguineal ties count for little until they have been realized through the contributions of work, wealth, and consociation.

Thus we can see that, in contrast to the situation in classical lineage models, membership in yame is neither exclusive nor ascribed: "it is the use of kinship terms through the relationship between name sets that is ascribed and not 'taking' the names themselves" (Biersack 1980, 78). Indeed, if we had to point to a unique essence of Ipili culture, it would be the fact that involvement with the activation of the unique and localized list of yame lineages is central to life, identity, and the coordination of action. This, rather than a specific cultural patrimony or a bright and clear ethnic boundary, is what makes Ipili people "the Ipili": playing the game of networking via yame, which is a distinct genre of practice and differs from membership in a preexisting leviathan.

Yame have been visualized in three major ways in writings about the Ipili. The first is the popular descent-based lineage model, represented graphically as a genealogy and summarized with the term "clan." We can now see why this approach fails on several levels: yame are not corporate in the way that classic clans are: bride-wealth, homicide payments, and other transactions are "not the responsibility of yame" (1980, 97). Rather, those transactions are the responsibility of an individual, who then mobilizes the members of his personal network (the fact that it is typically a "him" indicates the pervasive sexual inequality in Porgera) who work together to create the prestation (fig. 3.1).

In addition, truly corporate clans have an exclusive membership, while each Porgeran belongs to several yame (Burton 1990). Not only is "clan" affiliation nonexclusive, but Ipili do not consider it a virtue to identify strongly with only one clan. In contrast to a notion of pure and exclusive membership in an agnatic clan, Ipili seek to be middlemen operating between groups and using multiple affiliations to be where the action is. Thus often when outsiders consider someone to be "not really Tiyini" or "not really Tuanda," because the person's claims to that identity are not based on an unbroken line of agnatic descent, they are applying their own outsider ideologies of lineal purity to the Ipili. For Ipili, if someone did have "pure" and singular affiliation, it would be an unfortunate problem, indicating genealogical impoverishment instead of a potentially much richer and wider set of relationships. Thus despite the fact that anthropologists sometimes refer to yame as "clans" for the sake of convenience, yame have little in common with clans or corporate groups in any technical sense, other than the fact that they involve long genealogies.

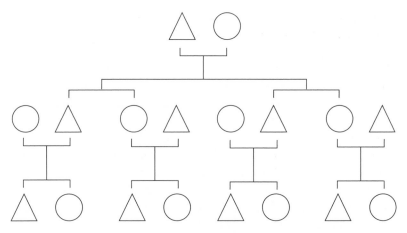

Fig 3.1   *Yame* as lineage: unilineal descent-based diagrams make it difficult to visualize the individual as a member of more than one cognatic stock.

The second model reverses the focus of a corporatist account to see yame as the raw material for ego-focused networks. According to this account, Ipili society is a network of nested "security circles" in Peter Lawrence's sense—"those persons with whom [someone] has safe relationships and towards whom he should observe stringent rules governing marriage, diet, and political obligation" (1984, 28). Here, cognatic stocks are the means of creating an individual's connections (fig. 3.2).

This egocentric approach visually suggests that the individual rather than the group is central in Ipili social life, which runs counter to widely reported beliefs about personal interdependence both among the Ipili and in Melanesia more widely. Furthermore, it does little to explain how individual security circles mesh. Finally, it is not clear that this is how Ipili themselves understand their relationships. Although it is a clear improvement on lineage model, it still leaves something to be desired.

These two approaches attempt to understand Ipili sociality in terms of familiar Western dualisms of individualism and collectivism (Parsons 1961, 85–97). A third way to conceive of Ipili sociality is to take literally metaphors of it as reticulated and rhizomatic (Goldman and Ballard 1998) and visualize it as a network. Tropes of networking have long populated Melanesianists' thinking about social organization, myth, and conceptions of the person. However, few Melanesianists have actually undertaken to use graph theory to conceptualize Melanesian sociality in more than a metaphorical way (see, for instance, Lederman 1986; for more literal uses, see Terrell 2010; Sillitoe 1979).

[handwritten marginal note: Ipili sociality as network]

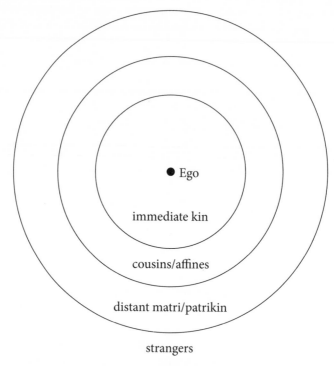

Fig 3.2 *Yame* as security circle: egocentric models obscure the centrality of cognatic stocks to everyday life.

Biersack has argued for the use of this metaphor (1995b, 233), but her diagrams take the form of Venn diagrams of overlapping yame. This approach does a good job of visually demonstrating the concept of overlapping yame membership, but it also has several drawbacks. It presents yame as groups—albeit overlapping ones—with clear boundaries. Individuals are absent. As a result, it reinforces a focus on yame as a sort of group. In addition, these diagrams lack ethnographic specificity: They are abstract representations of a principle of social organization, not actual depictions of any existing network of people. Nor could they be, given the complexities of actual overlappings, which could probably not be accommodated in this format. Thus, Biersack's graphical representations do not do justice to her careful and ground-breaking written accounts of Ipili kinship (fig. 3.3).

A better way to depict Biersack's important conceptualization of Ipili kinship, I would argue, would be to literalize metaphorical uses of network to describe Ipili sociality. Rena Lederman writes that for Mendi people, "'auton-

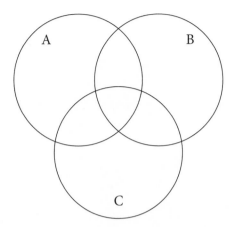

Fig 3.3   *Yame* as set: making the overlap between cognatic stocks obscures the existence of individuals.

omy' . . . is rooted in . . . a matrix of intensely social obligations" (1989, 235). I've used such a matrix (an adjacency matrix, to be precise) to describe Ipili sociality, a system in which people are individuals because of—not in opposition to—the network edges that run through them. Figure 3.4 is a visualization of an adjacency matrix of yame affiliations in Tongeanunga hamlet in Paiela in the 1970s (Biersack 1996b, table 3). Here, each vertex (or node) is a person, and the edges (lines) that connect them are shared *yame* affiliations. These edges are "weighted": the more *yame* two people have in common, the thicker the line that connects them. I have also used a standard spacing algorithm that arranges clusters of closely related people together. As a result the algorithm has placed person 4, whom Biersack reports is the most prominent person in the hamlet, at the center of the network.

Here, yame are seen not as corporate boundaries enclosing a space in which individuals belong, as in a Venn diagram; nor are they lineal, as in a corporatist model, which cannot diagram an individual's multiple connections to different yame; nor are they providers of connections for an ego-focused network, centered on the individual. Rather, yame are represented as edges that do not enclose the space of a corporate form but connect individuals into constellations of relations. Density and overlapping membership may still be represented by visualizing yame networks in grouped forms, using standard weighting procedures from graph theory.

Presenting Ipili society in this way may seem like quibbling over details of visual models, but I believe it has concrete importance. Such an account

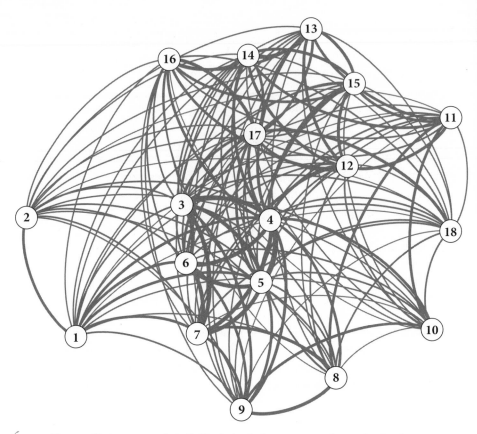

Fig 3.4 *Yame* as network: individuals (nodes) are connected to each other by *yame* affiliations (the lines, or edges).

creates easily understood models that can be displayed to makers of law and policy to explain why Ipili sociality is not clan based. It gives us a method of accurately mapping empirical cases of connection without buying into lineage-based models. It allows us to create a social-mapping model of sociality that articulates with anthropological theories of relationality that have grown remote from the particulars of residence and consociation. Finally, this reticulated understanding is much truer to Ipili idioms. Indeed, graph theory and Ipili often use the same metaphors—for instance, of people being "bridges" (*toko*) or "middle men" (*tombe akali*).

As we've seen, consociation is required to actuate yame connections in order to mobilize people to undertake coordinated group activity. For this reason I believe we ought to think of yame as meaning something similar to the classic network-theoretic concept of "action set": "a "quasi-group" assembled out of a broader network by a particular person or persons who becomes the shared focus of whom or for the sake of whom this current assemblage of people is acting" (Mayer 1966).

This makes sense of the fact that "clan" names in Porgera are simply the names of apical ancestors: "clans" in this case are sets of people gathered for an action—a lawsuit concerning land, a compensation payment, a census—by virtue of their genealogical connection to the apical ancestor. It is also not uncommon to hear people refer to "Daniel yame," meaning not the descendants of Daniel but the assembly of people—united on the basis of consanguinity, affinity, and friendship—whose mutual imbrication is a result of Daniel's central position in their social networks and who might thus work together for a particular purpose, such as helping him make a brideprice payment.

Seeing yame as the basis for action sets also explains the use of yame terms to designate assemblages that participate in political contests within the valley. People often use "Tiyini yame" to refer to a group of people galvanized into assembling together on a particular occasion based on a shared tie to Tiyini—a much smaller and occasion-based collection of people than the larger and virtual set of all people who are Tiyini yame. For instance, during the Yakatabari negotiations many people referred to the faction opposing the PJV as "the Tiyini"—despite the facts that one of the leaders was an agent for Angalaini, and that some of the most influential of the Tiyini agents were not active participants in the action set. "Tiyini-ness" became a basis of the mobilization of personal networks, not an exclusive and clearly defined corporate group. And of course most grassroots Tiyini were excluded from the negotiations altogether.

Finally, it should be noted that in contemporary Porgera yame is used to mean just about any sort of group—I have heard it used to describe groups of security guards and church congregations. This use may suggest that yame means "group" without any connotation of "descent," but in fact this is not quite right. It seems likely that Porgerans see these groups not as corporate groups but as temporary action sets that are ephemeral and only one of many possible arrangements of people. What Eurochristians think of as groups or leviathans are conceived of by Ipili as action sets, or temporary roles—of which an individual could always have more than one. Indeed, as we have seen in the previous chapter, the history of the valley supports such a view. And as we shall see in the next chapter, a method of mobilizing,

using, and then discarding groups for collective action is not unusual in
Papua New Guinea.

Directionality in *Yame* Networking

There is more to life in Porgera than just consanguinity. "Kith" (Blehr 1963)
are an important part of Ipili networks as well: affines, *epo arene* (friends of
friends, or people who share kin ties with someone you share kin ties with),
and friends. This network model could be expanded to add additional sorts
of connections between nodes in order to accommodate these ties, but I
think it is important to note that Ipili have already anticipated me in this regard. Network change in Porgera is "directed" (Kilduff and Tsai 2002): Ipili
"favor dense networks, which consolidate and centralize society" (Biersack
1996b, 34) and actively seek to arrange their networks through controlling
marriages in such a way that affines and unrelated friends (or rather the
friends' children) become kin.

In local parlance, this is described as a merging of yame until everyone
is so interrelated that the incest taboo prohibits further marriages. Indeed,
Biersack paints the desire for such interconnection as an almost eschatologi-
cal desire among Ipili people, who associate this state with an apocalyptic
scenario of future prosperity (Biersack 1996a; see also Golub 2006).

In Porgera, this means that Ipili actively seek to draw powerful outsiders
into their personal networks and keep them there. The goal for dealing with
outsiders is to incorporate them into local communities and then extracting
value or "life" (in the terms of the service economy) from them as reciproc-
ity for hospitality. This strategy has probably been exacerbated by the history
of gold mining in the valley. As we saw in the last chapter, the Ipili have a
long history of incorporating powerful outsiders into their networks in order to benefit from their presence, and indeed the children of outsiders did
play an important role as Ipili. This explains why Ipili, over and above the
promise of money and other benefits, were eager to "host" a mine. Indeed,
Porgera is the site of the only mine in Papua New Guinea whose inhabitants
not only didn't mind, but actually demanded, that workers at their resource
development be accommodated in the valley with them in a multiracial
township.

You do not have to be in Porgera very long before the networking pro-
pensities of Ipili make themselves obvious. Ipili linger over details of people's
name-set affiliations, possible connections among people, methods of drawing ties between people, and so forth. Ipili enjoy discussing the twists and

turns of their genealogies and constantly mull over the fine details of their own potential heritages with an excitement and nostalgia that is somewhere between Talmudic exegesis and the American tendency to discuss in detail the batting averages of the great left fielders of the 1930s. Finding and mobilizing these connections is thus an art, and the situation is one of entrepreneurial agency: Ipili are networkers not only in the context of social structures but also in the more prosaic sense of the term—inveterate handshakers and let's-do-lunchers, they are always on the lookout for new allies and new places where they might find them. Ipili enjoy meeting new people; they constantly seek to expand their social networks and will engage in constant meeting and greeting whenever they are presented with the opportunity.

[handwritten marginal note: (similar to Senegal?)]

Anthropologists are gun-shy of schools of thought such as the transactionalism I have drawn on here because it emphasizes individual, entrepreneurial action, an emphasis rooted in its Euro-Christian genealogy (Sahlins 1996). I would note that the approach I have taken here does not reduce Ipili to economic maximizers. Networks of yame affiliations are not the result of volunteerist, resource-maximizing individuals who use them. Rather, they are the result of history, the previous generations who have slowly and laboriously "made kinship" (Biersack 1996) by arranging marriages, raising children, and creating alliances. Leviathans look for ordered, demarcated institutions whose officeholders they can identify—"the true landowners"— but the real nature of Ipili sociality can be found not in a delineated ethnic group, but in a culturally specific method of tying people together, the need to play the yame game. Biersack puts it this way: "The system as such . . . is best understood as a set of activities, resources, and strategies . . . that political entrepreneurs deploy to shape and manage their world in the name of a collective good" (1996b, 45). It is "a project rather than a structure" (1995b, 233; see also Sartre 1963), or not only a set of cosmological principles but also an ensemble of genres of action.

Land

An excellent example of yame connectivity comes from people's relations to land. Porgerans divide the surface of the earth into two layers, the underlying "bone" (*kulini*) and the "skin" (*umbaini*). At the most general level, there is a clear and intimate relationship between the bone of the ground and a particular cognatic stock. Thus the Waiwa have two tracts of land, one of which is named Waiwanda. Similarly, the Tuanda "own" Apalaka, the Tiyini "own" Yarik, and so on. During large prestations people chant the name of a river or mountain from their territory as a sign of which stock they are from, and hence from which stock their hosts are about to receive pigs. Each yame also has a set of sacred sites on their territory where various spirits associated with the line are said to live, and where sacrifices to those spirits are made.

Thus it is straightforward to say that "the Tiyini own Yarik," but the catch lies in figuring out who precisely gets to be "the Tiyini." As we have seen, the Tiyini are not a clan in the sense of some sort of bounded, corporate group with a determined and exclusive membership: any of the descendants of Tiyini have a claim to be Tiyini. But having a possible relation to Tiyini is very different from living at Yarik and making gardens there. Although there are many people who could not be completely discounted in any future dealings with the bone of the ground, many—indeed, most of them—rarely ever reside full time in Yarik. Indeed, as Biersack notes, "it is impossible to localize cognatic descent groups" (1996b, 25).

Thus saying that "the Tiyini" own Yarik is perfectly true but doesn't get one very far. Despite the intense emotional charge in Porgera surrounding land, identity, respect, and entitlement, actual claims to the bone of the ground are widely diffused and abstract: it is very clear which stock owns the bone of a particular territory, but who exactly constitutes that stock is something that is locked up in the ambiguity of Porgera's network-driven social system. For this reason land disputes in Porgera rarely focus on which stock owns land in principle. Rather, the question is who will successfully be subsumed as a member of that stock.

Issues of landownership are complicated by Ipili conceptualizations of residence. Porgerans distinguish between *tene* and *wana* when they talk of residence—that is, between residents on land whose claim to the bone of its ground comes from their father (tene) and those whose claim derives from their mother (wana). Tene have a morally superior claim to land because of a patrilineal bias in the system, which downplays the enatic connections of wana. As the literature on this distinction in Enga (Barnes 1967; McArthur 1967; Meggitt 1965) makes clear, however, the distinction is not about lineage relationships because it refers only to the gender of one's immediate parent rather than an unbroken line of agnatic or enatic descent—this generation's set of wana will produce tene children if they marry local people. This method of mobilizing a yame affiliation means that unbroken descent on a piece of land, or a genealogy populated only by males, is not necessary to develop a deep attachment to land, despite what appears at first to be a patrilineal bias in the system.

In Porgera, then, much of what is discussed in the idiom of agnation is actually about coresidence. Thus it falls in the category of gender- and lineage-related explications of behaviors that anthropologists might want to classify as "the activation of agnatic ties through consociation." When Ipili discuss these categories, they do not, as some other Melanesian peoples might, speak of children as "not having the blood of the father" or "not being of his semen." Instead, they speak of "eyeball time." "I never see those people," they say, "they live with their mother in their father's place. They never come around here."

In fact, in distinct contrast to common stereotypes of stationary, land-enamored indigenes, "eyeball time" and consociation are central to Ipili goals of network activation and expansion. In their quest for multiple affiliations, Ipili often travel away from their natal area—after all, that's the one constituency that is typically the most nailed down. The ideal big man is a roving polygynist who rotates between wives and (hence) his in-laws as he keeps circulating. This goal "is best attained under a pattern of itineracy in which people . . . 'come and go' (*pua ipu puu*), having houses, gardens, and trees . . . in different places, and visiting different segments of their network serially" (Biersack 1980, 97). Thus "the emphasis is, if anything, on itineracy rather than on residence" (1996b, 25) and the aim is to travel "in a wide orbit, visiting, residing, and/or gardening among affines and consanguines" (1995b, 240). Far from residing in a single place and having a single connection, Ipili are on the move so as to consociate with as many members of their network as possible. The ideal Ipili big man is constantly on tour.

In fact, since Ipili seek to "eliminate or overcome descent unit boundaries as network boundaries" (1980, 101) rather than to create coherent one-"clan"-per-territory localization of descent group boundaries, they believe that "clans should be dispersed; they should intermingle with members of other clans" (1995b, 239). Thus if one cannot use mobility to visit others with shared yame affiliations, one can reside with them on a particular piece of territory: "The local group is therefore actually translocal in its affiliations, and the communities that Paiela residential policy . . . produces are cosmopolitan rather than parochial . . . What is localized in Paiela hamlets is not a descent group . . . but an open-ended—even, by virtue of the recruitment policy and the incest taboo, a self-expanding—segment of an affinal chain" (40). It is not only normal to have nonagnates residing on a piece of territory, it is an explicit goal.

The land rights of resident nonagnates ought not be underestimated. The skin of the ground is something that people have rights to use and transfer on the basis of their individual security circles. Individual plots in a territory can be given by one person to another for use, and, in some sense, ownership can be conferred as well—keeping in mind that it is only ownership in the skin (that is, usufructory rights to the surface of the land) and not in the bone of the ground that is being transferred. The actual distribution of rights of use and occupancy of the surface of the earth is a complex mosaic that is a result of the interaction of numerous people's personal networks. Sometimes, land inheritance can be as simple as a woman passing gardening ground on to her daughter. But in most cases matters are very much more complicated.

In sum, there is a double form of ambiguity in land ownership. On the one hand, there is a vast number of people with a claim to the bone of the ground that is very deeply felt but weakly vested, since the vast majority of those people have not turned their possible identity as a member of a landowner stock into an actual one, and many of them may not even know of their genealogical connection to that land. On the other hand, there are people deeply embedded in a residential group who have definite rights to the skin of the earth, rights that no one can deny even though they are based on "eye-ball time"—work and coresidence—rather than blood ties. These consocial links are definite and indisputable, but not as strong as the more enduring claims to the bone of the ground. Thus, the art of making claims to land in Porgera is, at the practical level, far from the simple model of clan Y owns land Z.

Ethnography in highlands Papua New Guinea is haunted by the argument that sociality in the area is loose. We can see now the ways in which this is, and isn't, the case in Porgera. As Biersack points out, network topography is tight, and people work to make it tighter. Equally, the principles and life-world categories of meaning the Ipili use to build these networks—the cultural structure, in Sahlins's sense—are remarkably intact and have not only been transformed to keep them relevant, but also have forced global capital to restructure its system of recognition to meet their demands. There is no "looseness" in the system in this sense. What is loose, however, is the link between general category and particular case.

Apalaka, A Relocation Settlement

When we turn to the actual ethnographic case of life within the SML territory, it is difficult at first to see the fluid, agency-driven network I described in the previous section. Instead what we find are entire villages built on the basis of lineage models of descent and residence. A closer look at one of these relocation communities, Apalaka, and its sister site, Waiwanda, will reveal that despite the seemingly potent regimes of centralization, homogenization, and standardization that the mine can harness, the relocation communities it has constructed still do not reflect in their composition the corporate principles that guided their construction. These communities, the black boxes out of which "the Ipili" emerge, can be opened to reveal the untidy, noncorporate processes at work within them.

When the mine was being built, the members of landowning yame living within the SML territory were relocated to an area of their choice. Some people were relocated far from their former neighbors, but most chose to live in nucleated settlements built around an *ama* (a cleared area or central meeting place). In fact, the history of relocation is complex and includes several bouts of house building as the mine acquired land—initially for the mine and later for its growing waste dumps. The results, however, are straightforward: densely populated nucleated settlements, each of which is centered on a public square, located on a distinct territory, and associated with a particular "clan." Thus the Tiyini live in Yarik, the Tuanda live in Apalaka, the Waiwa live in Waiwanda, the Pulumaini live in Kulapi, the Angalaini live at Mungalep (much of which was adjacent to, but not in, the SML territory) and the Mamai live at Panandaka (for more on the Porgera relocation, see Banks 1999 and Bonnell 1999; for relocation in Papua New Guinea more generally, see Asian Development Bank 2000, 55–73). Ironically, even as anthropology and other disciplines critiqued the hypostasized "villages" of the area studies literature in the late 1980s and early 1990s, the Porgera gold mine was building exactly these sorts of settlements, one per clan.

Apalaka, the community where I lived, was one such relocation community—the ostensible home of the "Tuanda clan." Like all Ipili, the Tuanda are part of a larger, regional lineage diaspora. In the case of the Tuanda, genealogies relate that Apalaka was settled when Tuanda left his home in Hoyebia in the Tari basin (north of the town of Tari and near the location of Robert Glasse's original fieldwork) and settled in Apalaka, although not before establishing communities in Enga territory around Mulitaka. Some claimed that if I traveled to Hoyebia, I would be able to trace the Tuanda diaspora all the way southwest to Lake Kutubu, where the landowners of the Kutubu oil project "were also Tuanda." Although the connection to Hoyebia and Mulitaka seemed certain to me—I met people who were from there and who visited there and confirmed it—these farther-flung ties to another lucrative resource development project were harder to prove. At any rate the Waiwa, the "clan" that was part of the Waiwanda area adjacent to Apalaka, claimed much more clearly to have ties only with groups in Paiela and the Tari basin and did not claim connection to any group in Enga.

Historically, Apalaka is a settlement of some antiquity—it appears as "Abaraka" in John Black's 1938 diary of his patrol into Porgera. This does not mean that the Apalaka that Black wrote about is identical to the settlement where I lived, however. Most of where Apalaka was originally located is now covered by the Anjolek waste dump, a large, erodible dump that carries waste rock from the open pit down to the Kaiyia River (for geotechnical aspects of the waste dump, see G. Parker 2004). Today Apalaka is a cluster of relocation houses and the improvised residences that grew up around them. Perched on the slopes that emerge out of the waste dump, Apalaka is basically a bulging pocket of land bounded by the waste dump on two sides and the open pit of the mine on a third side. In addition to Apalaka, this pocket of land is home to two other settlements. Ekanda, upstream of the main settlement, is a break-off community founded by the brother of one of Apalaka's two Landowner Negotiating Committee (LNC) members. Up the slope from Apalaka is an area known as Waiwanda, which extends to the uninhabited ridge top. On the other side of that ridge line is the relocation settlement of Yarik. Here I will focus on Apalaka and Waiwanda.

We can say that each territory is associated with a particular "clan" and its constitutive "subclans." Apalaka, for instance, is the home of the Tuanda, while Waiwanda is the home of the Waiwa, and Yarik is the home of the Tiyini. These territories are then subdivided along subclan lines. Thus (very roughly) the Tuanda Ulupa own the land between the waste dump and the Apalaka *ama*, while the Yapala own the land between the Apalaka *ama* and Waiwanda. There is only one subclan of the Waiwa, the Yaliape, in Waiwanda—the other subclan lives outside the SML territory. My house during my stay in Porgera was in Waiwanda proper; since Waiwanda is a satellite community without an *ama* of its own, I took as my field site both Apalaka and Waiwanda, and I was considered to be affiliated with both the Tuanda and the Waiwa. When people asked me where I lived in Porgera, I would answer Apalaka and specify Waiwanda only if my interlocutor had lived in the valley for some time or knew quite a bit about it—it was roughly equivalent to describing yourself as being from Manhattan as opposed to Alphabet City. As a result, for much of this chapter I will use the term "Apalaka" to refer to both communities collectively.

The Tiyini, Tuanda, and Waiwa are not just any clans. They are the triad at the core of the seven landowning groups. As we have seen, the Tiyini are not only the owners of the land on which Porgera's open cut mine is located, but they are also closely associated with the serpent Kupiane, the mythical origin of the Porgera ore body. The genealogies of both the Tuanda and the Waiwa involve migrations to Porgera, and both groups record their early ancestors as arriving in Porgera and marrying women from the Tiyini, thus making the three groups interrelated and the truest of the true landowners.

Apalaka's Sights and Sounds

As we saw in chapter 1, it is hotly contested whether or not these reloca-tion communities are healthy and safe places to live in and, if they are not, whether the PJV or local people are to blame. Because these communities are located within the SML territory, the extent to which they are being affected or "squeezed" by the mine is a topic that can be addressed only by someone with extensive expertise in assessing the ecological and environmental im-pacts of gold mining on a community. Experientially, however, I can report that people in Apalaka do feel surrounded by the mine. It is difficult to con-vey to the reader the extent to which relocation communities feel hedged in by mining operations: the sense that one is surrounded by waste, hemmed in, limited in resources, and removed from life in the rest of the valley.

These relocation communities are not like other areas of Papua New Guinea that I have visited. The view downhill from practically every area of Apalaka is of a massive expanse of waste dump—a flat moonscape out of which a few brave weeds poke. The vast surface of the waste dump alternates between soil-like firmness and the consistency of quicksand. People often venture out onto it to try to find gold in the rock (always unsuccessfully, as far as I know), while children swim in the large pools of gray rainwater that collect in depressions on its surface. When blasting operations are regularly scheduled, it is possible to set your watch by the tremors that accompany them. Similarly, the mud—which is ubiquitous in Porgera and even more omnipresent in the SML territory—along with what expatriates describe as the "squalor" of the relocation communities make these places fairly grim. The incredible density of settlement makes them crowded, and the pres-ence of cash means the presence of purchased foodstuffs, which leads to the creation of garbage for which no sanitary system exists. There is no suf-ficient supply of firewood, and a jury-rigged system of electrical cables ex-tends from relocation houses connected to the power grid supplying the mine to relocation houses and bush houses that would otherwise be without power. These new communities are too high up for, and on terrain that is too poor, for much agriculture to take place (although gardens are still planted). Anyone who has had occasion to live in Apalaka will find Glenn Banks and Susanne Bonnell's (1997) assessment of the plight of relocation communities to be convincing indeed.

The community in which I lived, in other words, was considered dangerous, dirty, degraded, and squalid by expatriate mine employees and others who visited it. At one point a high-school student from East Sepik Province came to visit her brother who had married a member of the community there. When I asked this smart and modern young woman what she thought of the place, she replied, "I can say these people live like animals." Drinking bouts, gambling, prostitution, and violence against mine employees are said to lie in store for any who venture up there. Many outsiders consider the relocation communities to be at the forefront of the decadent, self-destructive behavior of Ipili who receive money from the mine. They point to outrageous expenditures on alcohol and increased rates of polygyny and domestic violence as two of the most obvious ways in which Ipili have misused the money they have received from the mine. In addition, the steady influx of immigrants from other areas is a major engine of social change in Porgera and threatens to turn Porgerans into strangers on their own land. Although stories of prostitution in Porgera have, in my opinion, been greatly overestimated (at least during my fieldwork), the rest is more or less true—on one occasion when a PJV vehicle drove into the village after dark (to drop me off after a meeting at the mine site), local people threw stones at it.

Thus these communities remain black boxes for the government and the mine: although densely populated by Papua New Guinea standards, they are so unwelcoming to outsiders and mine employees that it is difficult to gauge exactly what is going on within them. Even the social science work that has been done, such as that by Banks (1997), is based on brief survey work and, although well done, does not paint a detailed picture of life in these places that long-term participant observation can provide.

With all of this in mind, let us now turn to the actual inhabitants of Apalaka and Waiwanda. Although the settlement of Kewanda—which is visible on the hills on the other side of the waste dump—is also technically in the SML territory and includes a few relocation houses, Apalaka is the relocation village farthest from the government station. The unsealed, all-weather road to the community is maintained by the mine, but landslips frequently make vehicular transport up to the village impossible, halting the privately run buses that provide service to the village and the shuttle service that mine contractors run to relocation communities to bring the local mine employees to work.

Apalaka itself is at the top of a high and steep hill, reached by a grueling climb. As one walks up the hill one passes settlements on either side, including the seldom-used community school. The road ends in the main *ama*, which is lined with "tradestores"—the ubiquitous mom-and-pop metal shacks that represent entrepreneurial activity to most Papua New Guineans. In addition to selling cooking oil, canned fish and meat, soap, tea, guitar strings, and mercury (for refining gold), some tradestores also have pool tables, and a few have VCRs and televisions that show movies to eager audiences. The Ipili taste in film is erratic—*Superman* was too corny, *Fight Club* unfathomable. The most popular films during my time in Porgera were *Kickboxer* (with Jean-Claude Van Damme, whom Porgerans believed to be named Frankie), *Anaconda* (starring Jennifer Lopez and Ice Cube), and the documentary *The People of Porgera*, which offered villagers a glimpse of deceased loved ones.

In theory, all Ipili love the idea of owning and running their own business. In practice, however, most tradestores in the settlement were not actually open for business. Half operated sporadically when they had stock, and four or five were open regularly. But there was only one tradestore in Porgera that was consistently open, and that one was owned by an enterprising Huli man who had settled in Porgera years before. The inventory of the other stores suffered from the pressures of hungry but penniless relatives to whom food could not be refused, the difficulties of transporting goods up to Apalaka, and the more competitive prices at the government station, where more serious businessmen sold wholesale. Thus most tradestores were closed and locked up or served as places where the families that owned them could sell betel nuts, cigarettes, *palawa* (similar to fried dough), and popsicles and could relax without having to hike up to their houses (for more on tradestores and business in Porgera in general, see Banks 1999).

In more traditional Ipili communities people live in homesteads dispersed across the landscape, separated from each other by gardening ground. People value their privacy in Porgera as well, but they live in much closer quarters. It is considered unacceptable to be able to see another person's house from your own. In general, it is not acceptable to visit someone's house without warning them beforehand of your visit. Any movement in one's house area after dark is a cause for alarm and is met by the use of force. Occasionally when I, the clueless anthropologist, took a wrong turn and stumbled into a neighbor's compound, I would be met by angry men with machetes. As I found out in the course of my census work, even those residents of Apalaka who had lived there since it was created had never visited large areas of it, including the homes of people with whom they were acquainted.

As a result, the paths that led out of the ama up to people's houses are often so overgrown that the canopy has spread overhead and created a tunnel. Houses are surrounded by fences and hedges. This fact, combined with the steep and uneven geography of Apalaka, could make finding one's bearings very difficult. The flip side of this was that identifying and delineating Ipili households was relatively straightforward, since they are literally bounded off from their neighbors. Typically they are clustered in compounds based around one or more relocation houses that had been built together. Alongside these, numerous houses of bush material—typically referred to as *haus kuk* (cook houses)—were constructed. The most important reason that Ipili built these structures, they told me, was to ensure that in the "next relocation" (whenever that might be) they would receive a permanent material house in exchange for it. Many also prefer to sleep in bush houses rather than in their relocation houses. Cynical mine employees determined to squeeze every ounce of irony out of the situation inside the SML territory often raise their eyebrows at the fact that people are so eager to have another relocation house in the future, when they appear to prefer bush houses to the relocation houses they already have. I briefly discussed dissatisfaction with relocation houses in the previous chapter. Here I will merely note that in my experience they are in fact quite cold compared to bush houses, which can be heated with less fuel and so are more comfortable for older people who need more heat. In general, bush houses are places where visitors could stay, people could cook using an old-fashioned stove, and old people could sleep comfortably.

Community Dynamics in Apalaka

Moving from an ethnography of life in a relocation village to an analysis of life in a relocation village is difficult. Even basic questions about the population of these areas are difficult to answer. It is almost impossible to overstate the mobility of people within the SML territory. As we've seen, Ipili have strong predilections for itinerancy and multilocal residence, and these combine with Porgera's status as a regional hotspot to make even apparently simple questions like "How many people live in Apalaka?" very difficult to answer. Even relatively poor landowners move between houses within their relocation settlement, move to other villages inside the SML territory, and go on weeklong trips west to Paiela or east to Enga—or even further afield. At the same time, visitors are so frequent that it was not always easy to tell the visitors apart from the residents.

Distinguishing between migrants and residents is difficult because Apalaka as I encountered it was barely a decade old. It does not make much sense to speak of "migrants" and "nonmigrants" in terms of some sort of long-term residence on the land. Most of the Tuandans now living in Apalaka had migrated out of the original village in order to be closer to the mining camp that operated at Alipis in the 1980s. Thus "relocation" to Apalaka was not so much the shifting of an established residential group from one location to another as it was the creation of a village out of the people who had—with the exception of a small group—not lived there for some time. Technically, any one in Apalaka over the age of ten is an immigrant. Finally, residence in the SML territory was highly politicized, since being a resident or landowner entitled one to various forms of compensation and benefits, which meant that Ipili tendencies toward secrecy were even more pronounced than usual when it came to issues of land tenure and household membership.

As a result of all of these difficulties, my attempt to conduct a census of Apalaka and Waiwanda took place at the very end of my fieldwork, after almost two years of residence in the area. At that point I had already visited many households and knew most community members (and frequent visitors) by sight. The mine had recently hired a company to produce orthorectified aerial photography of the entire SML area and allowed me to make a copy for my own use. I used it to systematically walk through Apalaka and Waiwanda, making sketch maps of each homestead area and marking all bush houses and structures made of permanent material. Over the course of a few weeks, I then visited each household and asked who lived there. Most people were happy to answer, partially because they trusted me, but also because they were eager to have their claims to land recorded in every possible forum imaginable. A few even offered to share with me their malu, or genealogical entitlement to their land. This was, in general, secret, very sensitive knowledge, and I declined to record it when offered. Many people who were visitors or immigrants to the area might have shied away from official census takers, but since I was myself a visitor, these were often the people I knew best—it was the solitary families who preferred to pursue gardening that were actually the hardest for me to reach. In sum, then, although the assignment was a daunting one for a first-time fieldworker, I feel relatively optimistic about the quality of my results.

Table 1   Population of Waiwanda and Apalaka

	Waiwanda	Apalaka	Total
Men	62	334	396
Women	70	345	415
Total	132	679	811

Because residence in Porgera is highly politicized, I do not want to present detailed findings from my census beyond what is absolutely necessary to discuss, at a general level, community dynamics in Apalaka. Table 1 shows population statistics for both Apalaka and Waiwanda. You can see immediately that Waiwanda has a much smaller population than Apalaka. There is a slight gender imbalance in both villages in favor of women. My data show roughly 811 regular residents, although it is difficult to say how many "households" there are. Some "households" were houses that were home to only two or three people who preferred their privacy. Others were composed of a compound of six or seven bush houses surrounding a single relocation house and might house more than sixty people.

Difficulties in Finding "Landowners" in Census Data

Can we find in Apalaka a clear group of people who count as "landowners"? One would expect that the answer would be yes: discourses within the valley regularly contrast *epo arene* (translated either as "guests" or "squatters" depending on the speaker) with "real landowners." In fact it is difficult to accurately formulate a definition of *epo arene* that could be used as a stable category for understanding social dynamics in Apalaka and Waiwanda. This is not because the term is not used—it is, often—but because it is "essentially contested" (Gallie 1955). As a result, the term on the opposite side of this dichotomy, "landowner," is equally amorphous.

Table 2 provides information about the residents of Apalaka and Waiwanda who lack a consanguinal relationship to Tuanda or Waiwa. Depending on how one defines *epo arene*, either 222 people out of 811 (27.3 percent) are outsiders, or 293 people out of 811 (36 percent) of the population are not in

Table 2   "Outsiders" Living in Waiwanda and Apalaka

	Paiela	Non-SML[1] Porgera	Ethnic Engan	Ethnic Huli	Other/ unknown	Total
WAIWANDA						
Husband marrying in	4	1		3	1	9
Wife marrying in	5	3	2	1	1	12
Relative of husband marrying in				3		3
Relative of wife marrying in	1					1
Epo arene man						0
Epo arene woman				1		1
Epo arene child						0
Waiwanda **Total**	10	4	2	8	2	26
APALAKA						
Husband marrying in	19	5	7	7	3	41
Wife marrying in	18	11	16	3	7	55
Relative of husband marrying in	1				3	4
Relative of wife marrying in	3	1	4			8
Epo arene man	1		9	7	6	23
Epo arene woman			8	3	3	14
Epo arene child			21	2	2	25
Apalaka **Total**	42	17	65	22	24	170
Total	52	21	67	30	26	196

[1]SML is special mining lease territory.

some sense "landowners." I will begin by discussing this first statistic and then explain the sociology and politics of *epo arene* that could be used to produce the second statistic.

This high percentage of outsiders is not surprising since the total includes spousal affiliates—men and women who have "married in" to the SML territory (although it does not include Tuandan spousal affiliates in Waiwanda and vice versa) and who it would be difficult to consider illegitimate immigrants. Spousal affiliates are drawn mostly from outside the territory for several reasons. First, the populations of most yames in the territory are heavily intermarried, so further marriages might be incestuous. Second, Apalaka is the end of the road, and Tuandans with spouses from within the territory often choose to reside on the spouse's land because it is closer to the road and the government station. Finally, marriages that occur between landowners are often polygynous unions, in which men take additional wives in order to secure their position as members of all seven landowning clans. These men are typically multilocal, and although they often visit Porgera to network with their wives and affines, they do not sleep in the village often enough to be considered "resident" there.

The two figures indicate immediately the difference between Waiwanda and Apalaka. Waiwanda is a more rural enclave of a less powerful stock that rides on the back of the more densely populated Apalaka. It is not surprising, therefore, that there would be considerably fewer epo arene in Waiwanda than Apalaka. Table 2 indicates clearly that one of the most common classes of people who move to Apalaka are Paielans who are marrying "up" to Porgera. The high number of men who marry Porgeran women and then reside in Porgera clearly indicates what on-the-ground fieldwork confirms: these men were leaving low-prestige rural communities and coming to the more urban and high-prestige SML territory. Porgerans see their country cousins as hard workers who know how to do things like make bush houses—tasks at which landowners in the territory were inexpert. No other ethnic group in the study had as many men choosing to reside uxorilocally as the Paielans.

The table also indicates the predominance of Engan women coming down the highway to settle in the SML territory as spouses. Although I did not attempt a rigorous tabulation of these women's place of origin within Enga, in my experience almost all of them were from the Laiagam area, or other points between Laiagam and Porgera in west Enga. Paielan women continue to marry Porgeran men, as they always have done. Porgerans from more distant lineages such as those in the Lower Porgera Valley or Tipinini also frequently marry in, usually because landowners in the SML territory do not have preexisting consanguinal ties with those areas and hence can marry them without worrying about adding a possibly incestuous tie to their kinship portfolio.

Despite the opinions of the government and the mine about Porgera, these findings indicate that it is relatively uncommon in Apalaka for in-marrying spouses to act as "migration anchors" who are followed to Porgera by members of their natal community. The image of a woman's entire family moving in from Laiagam three weeks after she's married a Porgeran man isn't borne out by the data. Indeed, the number of "true" epo arene—people who settle in Apalaka without direct consanguinal or affinal connections—is relatively small: 40 out of 811 people, or just under 5 percent of the population. These people are often friends or clients of powerful Tuandans. The members of one family of Engans from Laiagam, for instance, were referred to as "work men" for the powerful landowner who hosted them, indicating their subordinate status as clients.

Ambiguities in *Epo Arene* Status

In fact, it is telling that the largest single class of people in Apalaka today who lack any kin ties to the Tuanda and Waiwa stocks are not people who have migrated there at all, but children born in Porgera to immigrating Engan parents. This mirrors the crucial and more general dynamic we are seeing of massive generational growth that is not offset by infant mortality or outmigration.

Another question is whether or not children of immigrating Engans are considered to be Tuandans. As I mentioned above, the problem of defining "the Ipili" as a clearly bounded ethnic group makes it difficult to decide what—other than a commitment to the community—makes one an *epo arene*. The Marinaka are a clear example of this definitional difficulty. In this case, the "clan diasporas" provided a charter for inmigration. The Marinaka, considered one of the "brother groups" of the Tuanda, live down the highlands highway in the area between Porgera and Laiagam. In the late 1960s and early 1970s Ambi Kipu (a powerful patron and one of the Tuanda's members on the LNC) befriended a Marinakan man, who eventually came to live with him in Porgera. This man served as the anchor for a wave of Marinakan migration that led an entire community of ethnically Engan citizens to settle in Apalaka. Or are they ethnically Engan? After all, they are related to Tuanda himself. The point here is that regardless of the status Marinakans may have had in the past, today they form a sort of minicommunity of second-class citizens. They are not considered to be "true landowners" and do not have access to money or job opportunities—despite the fact that they have lived in Porgera as long as most Porgerans have. Thus, depending on whether or not they are classified as epo arene, the percentage of "outsiders" in the community could be as high as 36 percent.

Finally, it is interesting to note that much of the movement of "outsiders" perceived in Porgera is a result of migration to the valley that makes use of the mine's reified notion of "landowner," but not the terms of the Porgeran community. One household in Apalaka is based around a married couple of two Tuandans, whose union was considered incestuous by the rest of the community. Disgraced, they still live in the village but have little to do with it and are rarely seen in the ama—I was surprised, in fact to find how large their household was when I visited there during my census work. Their children married people from Waiya, a fringe Enga settlement that Jacka described (2003, 289–303). Previously a center of population, Waiya is today distant from the highlands highway and relatively underpopulated. In fact, many men and women from Waiya moved to Apalaka. To a certain extent, then, we can say that Waiya was absorbed by Apalaka. This population does not strictly fall into the category of epo arene because people used affinal connections to come to Apalaka. Nonetheless, people from Waiya are considered by many Apalakans as tolerated but unwelcome "outsiders" who are part of a disgraceful household—in some sense less a part of the community than are Engans and Huli who have strong histories of coresidence but lack affinal and consanguineal ties.

Rentier Leadership in Apalaka

Like other Ipili, Apalakans and Waiwandans actively attempt to incorporate powerful outsiders into their security circles. Unlike other Ipili, however, landowners in the SML territory can offer outsiders incentives such as royalty checks and access to jobs. This provides a mechanism for landowners to convert those who would otherwise be friends and acquaintances into subordinate clients. In order to explain this dynamic more fully, and the implications that it has for how people are subsumed into the category of epo arene, it is useful to contrast the situation in Porgera with the "rentier leadership" described by Burton (1997) in the Upper Watut Valley, in Morobe Province.

Burton's discussion of rentier leadership is drawn from his study of landowners enriched by prospecting and mining activities undertaken near the

Hidden Valley prospect in the Upper Watut. Burton argues that in the Hidden Valley area, senior men use their control over land to become "patrons," a term he deliberately uses for its English connotations of "a reasonably expansive fellow, a sponsor" as well as the "stern figure not to be argued with" of the French usage, with its connotations of "not-to-be-brooked autocracy" (5). This control puts them in conflict with other relatives who have claims on the land, and patrons then gain and maintain power by allowing non-owners to settle on the land in return for their deference and allegiance. Typically, the patron also operates a sort of embryonic tributary system in which he receives a portion of the food, firewood, and other resources produced on that land (8–9). Just as Claude Lévi-Strauss sees house societies emerging out of egalitarian kinship arrangements (1987, 1982), Burton suggests that the rise of a patron marks the formation of a semi-institutionalized personal power that emerges from, but surpasses, kin-based ties. The key here is that inequities that would normally be leveled by fissioning processes (as when disgruntled junior relatives found their own settlements) solidify in the context of resource development: "In pre-colonial times . . . the inequality I have described would have been temporary and unimportant . . . But this circle is now broken and settlements are permanent. As a consequence, as secondary landowners are removed from active participation in village decision-making, a stratification of rights has occurred" (Burton 1997, 9). Burton's prediction that "it may be that he [the patron] is a creation of the post-colonial period with its growing emphasis on the ownership of resources" (9) appears to be borne out by the situation in Porgera, where a similar stratification is taking place. However, there are differences between the kind of settlement in Apalaka and the one Burton describes in the Upper Watut. In the Watut, the rentier leader's position is tied to claims to land that are legitimated by reference to some sort of genealogical charter. This source of legitimacy is thus based on kinship and genealogy despite the fact that the rentier leader's interests are often at odds with those of his kin:

> The patron heads his patriline, but far from ruling it, he is likely to be permanently at odds with most of it for quite a lot of the time. This is because it lacks the features of group solidarity that it would have if it were clan-like. Nor do patriline "brothers" owe a debt of allegiance to the head, as clients are expected to. They should be loyal, but they offer a divisible loyalty at the best of times. The patriline is only a pedigree with rights attached to it, not a small bit of a corporate group. As for members of other patrilines who reside with the owners of the land the settlement stands

on, these people are simply clients of the patron and have limited rights to say or do anything. (8)

As Burton describes it, the patron's control of land can conflict with the interests of his kin when his position puts an end to the possibility that they might be able to use the open field of social arrangements in their own interests to secure the use of and rights to land.

Although Burton's description of genealogy as "a pedigree with rights" describes Porgeran malu quite well, there are differences between the Upper Watut and Porgera. In regard to land in Apalaka, we do not see the marked sense of conflict between the rentier leader and his kinsmen that Burton describes for the Watut. Rather, each Ipili household has become something of a rentier operation in miniature, with its own line of immigrant clients, typically affines but occasionally epo arene. In a few situations—such as my own, and that of the Huli storekeeper who was an important part of the community—these relationships could be reversed and individuals could find their positions eclipsed by the too-powerful outsiders they had invited into their communities. Indeed, the danger of this occurring and of the Ipili becoming strangers on their own land is a constant source of concern for those who write about them. On the whole, though, during my fieldwork Apalakans were successful in taking traditional ties of affinity, consanguinity, and friendship and remaking them into rentier ties of patronage.

In Porgera, epo arene today largely means the group of people who were formerly entangled in Ipili security circles and came to live in Porgera as still roughly equal guests of the Tuanda and Waiwa. Now, in the postmine age, they have become subordinates and clients to their Ipili hosts. The term "epo arene" once had the connotations of "friend" and "guest," but it is now translated into English as "squatter." This shift in the English translation of the term corresponds with the shift in the social dynamics of Apalaka. Much of this transformation has to do with inmigration, of course, but much of it also has to do with the way in which Ipili identity in the village is being refigured as a result of the local population's interaction with outside forces.

In the course of the Yakatabari negotiations we saw that the land on which the Yunarilama portal was to be opened was owned by Busane, a man who originally came by his land after moving from Tari to Porgera as an alluvial miner. It may have seemed strange that he should be considered as the "true landowner" instead of the Tiyini agents for the land. However, this sort of settlement is not an isolated incident. Another household in Porgera is based on a Huli miner who came to Porgera and settled. He has been part of the community for decades longer than most Porgerans have been alive. Equally, there is a large Engan household that has a long history in Porgera. It dates back to a founding father who was good friends with an Apalakan man. They contributed to each other's bride-wealth, and the Engan man came to settle in Porgera with his friend. He is now a grandfather, and three generations of Engans live in Apalaka. And who is to say that he is not a resident? The claims of these sorts of epo arene are very strong and demonstrate how seriously epo arene ties could be taken in Porgera prior to the coming of the mine. Do we say that these people are not "true Porgerans" and are epo arene?

Not everyone in Porgera is a rich landowner who gets around in a four-wheel-drive truck with tinted windows, but even within the relatively humble households in the SML territory, landowners are leveraging their identities to become rentier leaders. Indeed, they are not merely leveraging them, they are remaking them. When *epo arene* become "squatters" rather than "friends who have come to stay," a more restrictive definition of "Ipili" emerges, and the number of people who can be considered "outsiders" increases dramatically—to over a third of the population.

The Paper World

In the last section I examined the way that Ipili identity is used in Apalaka and Waiwanda. But Porgera is more than just the village, and Ipili identity can be employed in contexts that are still "local" even if they are not "the village." As I mentioned above, being a landowner in Porgera gives individual Ipili access to benefits that most Papua New Guineans can only dream of enjoying, such as royalty payments, other monetary compensation, and employment at the mine. The key, of course, is making sure that they can feasibly construe themselves as being "landowners." Yet, as the analysis in this section will suggest, the categories under which Ipili must subsume themselves are murky, ambiguous, and poorly structured. In fact, these categories resemble more closely the open-ended repertoire of relationship making that Ipili themselves practice, rather than the structured, routinized bureaucratic rationality that governments and companies like to believe is their typical modus operandi. Critics of high modern attempts to make local people "legible" might expect government institutions to refuse to see the complexity of Ipili identity. And yet Ipili identity is not coherently purified by official means of recognition because those means lack a coherent rationale about who to include and who to exclude.

On the surface, there is a paper world of names, identities, and criteria whose goal is to comprehensively list and describe who "the Porgera landowners" are based on criteria drawn from Porgeran custom. However, closer examination reveals to us that this paper world is neither panoptic nor comprehensive. In fact it forms a series of arenas within which claims and counterclaims for identity (and hence entitlements) are made. These arenas are not just scenes of activity and contest in a metaphorical sense: most of these claims are also made in particular physical locations, typically the government station at Porgera or the mine's community affairs offices. These locations thus represent the first step in the physical dissemination of knowledge about the Ipili out of the SML territory and into the broader world.

The government is a good place to start our tour of the paper world. Perhaps the most canonical list of Ipili landowners is the "Schedule of Owners" that was generated by the team that produced the land study. It was completed in 1988 and has been supplemented since then by two "Child Register" lists that are meant to update the total number of landowners. In another publication (Golub 2007a) I have described the creation of the schedule of owners and given an example of its internal incoherence. Here I will only briefly mention how this plays out in the case of Tuanda and Waiwa. As the title "Child Register" suggests, these lists appear to operate on a principle of consanguinity. Everyone who can trace a blood relationship to the apical ancestors of the clans in the SML territory is included. Thus the "Schedule of Owners" includes 608 names of people in the Tuanda "clan," while the 1994 "Child Register" includes another 510. The "Schedule of Owners" has 564 names for the Waiwa Yaliape, and the "Child Register" has another 411 names—far more than the actual population of Waiwanda. These lists were designed to be inclusive and to accommodate all Porgerans who had ties to the Tuanda and Waiwa ancestors in their cognatic portfolio, even if they had not activated them or resided outside of Apalaka—everyone, in other words, who could possibly be considered to have a claim to the bone of the ground in Porgera. The lists thus tell very little about who has activated these connections and thus might concretely be considered a Tuandan, much less who might be considered an actual resident of Apalaka.

The closer that one looks at these records, the more problematic they become. First, they include spousal affiliates, which complicates the idea that the main criterion for inclusion in the lists is consanguinity. Furthermore, the supposed segmentation of Tuanda into two "subclans" does not occur in this document; despite the fact that the document is supposedly the precedent for creating two Tuandan agents, the words "Ulupa" and "Yapala" (the two Tuanda subclans) do not appear in the "Schedule of Owners." Instead, it features a number of other entries in the "subclan" spot on the top of each page. For instance, we have "Kareya" and then a series of what are presumed to be sub-subclans—Kareya (Aiyengi), Kareya (Amini), and so forth—as well as a handful of names of other corporate groups.

Most tellingly, the subclan Marinaka (Lio) is included, and its "address" (that is, its location before relocation) is listed as "c/- Catholic Mission Kasap, Yangiyangi Village, Mulitaka Patrol Post—Lagaip District." This is, in other words, the Marinaka group that is part of the larger clan diaspora associated with Tuanda: Mulitaka is ethnically West Engan and outside the Porgera District. They are the same group mentioned above as a large "outpost" that lives in Tuanda—despite the fact that they are listed as landowners! The list includes ninety-four names, eighty-seven in Laiagam and seven people who live in Porgera proper, including one Marinaka man, his wife, and their three children. However, no Marinaka agent was ever appointed to serve in any capacity, the Marinaka are not listed as a subclan in the land study or the Porgera Agreements, and they are not listed in the "Child Register" of 1994. Between the "Schedule of Owners" and the land study, then, they apparently lost their status as "landowners."

Ironically enough, the "Schedule of Owners" is in some ways the most legally important document associated with Ipili identity, but it is also one of the least relevant. Although it was central to issuing the mine's lease, Ipili today gain little direct benefit from being included on this list. The copies of the list that I found were locked away in disused and dusty government files. Other forms of identity, such as being on the list to receive royalty payments, are much more relevant.

Royalties

For the Ipili whom I encountered during my fieldwork, the most important mode of being a landowner was not being listed on the "Schedule of Owners" but being on the list of people who receive royalties from the government. As we have seen, the Porgera Agreements mandate that a certain percentage of the government's royalties on gold sold by the mine be redistributed to landowners. As a result, landowners receive checks every three months based on the mine's performance. These checks thus represent a sort of permanent dole or pension to which every Ipili can aspire. The checks are distributed on a subclan basis and are tied to the total amount of land that each subclan owns in the SML territory. Thus, clans that have had more of their land damaged or destroyed by the mine receive larger checks. Royalties are also paid at two separate rates, one for adults and one for children.

The dynamic of the distribution of these checks is based on two facts. First, the size of the total payment to Ipili is linked to the mine's profitability. Hence it is theoretically in the Ipili's interest to maximize the mine's profits—a fact of which the mine often reminds them. Second, the easiest way to gain more money is to receive more checks.

There are several ways to do this. Since one can have multiple clan affiliations, the most obvious way would be to be listed on the rosters of every clan that one belongs to. Men who are not members of all seven clans—few men are—can round out their check receivership by marrying polygamously into the remaining clans. Since children receive checks, parents can grab a larger slice of the royalty pie by having (or claiming to have or claiming responsibility for) more children. As we shall see, since men often take the checks of their wives and children, a single man may therefore walk away from royalty payments with thirty checks or more. And these methods are only the legitimate and legal ways of getting checks. Overall, these strategies result in a sort of inflation. Adding names to the list decreases the amount each person receives (because the total amount for the clan must be divided among more people) but as long as you can add names to the list faster than others in your clan can, your payout increases.

How, then are these royalty lists compiled and processed, and how are the checks paid out? Theoretically, the lists of landowners are taken from the original land study. The lists have grown over time as periodic censuses of children have been conducted to add the names of newborns and infants. Additionally, landowners can appeal to the local government to add the names of people whom they have approved—typically, newly acquired affines—to the list. The local government is, in this case, personated by a long-serving *kiap* who was one of the people who conducted the land study. This person is himself a Porgeran, and, when he is visited in his office with a request to add a new person to the list, he will do so if the person is vouched for by someone he knows.

These additions to the list are added to a Microsoft Excel database in the Porgera Development Authority's office. When royalty money is transferred to the relevant Porgera Development Authority bank account, checks are printed out on the office laser printer. The resulting stack of paper is then brought to the government office building and, over the course of a week or so, the checks are handed out on a clan-by-clan basis. Queuing up—or indeed, any form of public order—does not come naturally to the Ipili, so the government officers sequester themselves in a windowless room and hand the checks out through a small hole with a security grill in order to prevent any unpleasant incident. With a landowner representative observing, the government officers hand out checks and get people to sign receipts for them. When individuals receive their checks, they cash them at the local branch of the Bank of Papua New Guinea (or other, less official, places) and then are free to spend the money on whatever they like.

The distribution of royalties results in a progressive three-day-long party in relocation communities that moves from one location to another as money runs through each community when its turn comes up in the order of check distribution. Thus if the Tiyini receive their checks first, there is a huge party at Yarik, which then shifts to Apalaka as the Tuanda begin cashing their checks, and so on. What is done with the royalties? It is difficult to track this money given the complexity, secrecy, and speed with which checks are cashed and the money is spent. Anecdotally, it seems to me that the spending took a few common forms. First, gambling is popular, and I've witnessed pots of enormous amounts of money up for grabs in public card games that occur during royalty parties. Second, of course, is splurging on beer and alcohol. Third, money is given to friends and affines. Fourth, money is used to pay off debts in tradestores for food purchased over the past quarter. Although this last form of expenditure is the least obvious, many people use the majority of their checks to pay off debts at tradestores for store-bought food since their gardens cannot grow enough food to sustain them. During my fieldwork few people saved their money because they felt assured of an income from the mine, and because Papua New Guinea's currency was rapidly losing value against the dollar, which meant that imported goods (that is, most goods) became more expensive. In sum, splurging was rational.

Theoretically, the royalty lists are compiled based on the "Schedule of Owners." The truth is somewhat different. Despite the existence of twenty-three landowning subclans, there are twenty-one different royalty lists: the two Waiwa subclans have been collapsed into one (not surprising, since according to the land study the Lunda do not have any land inside the SML territory), while the ever-amorphous Pulumaini have been reduced from five subclans to four. Although it is not clear where the names on the royalty lists come from, they surely do not come from the "Schedule of Owners." As we have seen above, the schedule counts 608 adult Tuanda plus the 510 children on the 1994 "Child Register," along with 564 names in just the Yaliape subclan of the Waiwa and another 411 names on the "Child Register." However, the list of royalty payments from the second quarter of 1999 lists only 179 adult Waiwa and 169 young adults—which includes the Lunda—while the Tuanda number 480 adults and 644 young adults.

Untangling the actual distribution of these checks proved to be quite a task, and I will offer only the most cursory of remarks about the problem. Let us examine for a moment the 284 checks distributed to the adult members of the Ulupa subclan of Tuanda. According to the signatures on the completed payment sheet, these 284 checks were distributed to 94 recipients. The highest number of checks a single recipient received was 38, while the lowest was (not surprisingly) 1. Thus each person receives roughly 3 checks on average. In fact the distribution of checks is skewed—some people receive many, while most receive few. Of course, this could simply mean that one person is taking the checks for an entire family and distributing them back in the home, but this goes against Ipili egalitarianism as well as the rationale for having individual checks in the first place. There are some procedural issues that accompany handing out the checks. Some may be understandable: the government officer who is responsible for witnessing the check distribution receives one himself in his role as a landowner (which he is), despite the fact that someone else technically should have countersigned as a witness for him. Other issues are more suspicious: one Tiyini agent is listed twice on the Tuanda list—perhaps because he married two Tuandan women, but the rationale is not clear.

It could be argued that the small number of people on the royalty lists is based on a principle of residence in an area, rather than on consanguinity. But if this is the case, why does the government employ two different standards for defining who a landowner is? It appears that these royalty lists are also being used as a way to transform people drawn into the security circles of prominent Apalakans into clients. Names can be added to the list by anyone who is already on the list, providing that they can pass the relatively easy test of the local kiap. Although this man is very obliging when it comes to adding names to the list, he is also very familiar with Porgera and the SML territory and thus is a fairly accurate—if personal and intuitive—assessor of whether someone is a "true landowner" or not.

Thus as far as royalties go, being "a landowner" amounts to little more than already being on the list and knowing the kiap, and there is little overlap between the "Schedule of Owners" and the royalty list. The two different levels of checks are theoretically based on the age of the recipient, but in fact they represent how well liked you are by the landowner sponsoring you, and thus whether you are deserving of a large or a small check. Often, these checks are collected by the landowner, who retains a portion of the money before passing the rest on to his clients.

Compensation

Landowners are paid compensation for land that is damaged by mining operation. Banks (1997) has discussed compensation payments using mining company records that I do not have access to, and my own experience following individual land claims is ultimately too private to discuss here. For these reasons I refer readers interested in a detailed discussion of compensation payments to Banks's work and will make only a few remarks here.

As we have seen, large-scale dealings with the mine, such as the issuance of the SML or the creation of new and unscheduled works within the lease's territory, are dealt with by the LNC. Most of the time, however, Porgerans interact with the company at an individual level. Porgeran landowners actually live in the SML territory; their houses and gardens are technically located on land that the mine has the right to use. The mine can work on this land and destroy improvements on it without the permission of the person living there. Or rather, technically that person has already given permission to the mine via his or her representative on the LNC who signed the agreements of the late 1980s—technically, the land has already been leased from residents. Landowners must, however, be compensated for their lost land and damages to the improvements that they have made on it. The amount that they receive as compensation is not negotiable—the rates, including the construction of new houses, are set by the original agreements negotiated in 1989. But the mine rarely seeks any land that it is not already using. Although compensation claims took the form of massive payouts during the mine's construction, today they are paid out mostly when mine-related activities cause inadvertent destruction of landowner properties—for instance, when a landslip is caused by explosions at the mine site, or a waste dump creeps over gardens. The result, obviously, is a strong incentive for landowners to build houses and plant crops in areas that are likely to be disrupted by mining.

Additionally, landowners are entitled to an annual rental fee for their land. This is considerably less money than the royalties and is less frequently paid. As a result, it is not something people spend a lot of time thinking about. In fact, this payment is referred to by landowners as *monge muni* (literally, "frog money"), and the popular conception is that this money is paid to them for the disappearance of wildlife from their areas as a result of mining. It should be noted, however, that rental and compensation fees are paid to people who are resident on the land being rented or compensated for. Thus these payments are made on the basis of residence rather than genealogical descent, while at the government station it is genealogy, not residence, that makes one "Ipili."

Employment

Employment at the mine is highly sought after in Porgera. Jobs are rare in Papua New Guinea, the mine pays well, and there are often benefits associated with working for it such as free clothing that is both durable and prestigious, in the form of mine uniforms and boots. Working for the mine also has the potential to lead to further employment. However, there are not many openings at the mine. Furthermore, given the nature of the highly mechanized mining that goes on in Porgera, many applicants are not fully qualified for technical positions inside the plant. As a result, competition for jobs is fierce.

The Porgera Agreements have obliged the mine to hire according to a strict standard. Given equal skills, Ipili are hired preferentially over Engans, Engans over other Papua New Guinean nationals, and Papua New Guinean nationals over expatriates. The mine in turn seeks to demonstrate its compliance and standing as a good neighbor to people in the valley by hiring as many Porgerans as possible. Doing so is also in the mine's best interests. First, hiring locals is cheaper, since they do not require housing. Second, local hires increase the percentage of national hires and thus decrease the mine's costs of adhering to a "Fly-In-Fly-Out" agreement signed in 1998 that requires it to maximize national hires. Finally, local employment is seen by the mine as a social benefit and can be portrayed as part of its "positive social impact" and commitment to sustainability and positive outcomes for all stakeholders in the mine. Being "Ipili" thus increases the desirability of applicants for mine jobs.

How, then, is this identity vetted? The mine has a long-standing policy of refusing to engage in the business of identifying landowners. All such identifications, it insists, must come from the community. This minimizes the mine's entanglement in landowner politics and allows it to present itself as an institution concerned with supporting the autonomy and self-determination of indigenous peoples. The result, on paper, is a system that relies on something like the following principle: inhabitants of the SML territory—in my case, Apalaka—appoint by popular acclamation a member of the "hiring committee." They then tell the mine who their representative is, and the mine grants that person a small stipend for his service (the representative is always a man). In return, the member of the hiring committee is responsible for distributing employment forms to people within his area and vetting them to the mine by—I believe—including with the completed application a statement of his recognition of them. The system thus applies a choke point to the interpretation of identity in Porgera. A single local gatekeeper simplifies the process by which the identity of a person—as agreed to by the consensus of their consociates—is vetted by a single person.

It is quite difficult for a community to remove a member of the hiring committee. Convincing the mine of a community's change of heart requires a fair amount of persuasion. Even more difficult, it requires the consensus of the local community as to what course of action to take—something rarely achieved in Ipili social life. Finally, it takes overcoming the active opposition of the current officeholder, who by virtue of that fact (and also probably for other reasons) is able to exert at least some influence in the community.

There are many advantages to being a member of the hiring committee. Members' sinecure nets them a small income that requires virtually no work in return. In addition, their position is ripe for exploitation. In the case of Apalaka (and, by hearsay, elsewhere in the valley) people seeking employment in the mine have to purchase the application forms from their local committeeman and pay him again to submit completed applications to the mine. This expenditure of money often involves the creation of some sort of relationship through which the committeeman and the applicant would both plan to benefit in the future. The situation is structured, in other words, to give members of the hiring committee many reasons not to be honest and to put them in yet another position of rentier leadership, in which they become more powerful than other residents.

What sort of incentive scheme exists to get Tuandans and Waiwandans to work for the mine? They are the people whom the mine most seeks to employ, but they are also the least likely to apply. Not only are they less educated than Engans on the whole (given the short history of formal education in the valley), but they have little reason to seek work. The hours are long, and although the wages are welcome, most landowners in the SML territory can rely on revenue streams based on their status. In addition, other sources of income are available—being compensated for damaged ground, for instance, or successfully bringing a legal action against the mine. Finally, as far as Ipili are concerned, the whole point of having the mine in the first place is that they won't have to work at all. So jobs' desirability is outweighed by the facts that they are expensive to get and pay little money for lots of hard work—especially for someone already receiving royalty checks. Thus it is often outsiders, rather than landowners, who find these jobs appetizing.

The result is a radical disjuncture between the state of local employment as documented in internal mine reports and the situation in Apalaka that they purport to represent. Mine documents provided to me by an anonymous source report the number of people in Porgera employed by the mine whose point of hire is Apalaka. This list did not, to put it diplomatically, mesh with my intuitions regarding employment in Apalaka. After looking it over I took it to someone qualified to examine it and assess its accuracy. He was a close friend who was both a long-time resident of Apalaka (although wana to the village) and a long-time PJV employee.

The results of our working through the list indicated that there was one "true" Apalakan—one person whose family had lived in Apalaka for some time—on the list: him. It was true that there were exceptions—another Tuanda who was tene to Apalaka had been suspended for misbehavior and did not appear on the list but would probably work again for the mine in the future. Another well-known local mine employee also lived in Waiwanda, but he was an inmarrying affine. Other Tuanda and Waiwa had been employed at the mine—shortly after I did this study, a Waiwa man was hired as a security guard—but very few stayed with the company very long. Lack of familiarity with industrial discipline, access to other forms of revenue, and the strong temptation to steal from the mine meant that people tended not to be employed by it for very long.

Who, then, did appear on the list of names? There was one large group: Engans and (less frequently) Huli who had moved to Apalaka, befriended local people, and managed to get work at the mine. After getting work, they inevitably moved out again—frequently to the government station, where they lived, often with communities of fellow clansmen.

The structures in place worked both to reduce the chances that Apalakans would be hired as well as to obscure an accurate representation of the origin of people who were hired as Apalakans. Being a "real landowner" in this case is focused on residence, or "point of hire"—rather than on descent. The way the mine structured its hiring committee—in theory, a noble attempt to allow the Ipili to determine for themselves who true Ipili are—merely provided an incentive for local people to use it as a mechanism to accumulate power and money for themselves.

Conclusion

In this chapter I have examined life in Porgera and shown how being Ipili can mean very different things in different contexts. Overall, I have attempted not to present one or more of these arenas of representation as accurate and the others as inaccurate. Instead, I have claimed that narratives of identity and kinship are told and retold as their institutional contexts change. "Landowners" exist in Porgera today as a group whose existence has been elicited by Porgera's wider institutional context, despite the facts that Ipili sociality does not map well to the descent-based criteria the mine and government use and that these criteria are often incoherent for reasons other than Ipili corruption.

The unruliness of practices such as preferential hiring, royalty payments, and standards for receiving relocation housing demonstrates that "landowner" identity is only tenuously related to how life is lived in the villages, however much this may be the idiom in which the delivery of these benefits is articulated. To a certain extent, the incoherence of Ipili identity is not often noticed in the valley, or particularly minded. The Ipili are used to unruliness. For those at a remove from the valley, however, these identities often harden into stereotypical forms in a way that has serious implications. We shall pursue these implications in the next chapter, in which I will examine what happens when narratives of landowner identity circulate outside of the valley to Papua New Guinea's capital, Port Moresby.

I will argue in the next chapter that Porgera is not a unique case: the nebulous nature of Ipili identity and sociality is not atypical of resource development areas in Papua New Guinea. Rather, it exemplifies a dynamic of elicitation and transformation that occurs throughout the country and perhaps even further afield.

The Melanesian Way

The social Super-Robot, mighty Leviathan in his behaviorist's paradise,
is a stirring vision, not devoid of a certain icy grandeur. But the Mind
remembers, as in a dream, its pristine thrills; and it turns its gaze away
from the Robot . . . The creative urge stirs once more. Intuition leaps.
The phantoms claim their own.
—Alexander Goldenweiser, *Robots or Gods*

"I would be less than honest if I did not say I am disillusioned,
disappointed, sad and even angry 25 years down the road," said
Bernard Narokobi, Papua New Guinea's first attorney general, at
a symposium celebrating a quarter century of independence for
Papua New Guinea (2000, 27). "The image we see of ourselves is
an image shattered, disillusioned, disappointed and despairing nation [*sic*]. It is an image of hopelessness and everywhere the feeling
is disappointment. The mood of the nation is that of frustration,
even anger, bitterness, and hatred" (25). Narokobi was not alone in
expressing cynicism about the country's future. At the same symposium Michael Somare, the first prime minister of Papua New
Guinea and father of the nation, delivered a paper entitled simply
"Where Did We Go Wrong?" (Somare 2000).

There were dissenting voices. Bart Philemon, then the minister
for transport and civil aviation, delivered a paper titled "Papua New
Guinea Has No Problems," in which he suggested that the media
should improve Papua New Guinea's image and self-confidence
by not reporting on crime and social problems. "These crimes,"
he said, "are urban based, which constitutes only 10 percent of

the population. The other 90 percent of the innocent population becomes the victim of such reporting." This "innocent population," he continued, is, "without doubt, enjoying the serenity of their villages, their mountains, their seas, their rivers, their beaches and their total environment, and are in concert with each other. They have plenty to eat, and are not begging for survival. This is the silent majority that is living without fear. They do not even care what is happening in cities like Port Moresby or Lae. Comparatively, in the global context, this is what I mean when I say Papua New Guinea has no problems" (Philemon 2000, 74). The anxieties and resistances expressed in these speeches are rooted in a variety of sources, ranging from the fading optimism of old age to the political and economic difficulties of postindependence Papua New Guinea. What Philemon and Narokobi share, however, is a similar image: that of the "innocent population" of Papua New Guinea that lives in rural areas and grows its own food. Where they differ is their diagnosis: one man sees those people as flourishing, the other as betrayed. For both, however, the "innocent population" is central to the nation.

The "innocent population" is known more broadly throughout the country as the "grassroots." In previous chapters I have examined one grassroots population, the Ipili, and the structures that enabled their feasibility. In this chapter I turn to an even wider context for Ipili feasibility—the cultural nationalism of Papua New Guinea. What commonly held notions about grassroots Papua New Guineans undergird the legislation, policy, and national sentiment that make the Ipili feasible? How do urban Papua New Guineans imagine the life of the grassroots, and what do they think they owe them? How are notions of "landowners" as the legitimate owners of Papua New Guinea's resource wealth entangled in independence-era images of the grassroots that were part of the nation's state-making project? In short, what sort of leviathan do urban middle-class Papua New Guineans consider grassroots Papua New Guineans to be, and how is Ipili identity enabled and elicited by this notion?

My argument in this chapter is that Papua New Guinea's innocent population must be understood in terms of the country's nationalist project, a project which desires both "development" and "tradition" but views these two things as fundamentally incompatible. As a result the grassroots play a central but ambivalent role in the nation's moral imagination. In the previous chapter, I claimed that the model of the grass roots enshrined in land law and policy does a poor job of conceptualizing life in Porgera. In this chapter I will argue that Porgera's case is generalizable: there is a disjuncture between the urban imagination of the grassroots and the reality of life in rural Papua New Guinea. Furthermore, I will argue that this disjuncture is dealt with not only in the narrow realm of law and policy, but also in the wider realm of the country's moral imagination.

Increasingly today, the country's positive self-image is tied to a notion of stable, unchanging, and peaceful tradition whose custodian is the grassroots. As a result both grassroots and urbanites find themselves caught in a dilemma: Grassroots who, like the Ipili, seek development, wealth, and modernity are excoriated by urbanites for betraying the nation's deepest values. At the same time, middle-class Papua New Guineans often feel that their desire for modernity must be a sign of their deculturation. This is not to say that there are no solutions to these dilemmas—there are many. But one gets the sense from Papua New Guinea's blogs and newspapers that these solutions leave something to be desired. Papua New Guineans' attempts to convince themselves that modernity and tradition need not be opposed seem fundamentally aporetic. In addressing both of these two dilemmas, this chapter broadens the scope of the book beyond Porgera to a wider set of dilemmas facing Papua New Guinea today.

As I will show, anthropologists recognize that the ideal of the innocent population reflects a deep cultural concern with order, amity, and unity which runs through many of the cultures of Papua New Guinea. But anthropologists have also found that in practice, Papua New Guineans are innovative, actively seek wealth, and are not necessarily opposed to conflict as long as it is productive. Papua New Guineans, I believe, exhibit the imagination and intuition described by Alexander Goldenweiser in his idiosyncratic masterpiece *Robots or Gods* (1931): they are too original in their thinking, as well as too changeable and dynamic, to maintain the static unity that so often claim they desire.

Roger Keesing noted decades ago that diagnoses of this sort put "scholars of Pacific cultures and history" into "a curious and contradiction-ridden position" because "the ancestral ways of life being evoked rhetorically" in fact "bear little relation to those ... recorded ethnographically" (1989, 19). As expert knowers of innocent populations, anthropologists who emphasize their dynamism seemingly gainsay the beliefs of educated Papua New Guineans, putting us in the uncomfortable position of telling educated Papua New Guineans that they do not know who they are, while insisting that we are paternalistic speakers of truth for our research communities.

But this dilemma, I will argue, is only an apparent one. In this chapter I attempt to summarize the scholarly consensus on Papua New Guinea and bring it into dialogue with contemporary thought in the country. Synthetic rather than original, my argument aims to demonstrate that there is a mode of scholarly connection with Papua New Guinea that can retain its epistemological confidence even as it comes off its pedestal. By telling Papua New Guineans what we have learned about their country, I argue, anthropologists can connect with communities and galvanize their imaginations. What anthropologists know about Papua New Guinea, I argue, can help Papua New Guineans imagine new and better futures for themselves.

Finally, this image of the Mind eluding Leviathan, of grassroots creativity fending off the icy structures that seek to stifle it, brings me back to some of the larger themes of order and spontaneity, creativity and regimentation, that have run through this book. In the end, the process of making the Ipili feasible speaks not only to Porgera, or to Papua New Guinea as a whole, but to much broader questions that must be answered by anthropologists and others who contemplate living in a world of indigenous modernities.

The Grass Roots in Papua New Guinea's Moral Imagination

It is fitting that Philemon made his remarks about Papua New Guinea's innocent population on the occasion of the country's silver jubilee, since Papua New Guinea nationalism is so closely tied to the independence period, when Papua New Guineans first came to see themselves as members of a single nation. Some have claimed that Papua New Guineans lack a sense of national identity, but I am convinced by Robert Foster's argument (2002b) that there is a widespread, if at times unconscious, sense of national belonging in the country today, a banal nationalism tied to commodity use and consumption. And even in cases where the shape and feel of Papua New Guinea's national culture are contested, this contestation highlights the fact that, as Ira Bashkow puts it, "people in PNG speak assuredly of two dissimilar worlds, European and Melanesian, as though the reality laid out before them continually forced upon them a choice between two contrasting domains of action: the modern urban, cosmopolitan world of money, personal freedom, and technology, and the traditional village 'grassroots' world of subsistence gardening, kinship, and ritual" (2006, 225). Marshall Sahlins would add that conflict does not indicate a lack of cultural coherence, but rather a "a larger, complex order, marked by a dynamic of contrasting moral and political domains," and thus an order "*in* and *of* the differences" which is itself amenable to analysis (Sahlins 2004, 186–187). For this reason, I would argue that

Papua New Guineans share a basic moral imagination—albeit a contested one—regarding Papua New Guinea's national ideology: a basic set of ideas about what sort of possibilities exist for Papua New Guinean lives, and how those ideas ought to be judged as good or bad. Central to this imagination, I would argue, is the distinction between the country's grassroots and urban areas. In order to understand the form that this distinction currently takes, it is important to trace it back to its origin: the independence period that Philemon, Narokobi, and Somare so ambivalently celebrated at the turn of the millennium.

Papua New Guinea's independence period ran from roughly 1964, when Papua New Guineans first served in the pre-independence House of Assembly, through formal political independence in 1975 to 1985, when the first state of emergency in Port Moresby was declared and the optimism of the early years faded. Throughout the decades bookending independence, artists, writers, politicians, and academics produced a lively discourse on the nature of Papua New Guinean culture and politics. These were strikingly multicultural engagements, and Australians and other foreigners in Papua New Guinea debated the country's future in journals such as *Yagl Ambu*, *Gigibori*, and *Bikmaus*.

By the late 1960s, decolonization projects worldwide had been going on for over a quarter of a century, and examples abounded of various "third ways" that had been tried in a variety of new nations that rejected both the Soviet Union and the United States as a model for the state that they might become. The high modernist enthusiasms of the postwar period were wearing off (James Scott 1998), to be replaced by the worldview epitomized by the "Buddhist economics" of E. F. Schumacher's *Small Is Beautiful*, published in 1973. Maev O'Collins and Peter King remember that the debate about Papua New Guinea's economic future "was at its height at a time when development planners around the world were beginning to question earlier assumptions that increased economic growth rates necessarily meant increased levels of well-being to the community at large . . . The publication of Schumacher's *Small Is Beautiful* was support and comfort to those who felt that social costs were being ignored" (1985, 368). Thus the architects of Papua New Guinea's modernity inherited a technocratic self-confidence tempered with anticolonialism and populist agrarian sentiments.

The result was a clear commitment to rural improvement and experimentation with a democratic socialism that embraced modernity—but within limits. "What was sought," wrote Anthony Siaguru, summing up the way many people in the country felt, "was a marriage of all that was good in customary ways with all that was good in modern ways" (2001, 171–72). In contrast to the "separate, lonely family" (Somare 1974, 5) of Western nuclear households, Papua New Guineans would not give up "the nourishment of our superior communal values" (Siaguru 2001, 172). "We shall not disrupt our traditional way of life more than necessary," Somare declared (1973, 4). Rural livelihoods were not to be denigrated or modernized out of existence. Rather, Somare's vision of development took the form of a sort of Melanesian pastoral:

> Improving the lives of the people means many small but important changes. It means that, when people work hard to grow crops, they can expect to have enough food to feed their families. It means that when a child is sick, there is an aid post close by where the child can be treated. It means that a woman can draw water from a village water supply and not have to walk miles to the river. It means that villagers as well as townspeople can enjoy community centres and entertainment. And it means, most of all, that every man and woman in Papua New Guinea is able to live with dignity, following a way of life that is not imposed upon us from outside, but a way of life developed from our own traditions. (Somare 1973, 1)

In the independence period, "real" Papua New Guineans were people who lived grassroots lives: "In all the 700 languages of our country, we have never needed words for air pollution, for slum, or for unemployment. Do we wish to build the kind of country that needs those words? We are not a city people, but a people of mountains, fields, and sea. And this we should remain" (1974, 3). Thus rural Papua New Guineans—the "grassroots," as they came to be known—became central to the national imagination, functioning like the familiar peasants of European nationalist traditions: simple, rural preservers of a cultural patrimony whose values undergird the nation. They are the *volk* in the Romantic mode: the authentic peasants, the people who maintain customs—the epitome of what is central to, not peripheral to, the lives of Papua New Guineans. "Village" and "town" became dichotomous terms, the one a locus for tradition, the other for culture contact and modernity.

Challenges arose, however, when Papua New Guineans tried to build a sense of national identity out of life in the village. As Lamont Lindstrom points out (1998, 145–53), many of the paths to unity taken by other new nations were foreclosed by Papua New Guinea's unique circumstances. For one thing, primordial national unity could not be guaranteed on the basis of a common ethnic or linguistic identity because of the country's cultural diversity; with no single coherent *volk*, Somare's mission "to weld together the multiplicity of cultures and languages that make up Papua New Guinea" (1974, iii) would not be easy. Despite abstract and hopeful claims that "for all the infinite variety of forms and styles . . . we share some very fundamental, basic attitudes to life that will enable us to make a modern nation state with a distinct identity and culture of our own" (Somare 1974, iii), it was never quite clear what those fundamental attitudes were, except possibly that they were the opposite of Australian or Western values. Some authors (Beier 1975) argued that a lack of clear-cut ethnicities would prevent ethnic divisiveness that would threaten national unity, but this still was looking at the glass as half full, rather than figuring out how to add more water.

Few Papua New Guineans directly experienced Australia's apartheid government in Port Moresby, and a lack of prolonged humiliation by white colonizers meant blackness or negritude could not be a rallying point for the country, except among those who had learned from whites that the identity was a stigmatized one. Although Christianity was broadly acceptable as a common denominator, an introduced colonial religion could hardly be used to oppose the colonizers. As a result, Papua New Guinea's nationalism in the independence period focused on cultural unity "through diversity"—the idea that what united Papua New Guinea was its "diversity" of "intact" cultures (Lindstrom 1998, 144). "The fact that we have many ethnic groups is in itself a Papua New Guinean way," wrote Narokobi (1975, 24).

Narokobi's *Melanesian Way*

It is worth focusing on Narokobi's work because he, more than anyone else in Papua New Guinea, shaped the country's image of itself and its culture. Narokobi's writings about the "Melanesian Way" sought to make feasible the concept of "unity in diversity." In the early 1980s he published a series of articles—reprinted as a book (1983)—in which he outlined the "Melanesian Way," a view of how Melanesian culture might best be adapted to (and thereby improve) modern society (see Otto 1997).

It is not an exaggeration to call Narokobi the Melanesian Emerson—his wide-ranging vision somehow managed to encompass positive valuations of both development and tradition, Christianity and indigenous cosmic orders. His vision of the Melanesian Way aimed to show people how they could both remain authentically Papua New Guinean and become modern. True, these seemingly intractable oppositions were finessed by Narokobi's insistence, both insouciant and mystic, that there was no point in defining his main term. "Because the Melanesian Way is a total cosmic vision of life," he wrote, "it is not only futile, but trite, to attempt a definition of it" (1983, 12). Still, in his ambition to create an authentically Melanesian form of modernity, Narokobi demonstrated a nuanced understanding of life in both town and village which has yet to meet its match in Papua New Guinea.

For Narokobi, Papua New Guineans could only have self-respect if they recognized that their past was as worthwhile, ancient, dignified, and full of achievements as those of white nations. His vision of that past was both primordial and pastoral. "There can be no PNG," he wrote, "until we come to grips with our ancient reality. We are a nation of villages" (Narokobi 1975, 6). Central to this vision of "a nation of villages" was a vision of orderly village life. Narokobi emphasized that "one of the special qualities about Melanesians is that we prefer reconciliation to conflict. Our traditional village politics was based on "harmony" which may or may not coincide with justice" (1974, 62). Happily, this sort of *ubi caritas et amor vicus ibi est* (where charity and love are, there is the village) also exemplified the values central to Narokobi's fervent Catholicism. In pieces with titles like "The Nobility of Village Life" (1974), Narokobi painted a picture of the grass roots that, while not unrealistic, was extremely optimistic about rural lifeways. "God is really a very wise Man," he wrote, "When He made our country, He made sure that we had villages or the "wanpisin" or "wanlain" (one people). We defended ourselves on that unit. We provided feasts on that unit. We worked together to build each other's houses and to pay bride prices as well as caring for each other" (Narokobi 1974, 57–58).

In contrast, Narokobi was critical of "Western" culture. By this he meant secular, urban living with its social isolation and conspicuous consumerism. His egalitarian Melanesian and ascetic Catholic tendencies came together in decrying secular Enlightenment values of individual autonomy and the idea that *stadtluft macht frei*—that urban areas are positive locations for human emancipation. Rejection of the village was, for him, also a rejection of Christianity. "Some of us so-called educated people think, 'I am educated. I am rich. There is no God. The Bible is wrong. Economic development has nothing to do with the Bible. Villages are nothing'" (Narokobi 1974, 58). In contrast, he argued that "development should consolidate that community living through which loneliness and despair can be eliminated. Community living should replace the senseless urban and individualistic living that flourishes in big cities . . . Cooperation, consensus, democracy blossom in small-scale communities. Participation and involvement are most effective in a small community . . . We must promote our cultures and reject some foreign cultural practices" (Narokobi 1975, 24). Importantly, this suspicion of modernization also meant a suspicion of elites, paradoxically a suspicion most deeply felt by elites themselves: "We feast on foreign institutions and fatten ourselves on the people's sweat and toil . . . I see technocratic, bureaucratic and elitist schools. Schools for the intelligentsia, middle class. These train us, you and me, who for the main part are sheltered from the burning needs of the masses. We hide behind laws and policies. We are defeated before we begin" (7). Narokobi's vision of Papua New Guinea would have been easier to implement if it had been simply an antimodernist project that used the language of primordial culture to brand high modernism as a tool of the colonizer. But Narokobi, a Christian, could not simply renounce the colonizer's gifts. Crucially, he sought to appropriate parts of Australian culture for Papua New Guinea's own purposes. Thus he embraced white technoculture while rejecting secular lifeways, a move that was to have an enduring legacy in Papua New Guinea's cultural politics: "Do I detest modernism then? Not really, but partly true. Yes, I want my people to play their ancient songs on modern pianos. I want my people to visit their relatives in motor vehicles. I want my people to have a feast under electric lights and cook their meals in electric ovens" (6).

Key here is the idea that Western influences could be safely and selectively appropriated: Christianity united black and white believers against a secular modernity, and, in any case, the values it was committed to were always already grassroots values. Technical systems such as electricity and transportation systems could be used in Melanesian projects without fundamentally altering the life of the innocent population.

Melanesian Sources of Enthusiasm for the Grass Roots

This valorization of the innocent population has some similarities with European nationalism in that both see their national patrimony as modular, internally homogeneous, and rooted in a primordial past. And just as historians have criticized the role that primordialism has played in Europe's nation-making projects, so have a certain subset of anthropologists taken issue with depictions of the innocent population and the Melanesian Way as inaccurate and ideological (Babadzan 1988). According to this account, acculturated Pacific elites romanticize the village partially out of their own ignorance, and partially to further their domination of their fellow citizens. These cynical interpretations of elite beliefs fail to appreciate the way that nostalgia about the village draws its strengths from "the village" itself. Images of the innocent population are not merely a product of postcolonial nation building. Rather, they have deep roots in Melanesian culture.

Many authors have noted that consensus is a key cultural value in Papua New Guinea. Because lack of conflict is morally valued, it is seen as central to efficacious communal action and overcomes the tension between a sociocentric model of the self and the egalitarian emphasis of Melanesian cultures (for a summary of this literature, see Leavitt 2001). Papua New Guineans dream of a life in which the tension between individuals is resolved through their concordance, and religious and development projects frequently make the creation of such unity their central focus (Lindstrom 2011).

Consensus remains something longed for rather than achieved in rural Papua New Guinea (and, of course, elsewhere). Still, this value is clearly one that preceded Western influence, and this desire for harmony and moral agreement probably is more often realized in rural areas than in cities. Indeed, for many middle-class Papua New Guineans, the village is a place of fond childhood memories, a safe place of nurturance markedly different from the often traumatic world of boarding school and the routine of the white educational system (Bosse 1994). And, of course, children do not experience the obligations and entanglements that adulthood brings in a village. It is not surprising, then, that the ideal "village" or "grassroots" Papua New Guinean life is viewed as one of unity and harmony by urban people, given the elective affinities between Melanesian concerns with unity and consensus and Western romantic notions of *volkisch* rural living.

Another major theme in Melanesian culture that feeds into beliefs about Papua New Guinea's "innocent population" is what Dan Jorgensen calls "Melanesian degenerationism" (personal communication), a thematization of decay, entropy, and degeneration (see also Ballard 1995; Biersack 1996b). As Thomas Strong notes, "sorrow is a common aesthetic or mood through which social life unfolds in many places in Papua New Guinea, and themes of decay and diminishment figure prominently in Melanesian cosmologies" (2007, 119; see also E. Schieffelin 1976). This includes a focus on the body as grown and, inevitably, decaying (A. Strathern 1996) and a focus on cosmic senses of the biodegradability (as Jacka 2007 puts it) of the landscape.

Similarly, it has often been noted that many Papua New Guinean cultures hold that humans are incapable of originality and conclude that all knowledge and practices, especially esoteric practices, come either from external sources or an ancient tradition which slowly decays as it is handed down over time. Myths, genealogies, magic, and other ancestral knowledge are seen as imperfectly transmitted over generations (Barth 1989). In some cases, the

[handwritten marginalia:] Consensus longed for

autonomous imagination (Stephen 1979; Herdt and Stephen 1989) brings novel techniques through trance, possession, or dreams.

In the Sepik River area, intragroup competition may lead to an entropic process (Errington and Gewertz 1986), in which novel (for them) forms of prestigious knowledge are imported and used in local strategies of aggrandizement (Harrison 1993). Frederick Errington and Deborah Gewertz write that "in the Chambri view of their entropic system, significant innovation—the creation of a truly novel way to gain access to power—is regarded as impossible. All that is possible is to preserve knowledge of the old techniques" (1986, 109) or import new ones from elsewhere. It is not surprising, therefore, that this view is transferred to the urban context, where a concern with "original culture" and its preservation have become central to national identity. In sum, given this degenerationism, it is not surprising that a "sentimental pessimism" (Sahlins 2000) about the golden age of village life could take hold in Papua New Guinea.

Papua New Guinea's Moral Imagination Today

Of course, Papua New Guinea's nationalist imagination is much more than the work of one thinker, even one as respected as Narokobi. Independence was a time when social change was a central preoccupation of Papua New Guinean writers (Gorle 1995), artists (Rosi 1994), and policy makers (Denoon 2005), and there was remarkable variation and ambivalence surrounding issues such as urbanization, village life, and Christianity. Some rejected the middle ground offered by Narokobi, seeking to valorize rural life and vilify the urban. Others took the opposite tack, emphasizing the dysfunctionality and backwardness of the village while being drawn to the bright lights of town. Since independence, perceptions of town and village have continued to evolve. During Papua New Guinea's independence period, for instance, agrarian populists hoped to create "a nation of sturdy smallholders following the Road of Business" (Filer 2006, 79). In the mid-1980s public attention was increasingly focused on resource extraction projects, including both high-profile failures (such as Bougainville and the forests) as well as up-and-coming projects (including Kutubu, Porgera, Hides, and Misima) and the culture clash between grassroots and urban life was explored in the widely read *Grassroots* comic strip (Browne 2006). As Colin Filer has convincingly argued, this led to a reconceptualization of grassroots identity that focused on "landownership." By the time the Porgera Agreements were being finalized, then, the idea that "the 'man in the street' is a man in a village or 'clan' or 'tribe' or other 'customary group'" (Filer 2006, 67) was a central part of Papua New Guinea's national imagination.

In this section I want briefly to outline the main lines of debate regarding what sort of moral valuation should be given to Papua New Guinea's "innocent population" and its city folk. Today, one might identify five main themes central to the village-town dichotomy, topics that are used as touchstones to evaluate village and town: Christianity, *wantoks* (social connections between intimates), law and order (the procedural regularity of bureaucratic institutions and a just and effective policing and judicial system), culture (in the sense of patrimony), and development (such as schools, roads, and hospitals). These topics can be viewed as good or bad. Table 3 schematizes some of the most common evaluations used in Papua New Guinea today.

Christianity is a good place to start, because it has strikingly little positive valuation of secular or non-Christian beliefs in Papua New Guinea today. Although urban secular modernity might be attractive to some members of the generation that reached adulthood in the independence period, on the whole Christianity is positively valued across the country. In some cases, this is due to the Narokobian idea that "the basic virtues of sharing, brotherhood, co-operation and friendship existed in Melanesia as much as they existed in Palestine before or since Christ" (1983, 49)—thus, Melanesian values were already Christian values. In other cases, however, Christianity is positively valued because it represents a break from the pagan and is part of urban modernity. This explains the emphasis in some denominations on dressing in formal clothing, the search for prestigious contact with foreign churches, listening to gospel and spiritual music, watching religious DVDs, and so forth. Younger elites, for instance, are often associated with evangelical and other nonmainline churches and look askance at both the atheism of some of the independence-era elites and the older churches who have sought to adapt their liturgy to local cultures and customs.

Each of these valuations has its opposite. A focus on Christianity as a foreign import leads to a negative valuation of the village as removed, backward, and uninformed about spiritual matters and global discourses of faith. However, a focus on the village as a source of piety leads to a valuation of the urban similar to the ideas of the great urban evangelical missions of America's nineteenth century: the city and its enticements are dangerous and lure innocent rural youth into ways of sin and decadence.

In contrast with Christianity, moral dichotomies of development—in the sense of schools, roads, and hospitals—follow a pattern that is found throughout the world: villages are seen as backward and undeveloped, and cities

Table 3   Moral Oppositions in Contemporary Papua New Guinea

	Morally positive	Morally negative
VILLAGE		
Christianity	Melanesian values have always been Christian values (*caritas, communitas,* etc.) Christianity improves benighted villagers	Grassroots are heathens or backsliders Christianity corrupts Edenic population
Wantoks	*Wantoks* are a safety net ("'no one goes hungry in Papua New Guinea'")	Greedy/extractive *wantoks* impoverish hard-working achievers
Law and order	Melanesian Way of dispute resolution, restorative justice	Tribal fighting, sorcery
Culture	Preservation of precious cultural traditions	Savagery and barbarism
Development	Authentic and unspoiled	Undeveloped/*bus kanaka*
TOWN		
Christianity	Christianity as a sign of development and imported white cultural modernity	"Brainwashed" by missionaries and forgetful of noble heritage
Wantoks	Freedom from *wantoks,* individualism and emancipation (*stadtluft macht frei*)	Anomie, no community, isolation
Law and order	Rule of law, rationality, impartiality, fairness	Government corruption, raskols and violence
Culture	No slavish adherence to past or selective maintenance of colorful but not taxing folk traditions	"Australian," acculturated, not uniquely Papua New Guinean
Development	Developed, cosmopolitan	Corrupted by decadent Western morals (alcohol, etc.)

are seen as morally good and developed. Alternately, these values may be inverted in a primitivist view, with the city seen as an impure location of assimilation and cultural deprivation and the village seen as the backbone of the nation's traditional values, an Edenic place of clean water and food whose high standard of living is derived from its lack of development.

As I've noted above, this dichotomy is one that seems a necessity to Papua New Guineans even as they feel a sharp ambivalence about it. Like Americans who adhere to dichotomies between individual choice and group membership even as they constantly attempt to overcome them (C. Fischer 2008), Papua New Guineans see this dichotomy as both undesirable and inevitable. Images of vaguely suburban villages filled with modern conveniences or— even more rarely—authentically Melanesian cities notwithstanding, Papua New Guineans have never quite found their *aufhebung*. It is only rarely that Papua New Guineans come down on one side of this argument. In some cases urbanites have fled their village homes, seeing them as dysfunctional. But this is not the sort of thing one is supposed to admit in Papua New Guinea. Alternately—and more rarely—there are Papua New Guineans who have called it quits, given up on modern life, and, like Candide, remained content to cultivate their garden.

Law and order is a third key component of Papua New Guinea's lifeworld. Deep-seated beliefs in the distinction between Western and Papua New Guinean lifeways are particularly on display here, where a strong distinction is made between procedural regularity and justice (a supposed hallmark of the West and its bureaucratic systems of government) and the Melanesian Way of conflict avoidance, "restorative justice" (Dinnen, Jowitt, and Cain 2003)—a process that supposedly lacks the regularity and logical coherence of Western forms of governance and is more emotionally wholesome and complete.

Unlike the ambivalence about development, criticism of the heartlessness and individualism of Western life is widespread enough in Papua New Guinea that even the most acculturated member of the urban elite feels that he or she has a heritage with inherently more *gemeinschaft* than that of white people. Cynicism about the heartlessness of Western life is made possible partly by the fact that true procedural regularity is quite rare in Papua New Guinea. Although many people believed in the "Rule of Law" (Filer 2006, 7) in the 1970s, the breakdown of most procedural regularity in the country (including in the police force) means that the negative view of law and order is more common than the positive one: if the system functions at all, it seems to treat the little guy unfairly.

That said, one of the most inadmissible, but nonetheless clearly perceived, truths in contemporary Papua New Guinea is that the village is not all that it is cracked up to be. Especially with the resurgence of tribal fighting and *raskol*-ism (gang-based criminality), many people feel that villages are places of dirty dealing (that is, sorcery) and conflict. This view, common in the expatriate community today and carefully examined in the early literature of the independence era, is nevertheless not publicly admissible today. Even Papua New Guineans who are critical of their own country do not find it acceptable for foreigners to make this criticism.

Wantok-ism—solidarity with kin—is another central trait of Papua New Guinea's national culture. Reliance on kin and giving and taking as part of everyday life is a key characteristic that separates Papua New Guinea from outside—especially white Australian—culture. It is for this reason that urban spaces are largely seen as free from wantoks, which means that the city is often figured as a site of alienation, isolation, and pathological solitude. At the same time it can also be seen as a location of freedom, autonomy, and liberation from village wantok ties that are draining, parasitic, and paralyzing. Alternately, for those who fear the anomie of the city, wantoks in the village are a source of caring, commitment, existential orientation, and support. One common transformation of the negative view of wantoks as extractive and draining dependents occurs when people transfer the location of parasitism from the village to the city. In this configuration, the city is where rural lifeways of obligatory giving are inappropriately applied, draining hard-working urbanites who are forced to host country cousins (see Bashkow 2006 for a good description of this). It is also common for negative readings of urban wantoks to bleed into concerns about corruption and the lack of law and order in cities—in this view, the wantok system parasitically bleeds properly run offices dry of resources when procedure is violated for one's wantoks.

Finally, at the most general level, the village-city dichotomy is used to discuss culture, or *kastom*, more generally. Typically the village is seen as a positive source of Papua New Guinea's vibrant traditional culture. Papua New Guineans strongly resist negative reading of the village as full of *bus kanaka* (barbaric, undeveloped savages). It is difficult for Papua New Guineans to negatively evaluate the lifeways of grassroots people—doing so contradicts national ideologies and sounds too much like the criticism foreigners level against Papua New Guinea, full of retooled tropes of the primitive, bloodthirsty, and savage. Old ways of life are seen as valuable bulwarks against the corrosive forces of modernity. This nostalgia for the village is everywhere in Papua New Guinea, ranging from idealized images of extended families in television commercials (Foster 2002) to the typical Papua New Guinean music video, in which traditionally adorned dancers perform heritage dances from the musicians' home village. This sense of the lost innocence of rural life is reinforced in urban areas, where Papua New Guinea's thin middle class grows up with the experience of urban violence and crime and without the experience of drudgery and claustrophobia that can sometimes accompany village life.

There are exceptions, however: some expatriates might still consider Papua New Guinea's savagery nasty rather than noble. Those who value connections with global Christian development might look down their noses at rural primitiveness. The result is Air Niugini syndrome: the tendency of sophisticated people, such as Air Niugini stewardesses, to be dismissive of unsophisticated bumpkins. In some cases those with a "sentimental pessimism" might see the village as a site of lost, destroyed culture, a "shattered Eden" (Errington and Gewertz 1995, 4–7). This is a popular view among older expatriates (including anthropologists), who might claim to speak the truth about Papua New Guinea to younger, urbanized Papua New Guineans. Mostly, however, the village is perceived as a positive site for "culture" in the sense of ethnic distinctiveness, if not always in the sense of "civilization" or being "cultured."

That said, the city is almost never a site of traditional culture. Rather, it is seen as the location where freedom from authentic culture is realized. It is really only in the hoped-for but unrealized synthesis of modern infrastructure and Melanesian values that the city, made humane by the Melanesian Way, is positively valued. This, alas, is a vision that is very far from being realized.

In sum, Papua New Guinea is a complex country with a long history of ambivalence about urbanization, rural life, and its own culture. Philemon's image of the "innocent population" falls squarely in the "morally positive village" part of Table 3, for instance, but it is more common for individuals to mix and match items from this table. A young Papua New Guinean educated in Australia who has returned to Port Moresby for work might have positive views of culture and law and order in the village, while also favoring the modern conveniences and freedom from wantoks provided by cities. On the whole, some general patterns can be discerned in Papua New Guineans' moral imagination. Indeed, they are not defined by a clear adherence to any particular pattern of choices as much as they are by the fact that they are confronted by these choices, instead of others, however ambivalent they might be about them. Such ambivalence demonstrates the existence and classificatory power of the categories themselves. Even in places where people are ambivalent about—or downright opposed to—a dichotomy between village and town, their ambivalence arises in response to this configuration of choices and the notion of the innocent population that it suggests.

The Melanesian Paradigm

This focus on the innocent population thus forms the context within which Porgerans and other landowners make claims for recognition and concessions and shapes the creation of law and policy in the country. Metropolitans imagine that Papua New Guineans have a "traditional culture"; that it is an appropriate basis for land registration; and that it is ancient, unchanging, and benign. John Burton has referred to this complex of ideas as the "Melanesian Paradigm": "It is the dominant national ideology in modern Papua New Guinea that its village societies include (a) a division of people into clans based on descent from an ancestral founder, (b) exclusively owned clan territories, and (c) 'true' leaders who capture the consensus of their community. This is notably seen in the ideological formation of people known as 'landowners' who have rights to certain things, usually in heroic opposition to some other groups or institutions of government" (1997, 1). Similarly, in an article subtitled "Myths We Live By," Michael Rynkiewich criticizes the common myth that "the landowners have held this land since time immemorial; and the landowners hold their land communally in clans; therefore, we just need to discover who the real landowners are and register the clans as a land holding group" (2001, 62).

Once again, Narokobi exemplifies these viewpoints. A lawyer by training, he was intent on demonstrating the legitimacy of Papua New Guinean lifeways and knowledge despite their oral and uncodified nature. As a result, his vision of grassroots life was one in which cosmology reigned. We might call this vision "weakly Andersonian" (Anderson 1991) because of the way Narokobi imagined village societies as externally bounded, internally homogeneous units that are "like nations": "Melanesia was constituted by various social and cultural units, or social 'orders.' . . . Each cultural unit was autonomous, possessed of its origins, and defined as to its territorial boundaries; and legal postulates. Each was complete in itself, yet interdependent with others on some aspects, as are nations of today" (1989, 17).

Despite Narokobi's assertion that "anthropology . . . is like a rape in which the rapist gets off and the ravished is penalised for having been ravished" (1983, viii), his corporatist vision of rural Melanesia is remarkably similar to that of postwar structure functionalism. Here, for instance, is Radcliffe-Brown: "A continuing social structure requires the aggregation of individuals into distinct separated groups, each with its own solidarity, every person belonging to one group of any set. The obvious instance is the present division of the world into nations. In kinship systems cognatic kinship cannot provide this; it is only made possible by the use of the principle of descent" (1950, 43). And here is Narokobi's sociology of village life:

> A village recognises itself as an independent, autonomous social unit and legal order. It exists by its own history, tradition and territory. Relations between people of a distinct social unit are of a different order from those of other social units. Self-recognition involves self-assertion of self-identity. The existence of such a unit is autochtonous [sic] and is self-executing (in that it does not depend on the state or any other higher authority). Identity constitutes the unit as a "corporation," an entity. The individual becomes a member of that unit by common identity criteria, including common socialisation and acculturation. One owes obligations to that community and expects rights from it. By virtue of membership one is bound by certain norms, values and accepted or prohibited modes of behaviour. Obedience to internal orderings is a necessary precondition to recognition of one among all. (1989, 21–22)

Morally valued for its social integration, lack of conflict, and unambiguous regulation of conduct, grassroots living seemed easily integrated into the policy arena. The result is what Filer calls an "ideology of landownership" that "asserts that 'clans' and 'land groups' are essentially the same thing" and that "these 'customary landowning groups' are the basic building blocks of Melanesian society" (2007, 161). Here, then, is the rise of the landowning clan as a leviathan.

Narokobi was one of the first to articulate this vision, but he was certainly not the last. Tony Power's work may represent the epitome of this approach. Power has worked for years throughout Papua New Guinea in a variety of influential positions, including as the first assistant secretary (for economic affairs) for the government of East Sepik Province and as a community relations expert at Chevron. Above all, he was the motivating force behind the Petroleum Act, which states that all land registration surrounding hydrocarbon projects must be made using the terms of the Land Group Incorporation Act of 1974 that he had a hand in drafting (Weiner 2007 is the best critical overview of Power's work).

As Power puts it, the Land Group Incorporation Act was designed to recognize the fact that "landowners will not suddenly become well organized in a manner that equips them to relate to a multinational company and the provincial and national governments" (1996, 136). To compensate, the act allows for the creation of Incorporated Land Groups, which will be both modern organizations and agents of custom. The idea is essentially to have a management committee composed of "traditional elders": "Associations should have an executive committee based on traditional political grounds. The 'Big-men'—leaders who are recognized by their group as having knowledge of the group's history and are given the authority by the group to speak its name—should be on the executive committees which should be constituted to represent all major groupings in the project area . . . *No pressure should ever be applied that would deny or fail to recognize the ethnic divisions that have existed for millennia*" (138; emphasis in original). Thus formal institutions need only be based on Papua New Guinean precedents in order to function: "PNG has 10,000 years of settled agricultural tradition and land management was and is an integral part of the Papua New Guinea community management. People know who owns what land" (136–37).

Power has most clearly grasped the similarities between the cosmological regulation of the clan and the corporation. According to him, the grassroots should be easy to incorporate because "the clan as corporate entity" is already operating as a bureaucracy (1988, 2). "The clan clearly is a corporate 'person,'" writes Power, and "in traditional times it acted as such in a natural fashion by the consensus of elders under the bigman term of leadership. Though conscious of its property rights, guarded unceasingly by force of arms, the clan never viewed itself as owner of real estate or property in a modem sense. The clan certainly saw itself as master of a domain—but not the owner" (2). The segmentary lineage system of the clan is similar to the hierarchical organization of a bureaucratic institution. Individuals are not said to "own" land but merely to have "usufruct" rights and to hold the land in trust for the next generation. The role of the "chief," "big man," or other traditional leader is clearly established, as is the unambiguous occupancy of that role by a certain individual. Thus both individual landowners and leaders are somewhat akin to officeholders who occupy a well-defined office for a span of time before being replaced by the officeholders of the next generation. Although standard operating procedures are not written down in files, customary rules are said to be universally known and to strongly prescribe action—land disputes, for instance, can be resolved through the application of well-known and precise standards for action, whose execution constitutes the daily activity of customary life.

It is confidence in the strength and solidity of these unwritten laws of custom that leads people to believe the key to success in land registration lies in an accurate translation of local knowledge out of the idiom of custom and into the idiom of a Western legal regime. As a result, finding "true land-owners" is seen to operate on a principle of clear translation, the transposition of unwritten but articulated rules for life into written artifacts.

Problems with "Cultures" in Papua New Guinea

The Melanesian Paradigm is a powerful tool because of the way it combines Papua New Guinean concerns with consensus, land, and cultural preservation with Cold War discourses of environmentalism, conflict resolution, and the third way. Today it continues to march forward under the banner of sustainability and environmentalism (West 2012). All of these movements rely on a Eurochristian imagination of the corporate form. However, a deep familiarity with Papua New Guinea and a healthy dose of skepticism are all that is needed to convince one that the Melanesian Paradigm has only a limited ability to capture the reality of life on the ground in the country.

Indeed, the country's history has been filled with other, more nuanced and ambivalent understandings of Papua New Guinea that have competed for space with the Melanesian Paradigm. As I mentioned above, many independence-era thinkers were suspicious of the nation-building projects that first drew on the trope of the innocent population. As Gilian Gorle has noted, much of the literature of this period was ambivalent about social change, seeing it as "inevitable: a painful and costly loss of innocence, an uncomfortable but unavoidable reality in contemporary life" (1995, 100). Many literary works probed the negative side of village life, such as the early classic *Maiba* (Soaba [1979] 1985). Others focused on the negative, colonial aspects of Christianity.

In the visual arts, intellectuals were aware that their ongoing cultural practices might be frozen and fetishized if they were made to serve the purposes of national patrimony. "Where," asked Jacob Simet, "is this Western attitude to art leading us at this moment? What is this culture that our politicians talk so much about—the culture they want to preserve so that it can give an identity to this country?" (1980, 216–17). In his study of *malangan*, he wrote that "very little or no Tolai art was ever intended to be preserved materially or removed from its setting . . . Also, I have noticed many new compositions and innovations in the songs and dances. I don't believe for a moment that this has only come about since the European contact. I think that Tolai art is a living thing, responding to each new situation. I fear that preservation by whatever means, if not very carefully thought out, may produce a Tolai art that will have lost its profundity" (216). Papua New Guinean intellectuals were not the only people to realize that the grassroots were not an innocent population suitable for use as exemplars of national patrimony. When policy makers of the late colonial and independence eras implemented policies of land reform they encountered problems that raised serious doubts about the adequacy of the Melanesian Paradigm. In 1952 the territory enacted the Native Land Registration Ordinance, which was designed to begin the process of developing a cash economy through the mobilization of land. Ward notes:

> The attempt broke down from naivety. Many planners have difficulty apprehending the fact that Oceanic land tenure systems are not based upon neatly bounded human clusters (clans or tribes) within tidy boundaries which simply have to be sought out, mapped and registered. The reality is that different levels of the society—individuals, families, extended families, "clans" and "tribes" commonly exercise different kinds of rights in the same land. Neither the human groups nor the territories in which they have rights, are neatly bounded. Asking them to define continuous external boundaries, sharply separating one group and its lands from the other, is to set a rather unfamiliar task. (Ward 2002, 2)

A decade later a new Land Title Commission "found itself heavily involved in resolving 'disputes.' There was still little recognition that disputation over rights to land is a normal part of PNG life, where tenure has to be constantly adjusted to take account of demographic flux, succession, marriage connections and local movements. Or that the demarcation of discrete individual, family or clan interests involves all those with intersecting interests relinquishing them to each other within agreed boundaries in an essentially new distribution of rights" (2). More recently the practical application of the Land Group Incorporation Act has also foundered as the law's idealized image of corporatist Melanesians prompted resistance based on actual kinship practices. In literature, the arts, and policy-making, then, there have always been thinkers skeptical of the Melanesian paradigm.

Anthropologists are amongst those suspicious of the Melanesian Paradigm. With the exception of short-lived versions of structure functionalism (which were influential in Papua New Guinea, as we saw in the last chapter), anthropologists have long emphasized the processual, historical, and boundary-spanning nature of cultural processes. We have argued that cultures are not "billiard balls" in Wolf's sense of being "internally homogenous and externally distinctive and bounded objects" (Wolf 1982, 6; see also Brightman 1995, Bashkow 2004, Lewis 1998, Sahlins 1999, Wolf 1988). In particular, American anthropologists as far back as Franz Boas (1962, 81–105) have thus always been critical of the nationalist imagination of culture that Benedict Anderson (1991) described.

But anthropologists have always also made a second, more particular claim: that Melanesian culture is especially focused on cultural innovation and importation rather than perduring cultural patrimony, migration and movement rather than primordial rootedness, innovative and porous ethnic identities rather than enduring and bounded systems of ethnic difference, and a focus on conflict and engagement rather than agreement and consensus. As we saw in the previous chapter, for instance, anthropological work on the regulation of conduct through kinship and customary norms paints a picture of Melanesian sociality that has little in common with the corporatist writings of Narokobi and Radcliffe-Brown. Here I will briefly touch on issues of trade, migration, and conflict before dwelling at greater length on the topics of ethnic identity and cultural patrimony that are most central to the argument of this chapter.

One common anthropological criticism of "billiard ball" models of culture is that they ignore the role of interconnections among local communities. In the case of Papua New Guinea, this criticism is particularly appropriate because anthropologists have produced massive evidence of trade in material and nonmaterial property across the country, beginning with Bronislaw Malinowski's analysis of Hiri and Kula trade and Margaret Mead's discussion of the Arapesh as an "importing culture" (Malinowski 1922, 1988; Mead 1938). The entirety of the country has been linked together by trade and exchange networks for hundreds, if not thousands, of years. This is one of the few areas where the Melanesian Paradigm agrees with anthropological reports, because Papua New Guinean nationalists use the existence of widespread trade networks to ground the concept of an incipient and primordial sense of national unity. Anthropologists, on the other hand, have used it as proof of the lability of ethnic identities and cultural patrimonies in the area (Harrison 1993).

Mobility in Papua New Guinea was not restricted to a few long-distance traders. Entire populations were on the move. "Historians of Melanesia . . .

underestimate the extent, frequency, and complexity of population move-ment," writes John Waiko regarding Oro Province. "Indeed, outsiders find clan histories—with their complex mobility, division, regroupings, alliances, and wars—almost impossible to follow" (Waiko 1985, 9). Joel Bradshaw, writing about the Huon gulf, says of migration that "every few generations, it seems as if a giant kaleidoscope reshuffles village sites, alliances and en-mities, and linguistic and cultural affiliations" (Bradshaw 1997, 238). Sum-marizing the literature on other parts of Papua New Guinea, he concludes that this "population kaleidoscope" is not unique to the coast (Bradshaw 1997, 239–242). Regarding the highlands, James Watson has argued that "a fluid personnel is no anomaly but the lifeblood of many CNGH [Central New Guinea Highlands] societies" (1970, 108). On the whole, then, Papua New Guinea is not a place typified by communities that have existed in their cur-rent location from time immemorial.

As I have noted above, anthropologists have long emphasized the impor-tance of consensus in Melanesian society, so it is understandable why the Melanesian Paradigm would seek to emphasize this aspect of Papua New Guinean life, even if ideals of consensus are more often honored in the breach than in the observance. This is not merely to point out that warfare was common in the period before Eurochristian contact; it is also to em-phasize that parity and equality are often achieved in Melanesia through opposition and contest. Competitive and egalitarian, Melanesians often see agreement as a process of opposition to be managed, rather than a state to be achieved once and for all. As Laurence Goldman has written of the Huli, "for indigenes, governments and developers in Papua New Guinea (PNG), the idea of a 'community without conflict' may be an objective which is neither socially imaginable nor even desired" (2003, 1). Rather, he emphasizes, "dia-logue, rather than closure . . . , was the processual essence of this system" (4).

As important as the topics of exchange, mobility, and conflict are, I men-tion them briefly here in order to dwell on two aspects of the Melanesian Paradigm that are central to this chapter: ethnic identity and cultural pat-rimony.

There Are No Ethnic Groups in Papua New Guinea

Pundits, policymakers, bloggers, and journalists all take for granted that Papua New Guinea is composed of numerous small ethnic groups. For in-stance, Benajmin Reilly calls Papua New Guinea "the world's most ethnolinguistically fragmented country" (2001, 167). This view colors law and policy in Papua New Guinea, as well as the self-understanding of its intellectuals. It is not, however true. In fact, in important ways, there are no perduring ethnic groups in Papua New Guinea. Even with the usual scholarly caveats that I will give below, this claim should give pause to adherents of corporatist models of the innocent grass roots.

Papua New Guinea is famous for its linguistic and cultural diversity, and it is tempting to look at linguistic maps of Papua New Guinea and mistake the bright and clearly bounded entities represented in them as ethnic groups. But, as Filer writes, "there is no sense in which it can be taken for granted that each culture in a certain region occupies a unique and exclusive space by virtue of belonging to a unique and exclusive local group. And yet it is precisely this assumption which a language atlas tends to foist on unsuspecting anthropologists" (1990b, 117). I will leave it to linguists to decide whether these maps do justice to the linguistic situation in Papua New Guinea (Rumsey 2010). What I want to demonstrate here is that there is no greater indication of the lack of enduring corporate groups in traditional Melanesian culture than the fact that there are few stable names of ethnic groups in the country.

Anthropologists have been far less successful than linguists in creating synoptic atlases of the country. The most ambitious attempt, *The Historical Atlas of Ethnic and Linguistic Groups in Papua New Guinea*, is still incomplete: Only three of the projected six parts have been published, and these three parts cover only New Ireland, New Britain, Bougainville, and the Madang coast, leaving almost all of the mainland of the country uncovered (in fact, the list of projected volumes does not include much of the south coast and Papuan regions). In the introduction the editor, Jürg Wassmann, notes the difficulties of compiling the work:

> Although anthropologists customarily refer to, and use, names of ethnic groups, tribal units in Papua New Guinea are vexing categories and seldom fit into neatly defined, named boxes. Often we merely find clusters of villages speaking the same language and displaying the same cultural properties, which, however, do not entertain the notion of belonging to, or being part of, a larger tribal unit. The linguistic and cultural boundaries of such groups are often fluid and difficult to delineate. In addition, when such units did receive a common designation, it often came from external sources: similarly structured neighboring groups, administrative officers,

missionaries, or anthropologists . . . A further, and irksome, problem one is confronted with when looking at the distribution of ethnic groups in Papua New Guinea is the inconsistency of naming. By this I mean that ever since the systematic documentation of, and research on, the cultures of Papua New Guinea began, different people have tended to call the same group by different names. In other cases, already defined ethnic groups underwent re-classification in a later period and were identified as being only a sub-group of a larger tribal unit. (1995, vii)

In fact, Wassmann's atlas is not a list of existing cultural groups in the country, it is a visual index of those groups' reification in the literature. This is not surprising to people in the country, since it is notoriously difficult to match up the name of the "ethnic group" in the anthropological literature with the terms used on the ground. In fact, it is a little shocking how many of the ethnic groups named in the titles of ethnographies were created for those works. There are numerous examples. The first line of Marie Reay's *The Kuma*, for instance, informs us that "the 'Kuma' have no name for themselves" (1959, 1). It appears that "Kuma" is a contraction of "Konumbuga," which is a term for people living on the south coast of the Wahgi River, and the actual subjects of her book are "clusterings of Yoowi-speaking people" (3), with Yoowi simply meaning "real speech" (1). The reader does not doubt that a coherent social scene is being reported on, but what is actually being studied is not an ethnic group called "the Kuma"—rather, it is one demographic cluster of one locality among many others.

After writing *Ku Waru* with Francesca Merlan (Merlan and Rumsey 1991), Alan Rumsey reports that "the label 'Ku Waru' is just one of a number of multiple, cross-cutting ways in which people identify themselves and their dialect for certain purposes, which Francesca Merlan and I have fixed upon in order to delimit the region that our ethnography pertains to. It has little or no cachet as a marker of social identity" (2010, 138). Like so many names of ethnic groups, "Ku Waru" is actually a place name—it refers to the cliffs that form a prominent landmark in Rumsey's area of study. Of the Maring— made famous by Roy Rappaport's *Pigs for the Ancestors*—Christopher Healey writes that "like so many labels for ethnic groups in New Guinea the name Maring has no currency among those it identifies" (1990, 28), and Edward LiPuma notes that "less than fifty years ago the name, the category Maring had no real indigenous resonance, the Maring only 'learning' that this was their collective name in the 1960s" (2000, 22). The name of the "Iatmül" in

Naven immortalized by Gregory Bateson is a kludge developed for convenience out of a complex intersection of groups and identities:

> I have adopted the name Iatmül as a general term for the people. But I doubt whether I am right in so doing. The people of Nimdimbit use the compound form Iatmül-Iambonai to denote the whole of the linguistic group, 100 miles in length. Iambon is an adjective referring to the "Upper River" and is applied equally to those who speak variants of the same language and to foreigners higher up the river. Iatmül, which I cannot translate, is the name of a very small clan in Mindimbit. In two or three other cases, names of clans are used as general terms for groups of villages speaking a common dialect, but I have never heard the word Iatmül used for the Mindimbit-Angerman group. (1932, 249)

On other occasions colonial rule, rather than authorial fiat, produced names for ethnic groups in Papua New Guinea (for a comparison with Africa, see Southall 1970). F. E. Williams writes that the term "Orokaiva" developed in the late nineteenth century as a result of colonial contact, noting that the people whom the colonizers called by that name "never possessed a sense of unity which would necessitate or justify a common name. One thing at least is certain, that they did not themselves use the name Orokaiva" (1930, 2). "The Wola have no all inclusive name for themselves," writes Paul Sillitoe, who argues that this is the rule, not the exception, when it comes to ethnic identity in Papua New Guinea. He adds that "efforts to impose logical categories where there are none . . . must inevitably result in some distortion. In this respect the names which administrators and others have given to people in other parts of Melanesia to indicate bounded linguistic groups are a lesson because translated they are silly; for example Siane is a greeting, Arapesh means friends and Gnau means no" (1979, 25). Sometimes this phenomenon degenerates to the point of farce. Michael Wesch, for instance, describes the Australian administration's difficulties in locating "the Kufelmin" in the inclement and sparsely inhabited upland of Western Province. "Kufelmin" is an indexical term used in this area to mean "people to the west" (2006, 98), and as a result

> as the patrols headed still further west, stopping in each valley to carefully map the tribal and sub-tribal boundaries, they asked locals who they might encounter next as they traveled west. The answer was invariably, the Kufelmin. As the patrols moved further west the inhabitants of each

valley claimed the Kufelmin were still further west. Even precise statements associating the Kufelmin with a particular river or other landmark proved false when this river or landmark was approached and the local inhabitants denied the designation, always claiming the Kufelmin to be still further west. They were described as a "mystery group" in the patrol reports. (96)

Eventually patrols reached the Indonesian border, where they could not pass, and thus "the Kufelmin" became the group on the other side—although, according to Wesch, an ethnographer working on the other side of the border was told by this same group that the real Kufelmin "were actually located 60 kilometers further west" (97).

This area is now said to be inhabited by "the mountain Ok," although Dan Jorgensen writes that there is little to suggest that the mountain Ok conceive of themselves as a coherent whole, and the term "mountain Ok" remains an outsider's designation rather than one used by the people themselves. Although it is doubtless true that the mountain Ok constituted something like a cultural area or a regional system in the Fly-Sepik headwaters, this is not the same as saying that it was a self-conscious identity (Jorgensen 1996, 193–94). Rather, such an identity developed in response to colonialism and global capitalism.

Even names of ethnic groups that are used widely in Papua New Guinea are relatively recent in origin. Epstein writes of "the Tolai" that "they lack most of the usual indices of political or cultural unity. They possessed no single common name for themselves . . . Today, the expression 'Tolai' . . . has won complete acceptance as a group designation, but this is of very recent origin. The earliest reference to it in this form that I have been able to discover in the literature occurs in an item contributed to the *Rabaul Times* by a correspondent in Way in the mid-1930s" (1969, 13). Tom Ploeg tells us that "the name Siassi is most likely of colonial coinage. Kovai told me it came into use when they were employed as miners on the Wau-Bulolo gold fields in the 1930s . . . the term was frequently used, mostly, if not always, in the context of development issues, when the relations between Kovai and regional and/or supra-regional agencies were discussed. Its frequent use, however, meant the unification of previously separate villages only insofar as the inhabitants of these villages were forced, by outside developments, to act together" (1993, 774). He concludes that "'Siassi' seemed for them primarily a name, a label, which they had acquired in the course of the colonial era and by which the outside world seemed to know them" (774).

This labeling by outsiders also happened to the Enga—who have an entire province named after them. Meggitt writes:

The term Enga was apparently first used by natives of the Mount Hagen–Tomba area to designate all those people west of the Hagen Range who speak variants of the one "Enga" language . . . with the establishment of Administration patrol posts and the gradual prohibition of interclan fighting after about 1940, Enga-speakers of different areas intermixed with each other and with non-Engan neighbors much more freely than in the past. They began to see themselves as one sort of people, distinct from Europeans and other natives such as Simbai, Mandi of the Mendi valley, Huli of the Tari basin and Ipili of the Porgera valley. In consequence, the term Enga is today gaining wider currency among the natives themselves, especially those of the middle and lower Lai valley. (1958, 254–55)

This is not to say that the "Siassi," "Tolai," and "Enga" do not exist as ethnic groups. They clearly do—now (LiPuma 2000, 22). Nor is it to say that these groups are made up out of whole cloth. As Jorgensen points out, these makings of ethnic groups in the colonial period combine with local understandings of difference to result in "a dialectic between a genealogy of local forms and wider historical processes" (1996, 190). Finally, it does not mean that Papua New Guineans are incapable of forming coherent groups—on the contrary, they do it with alacrity. As Jorgensen writes, "traditional times were times in which identities, communities and whole populations came and went with breathtaking rapidity" (2007, 69).

This trend continues into the present. Papua New Guineans often construct names for corporate groups by combining two more existing names. This includes soccer teams (Leach 2006) and political parties (Somare 1975, 51). But it also includes whole ethnicities. The Nayudos described by Christine Kocher Schmid were a new group composed of inhabitants of the adjoining Nankina, Yupna, Urua, and Som Valleys (hence "Nayudos"), created by a member of the parliament of the province in 1988, complete with flag and cultural center (Schmid 1993). A further example of this comes from an opinion piece by Peter Kinsharp (2010) in a Papua New Guinea newspaper. Kinsharp argues that the names of Hela, Enga, Jiwaka, and Melpa Provinces connote "our different language groups, cultural expressions and traditional significances of people living in those areas" (20). Hela Province does bear a name connected with the Huli mythological past (Ballard 2000), but all of the other province names are recent inventions rather than traditional names for languages or cultural groups. Kinsharp is aware of this, writing that "for Jiwaka Province, the word 'Jiwaka' stands for and is comprised of three major areas of the Wahgi speaking people. There are Jimi, Waghi and Kambia areas. 'Jiwaka' is therefore a word made up of the first two (2) letters of each of the three major areas, that is, 'JI' from Jimi, 'WA' from Waghi and 'KA' from Kambia, put together is 'JIWAKA' and it will now be the new Jiwaka Province" (Kinsharp 2010: 20). It would be easy to be skeptical of the "traditional" and "indigenous" nature of Jiwaka Province since it is an administrative division of a modern state named after a newly cobbled together ethnic group—hardly the stuff of ethnic primordialism. But the example of Jiwaka demonstrates exactly the difficulty faced by those who seek stable ethnic groups in Papua New Guinea: although Kinsharp's work is couched uneasily in an English-language discourse of tradition and indigenity, it is clear that he considers Jiwaka to be traditional and indigenous not because it is old and passed down, but because it is new and fabricated—by Papua New Guineans themselves. The limited success in finding ethnic leviathans in Papua New Guinea arises not from Papua New Guineans' lack of a facility for "cultural totemism" (Schwartz 1995) but rather from their great skill at differentiating people from another, which they do at a velocity that is antithetical to ethnic feasibility at a macro level.

Problems with Patrimony

This discussion of the dynamism of ethnicity in Papua New Guinea leads us to reconsider the other fixations of the Melanesian paradigm: cultural patrimony and heritage. We have learned from Boas that culture traits diffuse and are integrated into existing cultural patterns, and anthropologists have long used this fact to gainsay essentialized images of cultural patrimony (Linton 1936, 325–328; Handler 1988). But just as it is even harder than normal to find ethnic groups in Papua New Guinea, it is also harder to find cultures in the sense of a primordial patrimony handed down intact from time immemorial. Many anthropologists have argued that Papua New Guineans recognize—indeed, highlight—the novel and exogenous elements of their culture. Errington and Gewertz have written that "the Chambri explicitly regard their society as based on borrowing. They assert that most of their ancestors were of foreign origin; they recognize without embarrassment that many of their rituals were acquired from the Iatmül along with much of their esoteric knowledge. Moreover, they state that these rituals have been further modified through importations from yet other less powerful groups.

In addition, they say that important dance complexes, myths, flutes and talismans have come from a wide variety of groups" (1986, 99).

In her discussion of storyboards—a new form of tourist art—from the same region of the country, Roberta Dougoud notes that "the concept of what was traditional has been actively redefined, transformed, and dilated . . . in order to incorporate the new and the modern. On several occasions I discussed this shift with carvers, asking them to clarify whether the storyboards were modern or traditional, but they seemed not to see the incongruity which bothered me: for them the storyboards were invented at the beginning of the 1970s, but at the same time they were traditional" (2005, 261). She concludes that the question of the "invented" nature of this "tradition" was "irrelevant to the Kambots . . . they reflected on the fact that most of the designs represented on the boards as well as the myths illustrated had already been used by their ancestors and that even the new ones were derived from traditional figures. This was a way of claiming that the storyboards were their creation, but a creation made possible by the knowledge passed on to them from father to son by their ancestors" (261). This phenomenon is not limited to the Sepik. At the risk of exaggeration, I would claim that most of Papua New Guinea has a focus not on stability, fixity, and patrimony but on change, flux, and novelty.

Paula Brown noted of Chimbu in the 1950s that "there was always a search for variety, excitement and entertainment" (1972, 7). She writes:

> Despite persistent questioning, I could not elicit from any Chimbu certain sorts of traditions common elsewhere. They have no systematic cosmological beliefs. Nor had they stories describing, or even implying, a fixed order of the natural world . . . Chimbus, unlike many peoples in change, do not look upon the past as a lost golden age. Nor do they see their history and tradition as an irreversible movement from the primitive past to the progressive future. No such definite trend is recognized. It is rather as though they feel that the world is always changing and unpredictable. (Brown 1972, 5–6)

Merlan and Rumsey write that in Hagen, "the relative open-endedness of possible meaningfulness leaves ever more to be experienced and discovered," and this interest in open-endedness is tied to a "rapacious desire to experience and explore the novelty for what this might make manifest about possible difference . . . [an] uncovering of new, heretofore covert possibilities" (1991, 231). Ann Chowning notes that "the Lakalai genuinely value novelty for its own sake" (1969, 37). Bashkow writes that "Orokaiva have an ethos of cultural importation and experimentation; there is a constant scanning of the horizon for new forms of value" (2006, 187). Jorgensen argues that "there is something traditional about novelty" in Papua New Guinea, where a "vibrant, mobile, and heterodox spirit" and "the provisional and improvisatory nature of Melanesian cultures" (1994, 130, 131, 135) have created a people who can "generate radical transformations in thoroughly traditional ways. All of this is predicated on a cultural premise of incompleteness . . . the human order is always unfinished . . . such cultures remain alive to events and gain purchase on uncertain futures" (133). Rena Lederman notes that "Melanesians' apparently iconoclastic, improvisational cultural style of dealing with novelty" could even be "an alternative to postmodernism" (1998, 441). Summarizing much of this literature, Simon Harrison has argued that Melanesia is a region "whose peoples have been described as culturally highly acquisitive, actively seeking exotic and novel items of culture as valued and prestigious enhancements of the group or person" (2007, 39). Brunton, speaking more broadly of the region, has suggested that this makes religious and cultural life "unstable" or "volatile" (1989).

This is not to say that Melanesians do not think of themselves as devoid of fixity and heritage—we have seen above that this is not the case. But often their images of fixity contain within themselves a receptivity to the novel. I noted above that a belief in the ancestors is one indigenous reason why the Melanesian Paradigm is so attractive to Papua New Guineans, but this does not mean that their patrimony is timeless or unchanging. Writing more generally about the same point as Dougoud, Michele Stephen claims that "dreams, trances, and possession" provide

> means of direct communication with the ancestors and deities, they provide a continuing source of validation for new knowledge and cultural innovation: what men see in trances and dreams might in fact become social reality. This allows the existing framework of belief a flexibility which makes nonsense of any notion of "immutable" tradition, sanctified primarily by its origin in some distant past . . . Melanesians, in common with many other people, insist that they obey the time-honoured ways of their ancestors—and they speak the truth—what we forget is that they have a continuing dialogue with the ancestors, not a fixed, static body of tradition. (1979, 14)

No wonder, then, that one of the most beloved nicknames for Papua New Guinea is Land of the Unexpected—a slogan developed and discarded by the tourist industry but still often used warmly in casual conversation in the country.

Differentiation

What are we to make of a country whose people have no clear-cut ethnic groups—or rather, who create and discard them with such ease? A people who sometimes claim to hold fast to traditional knowledge but in fact seem to have little regard for patrimony at all? Melanesian ethnography has been an inspiration to theorization for a long time. In particular "Stragnerian" work (drawing on the writings of Roy Wagner and Marilyn Strathern) has been used to develop approaches such as "perspectivalism" (Viveiros de Castro 2004) or to develop theories of "partible" personhood (Mosko 2010). Such work is valuable, but directs attention away from Wagner's early work, which offers an explanation of the dynamism of Melanesian culture.

In *The Invention of Culture* (1975), Wagner provides an account of the "differentiating" mode of Melanesian sociality. Wagner describes this mode by contrasting it with "conventional" symbolic orders such as those of the contemporary United States. Conventional orders are "vertical" in the sense I discussed in the introduction: they imagine life to involve the subsumption of particular circumstances under general categories, making things in the world "tokens" of generalized Piercian "types," and they imagine semiosis to be a "drawing down" of general categories from an order often metaphorically "above" the here and now of everyday interactions. The result is a semiotic regime in which "Americans and other Westerners . . . [are] constantly trying to predict, rationalize, and order" the world (Wagner 1975, 88), creating a "busy busy world of responsibility and performance" (89). As a result, "this culture is in all its diverse aspects an enterprise of deliberately building collective and conventional orders, reducing or deciphering a world of phenomena, unique natural and historical events, to a rational and utilitarian pattern" (Wagner 1978, 19–20). Echoing Jacques Derrida and Judith Butler, Wagner argues that violence is done to the unique particularity of the world as it is elided in the name of subsumption (for more on Wagner's broader intellectual connections, see Viveiros de Castro 2008).

In contrast, Wagner claims, Melanesians are engaged in "a continual adventure in 'unpredicting' the world" (1975, 88) and focus on the ways in which the excessive particularity of any given moment resists subsumption under general categories. Conventions "are not intended to be 'performed' or followed as a 'code,' but rather used as the basis of inventive improvisation . . . The controls are themes to be 'played upon' and varied, rather in the way that jazz lives in a constant improvisation of its subject matter" (88). As a result, "the lifestyles of men and women are realized as innovations upon one another" (Wagner 1978, 29). Every moment is, as Sahlins might say, an "event" (1991). This is, in the words of Michael Silverstein and Greg Urban, an "ideology of textual newness," in which "the idea . . . of a continuously moving or evolving culture" (1995, 13) is central. In a differentiating mode, culture is temporally behind interaction, and human conduct creates a chain of associations that endlessly obviate what came before them. In this horizontal view of semiosis, "structure is . . . the residuum of metaphor" (Weiner 1988, 13) rather than the entity that regulates it.

There are reasons why Wagner's diagnosis of Melanesian meaning making has not attracted as much attention as other aspects of his work. For one thing, it is incredibly coarse: Wagner claims that differentiating regimes occur among "tribal, religious, and peasant peoples" (1975, 87), "the 'lower-class'" (89) and "the mature civilizations of Asia and the Near East" (1978, 27)—hardly a parsimonious generalization. Additionally, his idea that "no culture's idea of reality can be taken as absolute" (ibid., 21) makes him seem to be committed to a radical nominalism that at times appears to owe less to Immanuel Kant than it does to Philip K. Dick.

Still, there is no doubt that the large literature on creativity in Melanesia (Crook and Reed 1998, Leach 2007, Liep 2001, Lohmann 2003) influenced by Wagner's work indicates that, despite its eccentricities, it provides a useful way to think about grassroots Papua New Guineans.

Modern Melanesians

In particular, it suggests that we see Melanesians as quintessentially modern (Golub 2007a, 90). Such an approach has been tried before, in the 1990s, when Melanesianists combined the literature on the invention of tradition with the study of "other" or "alternative modernities" (Rofel 1999; Gaonkar 2001) to examine how Melanesians indigenized "the modern" to create "oxymodern" (Knauft 2002, 105) lifeways. This work was useful, but because it defined modernity simply as "the images and institutions associated with Western-style progress and development in a contemporary world" (18) it ended up focusing narrowly on the diffusion of Western cultural forms into Papua New Guinea. It is more fruitful to return to a more technical conception of modernity, one focused on historical semantics (Koselleck 2004) and more rooted in the modernist movements that were so important to anthropology in the early twentieth century (M. Fischer 2007).

Many authors have noted that Papua New Guineans, like European moderns, imagine social change to be radical and novel, to create a future different from the one previously expected. For instance, Dorothy and David Counts say of the Kaliai that "they foresee change, not as a process occurring by degree, but rather as a sudden qualitative transformation that alters fundamental relations . . . significant change is, by nature, catastrophic change" (1976, 304). Nancy McDowell writes that for the Bun, "historical time is structured into two periods with a chasm separating the before from the now. Only complete, radical change—a paradigmatic revolution—is possible. There can by definition be no gradual accretions or slow shifts in the organizing principles by which they live their lives and through which they perceive the world" (1985, 30). The overall picture is of people who recognize that radical change is inevitable—and who are often (but not always) willing to embrace it.

Lévi-Strauss famously argued against stereotypes of primitive peoples by insisting that some societies were simply 'cold' in the sense that they sought to avoid change. They were not "primitive," however, because they had complex aesthetics and social organizations that could be the object of anthropological connoisseurship. And yet at the same time, Lévi-Strauss's enthusiasm for art reveals the inadequacies of his view of cold cultural orders. Thus his appreciation of masks from the Pacific Northwest coast: "This unceasing renewal, this inventive assuredness that guarantees success wherever it is applied, this scorn for the beaten track, bring about ever new improvisations which infallibly lead to dazzling results—to get any idea of them, our times had to await the exceptional destiny of a Picasso. With this difference, however: that the daring feats of a single man, which have been taking our breath away for the past thirty years, were already known and practiced by a whole indigenous culture for one hundred and fifty years or longer" (1982, 4). Lévi-Strauss's vision of indigenous peoples seems paradoxical: on the one hand, they engage in unceasing renewal and inventive assuredness, but on the other hand, their culture is cold, fragile, and crystalline—slowly formed by generations of careful, artisanal work only to be dissolved in the boiling waters of modernity. It makes more sense, particularly when discussing Papua New Guinea, to simply jettison the "cold" part of this conception and focus on the modernism. We might hear in highlanders' "expectation of the potential revelation" of objects echoes of Baudelaire's painter of modern life who aims "to extract from fashion the poetry that resides in its historical envelope, to distill the eternal from the transitory" (Baudelaire 1964, 12). According to this account, we might call Melanesians not "oxymodern" but "modern," pure and simple. Like the flâneur, Melanesians actively seek novelty and surprise.

When looked at this way, James Clifford's "predicament of culture" in "a truly global space of cultural connections and dissolutions" where "local authenticities meet and merge in transient . . . settings" (1988) becomes merely provincial. As Strathern has noted, "Melanesians have never needed salvage ethnography. Their vision of the world had no problem with how parts fit together. There were no bits and pieces that had to be put back together again, for the sake of a culture to restore, a society to conceptualize. Save Clifford's predicament, I doubt nostalgia for either culture or society figures in their present cosmopolitanism" (1992, 99). As Richard Handler points out, this is really our problem, not theirs: "Authenticity . . . is a function of a Western ontology rather than anything in the non-Western cultures we study. Our search for authentic culture experience—for the unspoiled, pristine, genuine, untouched and traditional—says more about us than about others. Explaining anthropological notions of authenticity will give us yet another example of the startling degree to which anthropological discourse about others proves to be a working-out of our own myths" (1986, 2).

Anthropologists have long grounded their assumptions about the regulating power of cosmology in the purportedly species-deep need for social order. Thus even Raymond Firth, the first apostate from structure-functional orthodoxy, writes that "there is no doubt that for any society to work effectively, and to have what may be called a coherent structure, its members must have some idea of what to expect" (1963, 30). Keesing, seeking to find a grammar for behavior to match the order of social structure, dismisses the idea of "loosely structured" societies: "Where we find no neat, idealized kinship groupings, we have been prone to describe the society as 'loosely structured.' I cannot agree. A society might qualify as 'loosely structured' if people went around surprising one another" (1972, 24). Yet a Wagnerian account would argue precisely that: grassroots Papua New Guineans do seek to live lives in which they surprise one another by, in Merlan and Rumsey's marvelous phrase, "ransacking the world for novelty" (1991).

Melanesians Are Allergic to Leviathans

To summarize epigrammatically, leviathans do not exist unproblematically in Papua New Guinea because Melanesians are allergic to them. "The basic problems with the public service in Papua New Guinea," writes John Ballard, "is that the whole idea of bureaucracy and the values that are associated with it in terms of hierarchic organisation, specialisation, regulations and impersonality are all contradictory to the kind of values which Papua New Guinean societies have. . . . They are small scale societies and in which impersonality has no meaning . . . and in which regulations are in the form of customs which can be changed and bent to fit with human values and behaviour at any time" (J. Ballard 1975, 47). Leviathans fail because, as Foster puts it, "in PNG, many people . . . refuse to accept the idea of the state, to grant it the status of an expert system, a transcendent abstraction which commands trust, however grudging. Instead, they imagine the state as the particular officials who actually compose it" (2002a, 69). Foster describes this process as "putting a face on 'the state'" because "Papua New Guineans resist the 'lifting out of political relations from the exigencies of localized social interactions" (69). One might even go so far as to reverse this claim, arguing that it is not so much that Papua New Guineans "put a face on the state" so much as they resist other people's attempts to put the state on a face—to make human actors feasible representatives of leviathans (Benson 2008; Shever 2010). This is true not just of the state, but of every variety of leviathan.

This is not a surface phenomenon. Many ethnographies have illustrated the ways in which Papua New Guineans are keenly aware that the creation of collective subjects is a fragile achievement, not something to be taken for granted and always shot through with potentialities for reconfiguration. As Merlan and Rumsey point out, "a crucial part of what goes on at public exchange events is the struggle for control of the attribution of relevant agency, and of the significance of the event for various spheres of social relations" (1991, 14). This is because "the nature of the social identities involved in the transactions is under-determined . . . these identities cannot be established without careful study of the way in which the exchange events are 'represented,' both at the moment of transaction and in the ongoing social life of the people concerned" (16). In other words, a "persuasive interpretation of events" (Lederman 1989, 238) is required in order to determine if a collectivity is transacting a prestation—and who that collectivity is.

This accords with Donald Brenneis and Fred Myers's discussion of egalitarian communities across the Pacific. They point out that "speech events in situations where egalitarian relations prevail seem strikingly concerned with the construction and maintenance of a polity, with the constitution of a context within which interaction can occur . . . When one examines the evidence of these types of situations, one is struck by the extent to which a political arena is an achievement, rather than a category of analysis to be taken for granted" (1984). Brenneis and Myers insist that "the broader frame, the meaning or context established, is the polity in egalitarian orders, defining actors as political persons and specifying the sorts of relations that should obtain between them" (20). In her study of the Sepik, Karen Brison (1992) has argued that it is just this fear of the potential for social disintegration that leads large communal meetings to be so inconsequential—the danger of something actually happening at them is too great.

As I mentioned above, Claude Lévi-Strauss famously contrasted "hot" bureaucracies with "cold" cosmologies. For him, bureaucracies are "hot," the adaptive, all-encompassing, rational mechanisms of a restless modernity. "Our Western societies," Lévi-Strauss argues, "are made for change; it is the principle of their structure and of their organization" (1983, 321). These societies progress by incorporating change. Cosmology, on the other hand, relies on an immobilizing (and vulnerable) regulation by tradition. They are thus "primitive" societies, "which we might define as 'cold' because their internal environment borders on the zero of historical temperature, are distinguished by the limited number of their people and their mechanical mode of functioning" (29). "Cold" societies seek to "annul the possible effects of historical factors on their equilibrium and continuity" and thus avoid change in order to continuously replicate a positively valued past that is memorialized in myth and ritual. It is for this reason that Lévi-Strauss says that myth, like music, is an "instrument . . . for the obliteration of time . . . it catches and enfolds it as one catches and enfolds a cloth flapping in the wind" and thus "overcomes the contradiction between historical, enacted time and a permanent constant" (Lévi-Strauss 1969, 15–16).

Melanesians, I would argue, are "hot," not just in Lévi-Strauss's sense, but in Latour's sense: they prefer "hot" controversies to "cold" objectivity (1987, 30). This argument echoes Ben Finney's. In contrast to the racist paternalism of Australian colonialism, he suggested that highlanders were "pre-adapted to capitalism" rather than caught in the grip of a cold and unchanging culture that inhibited development (Finney 1973). Forty years later, it might be said that Papua New Guineans may be pre-adapted to entrepreneurship, but not to its institutionalization. Although there is a lot of truth in critiques of underdevelopment that place the blame on predatory international forces, there are also internal reasons why Papua New Guinea has never fallen in love with bureaucratic regularity: people in the country are too human, too empathetic, and too creative to believe that people can or ought to be turned into cogs in a machine.

In contrast with "hot" Melanesian sociality such as the Ipili's, the mine's bureaucracy is "cold" in the classical Weberian sense: it is a hierarchical organization with standard operating procedures designed to keep it open and running as efficiently as possible, complete with an office hierarchy, management based on written documents, and employees who distinguish between their official role and their private lives (Weber 1968, 956–57). The mine operates in this manner for many reasons, including, as Max Weber points out, that manner's "purely technical superiority over any other form of organization" (973). We are back to the close tie between the efficient coordination of action and the routineness with which people personate leviathans. The complex logistics and technical requirements of running a mine in a place like Porgera are met by bureaucratic organization: "precision, speed, unambiguity, knowledge of the files, continuity, discretion, unity, strict subordination, reduction of friction and of material and personal costs—these are raised to the optimum point in the strictly bureaucratic administration" (973).

"Reduction of friction," indeed—the mine's organization is literally prescriptive, with the work of its employees following prescriptions described in written standard operating procedures that are meant to exemplify what are now called best practices. As a result, the mine seeks to deny the historical particularity of, say, any historically unique toilet cleaning process in favor of a more efficient "stereotypic reproduction" of rules regarding the standard way to clean toilets—despite the fact that every toilet is utterly unique and particular and will never again be in exactly the same state as it is at the particular moment that a janitor experiences cleaning it. "Bureaucratization," Weber writes, "offers above all the optimum possibility for carrying through the principle of specializing administrative functions according to purely objective considerations . . . 'Objective' discharge of business primarily means a discharge of business according to calculable rules" and "without regard for persons" (975). Keeping the mine open depends on institutions that see people in their generality rather than their particularity.

Standard operating procedure is nomothetic in its subsumption of particulars under general categories. Indeed, Weber writes that as "bureaucracy develops the more perfectly, the more it is 'dehumanized,' the more completely it succeeds in eliminating from official business love, hatred, and all purely personal, irrational, and emotional elements which escape calculation" (975). The result is company discipline, or, as the Porgera Joint Venture refers to it, a "high performance culture": "the content of discipline is nothing but the consistently rationalized methodically prepared and exact execution of the received order, in which all personal criticism is unconditionally suspended and the actor is unswervingly and exclusively set for carrying out the command. In addition, this conduct under orders is uniform" (1149).

Like the ancient cosmologies that (attempted to) legitimate early states, bureaucracies (attempt to) present a picture of an all-embracing order that is reenacted and recapitulated in the course of everyday life. If Sahlins spoke of historical metaphors for mythical realities, perhaps we could say that leviathans are naturalized as local metaphors of mythical bureaucracies. It is through these bureaucracies that leviathans get put into black boxes, gaining agency and traction in the world.

At the top of these hierarchies are small groups of elites—collectively called senior management—whose decisions can change standard operating procedure. Like Sahlins's Polynesian chiefs, these people form an evenementially "hot" core at the apex of the bureaucracy that takes the form of a "reality management pool" (Murphy 1991) that decides what to do and then ensures that others implement their orders. A cold, obedient infrastructure harnessed to an evenementially hot executive structure creates the mine as a leviathan. This is why anthropology must "study up" (Nader 1972): for actors and researchers in the hot evenmential apex of bureaucracies, the arbitrariness of history making is apparent, and it is easy to "resolve social totalities into the projects of self-fashioning individuals" (Sahlins 2004, 142). When studied from a distance, the complexity of these interactions on the ground can be read as a James Scottian "Leviathanology," in which "autonomous cultural behemoths" appear unproblematically as big actors (142).

Thus we can see that bureaucracy is cold, a process of enrolling humans into sociotechnical networks of human and nonhuman actors that can effect action at a distance (Law 1986), both spatial and temporal, making it an efficacious leviathan. In a sense, we can say that the classic structural and functional view of landowners is in fact a misrecognized form of the West's own predilections for organization. There is a reason why kinship diagrams look like organizational charts: such charts are the paradigm for the diagrams. The charts are "cold" bureaucracy that project their self-understanding onto the other that they primitivize.

Of course, one ought not take the pretensions of leviathans too seriously. This image of a friction-free, perfectly functioning organization whose component people fulfill their functions with Borg-like precision is far from accurate. Nevertheless, it is the pretension of order that leads to order itself—and thus to the sense throughout this ethnography that although the landowners never quite managed to become a leviathan, the mine surely was one, even if the Ipili refused to accept it as such.

Landowners, Metropolitans, and Existential Authenticity

Some have understood Melanesian "heat" in relatively dystopic terms. Benjamin Reilly claims that the state of Papua New Guinea is "Africanized" or "failed" because of "ethnic conflict" (2000; see Chappell 2005 for a rebuttal). Filer has argued that the fluidity of social relations "menaces" a resource industry predicated on the bureaucratic, stereotypical reproduction of actions, which are needed to keep large resource extraction projects up and running: "Papua New Guineans make life unusually difficult for multinational companies because of the characteristic diversity and instability of political relationships between Melanesian persons, institutions, and communities which constitute their national policy process" (1998, 150). In this account, Melanesian "heat" means that "Melanesian communities have always been on the verge of disintegration, even in pre-colonial times, and it has always taken special qualities of leadership, in each succeeding generation, to prevent them from splitting apart at the seams. In pre-colonial times, such efforts were directed to the pursuit of warfare, the practice of initiation, and the organization of large-scale gift-exchange, but the rules of the game were no more permanent than the social groups whose continuity depended on the outcome" (Filer 1990a, 9–10).

Filer's discourse of abjection may be right about Melanesian allergies to leviathans, but just because "menace" is all about fluidity does not mean that all fluidity is menacing. True, the prospects are glum for Narokobi's dream of the village as suburb full of all of the technical infrastructure of the town but none of the human routinization. As science studies has demonstrated, technical systems are always in fact sociotechnical ones (Callon 1991), networks of both human and nonhuman actors. "Development"—in all of its currently existing forms—requires the leviathans that Melanesians are so averse to forming. Still, this openness to innovation can and ought be given a positive moral valuation in Melanesia just as it was valued in nineteenth-century Europe. Admittedly, seeing Melanesians as flâneurs rather than as savages is hardly a panacea for the many problems Papua New Guinea faces, but it might allow alternate visions with more room to imagine positive futures for the country than a vision focused on "disintegration."

There is good evidence that these alternatives are coming to light. Consider, for instance, what happened in the late 1980s and early 1990s when anthropologists developed a literature around the invention of tradition or, in its Melanesian mode, "*kastom*" (see Lindstrom 2008 for an overview). Too often, this literature took the form of defamiliarizing critique, an approach it

inherited from the British Marxists who originally deployed it against impe-
rialistic elites (Hobsbawm and Ranger 1983). Applied to the study of indigenous peoples and former dependencies, protestations of good intentions
could never manage to remove the traces of intellectual condescension and
political critique that clung to the model: its suspicion of elites, assumption
of epistemological authority, and belittlement (intentional or not) of non-
academic ways of knowing. In this literature, anthropology spoke truth not
to power, but to the indigenous.

At roughly the same time that arguments about the "invention of tradition" were being made, an approach was developed that enabled anthropology to become the study of the innovation of tradition. Today these projects
are widespread and often involve collaboration between Melanesians and
Western academics to find Melanesian methods of, for instance, managing
intellectual property (Kalinoe and Leach 2004) or cultural heritage (Geismar 2005). A Wagnerian focus on innovation might lead us to some refigu-
rations of the state of relationships in Papua New Guinea today.

Anthropologists have demonstrated over and over again that the result
of Papua New Guinea's attempts to "formulate a template of customary land
tenure informed by its ideology of tradition" has been "a series of experiments in clanship" (Jorgensen 2007, 59, 63), which can produce "landowning
clans on demand" out of grass roots who "have proven to be adept at fulfilling the expectations of legibility, and seem quite capable of inventing clans
if they turn out not to have any to begin with" (68). The result is what Summerson Carr calls "anticipatory interpellation": "reading how one is hailed as
a particular kind of institutional subject and responding as such" (2009, 319)
in order to gain recognition and entitlements from institutions.

There is a certain irony in this situation. In the age of industrialization,
Marx once quipped, workers came to the market with only their hides to offer and received the expected hiding. In the age of globalization, grassroots
Papua New Guineans come to Port Moresby with carefully prepared identities to flog, only to find policy elites who are less willing than Moneybags
(Marx's capitalist entrepreneur) to do the needful. The reason, ironically, is
that it is the urban center, rather than the "innocent population," that is under the mystifying influence of timeless tradition—or at least, their imagination of it. The efforts that grassroots Papua New Guineans make to become
the innocent population that cosmopolitans imagine them to be are labeled
inauthentic and corrupt. But in fact their willingness to innovate is the most
authentic thing about them. That willingness is a pure instantiation of the
Melanesian Way and exemplifies a penchant for approaching the new, rather

than relying on a fixed set of things that Melanesians used to do. It is a way of translating that is proactive, dynamic, and innovative, rather than a "cold" fixed content. This is what Narokobi meant when he wrote that "a determined pursuit of creativity will ignite in us the genius to be free" (1983, 6).

If I am right, policy making and implementation in Papua New Guinea could be improved if it recognized the creativity of the grass roots. Rather than insisting on "painting a frozen landscape whose 'landowners' could then be vetted or endorsed by the Minister of Petroleum and Energy as 'entitled project beneficiaries'" (Goldman 2007, 113), the nation could embrace models that were modern, innovative, and inclusive (Golub 2007b; Goldman 2007; Weiner 2006). This could start with something as simple as detaching land ownership from descent, as was tried in Southern Highlands Province (Goldman 2007). Recognizing that the capital is complicit in eliciting landowner identities is key here (Weiner 2006). People who are fixated on images of the innocent population will not welcome such innovation, of course, and even those who recognize that "the Melanesian Way may indeed be alive and well" to the extent that "local people are able to achieve recognition by fabricating new versions of who they are" worry that such fabrication is "guaranteed to raise questions, rather than settle them" (Jorgensen 2007, 69). This is true, of course—but the point in the Melanesian context is not to settle questions but to enable a healthy, dialogical process. Development forums and benefit-sharing agreements will tend to fail—regardless of how democratically they are designed—if their aim is to begin with a period of deliberation among stakeholders in order to produce a fixed consensus that is then bureaucratically implemented. More robust, I suspect, would be measures that called for continuing, institutionalized dialogue—which would keep the heat of Melanesian sociality from boiling over, as it were, rather than attempting to freeze it altogether. This is, after all, the route that grassroots Papua New Guineans have forced on metropolitans through litigation in the courts and direct action at resource extraction sites. Policy that legalized and recognized these de facto demands for ongoing consultation would probably work better than the procrustean schemes of current registration systems, even if it did not promise that we would know the outcomes of such deliberations in advance.

. . .

Grassroots Papua New Guineans are not the only people whose possible futures are foreclosed by the image of the innocent population. Urbanites also face specters of inauthenticity as they try to develop lifeways that are both middle class and Papua New Guinean. Weighed down by images of the innocent population, urban Papua New Guineans engage in extremely Melanesian methods of innovation and creativity to adapt to city life even as their explicit ideology of "the way Melanesians are" rules such innovations out of bounds. The result is either a guilty conscience or a decision to pursue a completely deculturated white modernity.

Focusing on innovation and process, rather than on patrimony and product, has important implications for how city dwellers can imagine their own modernity. Models of culture that emphasize a fixed and stable patrimony imply that any deviation from tradition is pathological. When a modernist concern for innovation moves to center stage, what is distinctly Melanesian about Papua New Guinean culture becomes its method of change, instead of the uniqueness of its contents. This opens up new possibilities for urbanites to imagine themselves as both Melanesian and developed.

Thus Papua New Guineans should be less fearful (or, contrariwise, less enthusiastic) about the price that modernity forces its adherents to pay. Traditional modernity is neither a paradox nor something reserved for the villages. Experiments in urban traditional modernity occur in Papua New Guinea in a variety of forms, ranging from house decoration (Beier 1978) to urban gardening contests (Battaglia 1995), where nostalgia for "the village" is productive of new kinds of sociality. Such experiments are common in Papua New Guinea because they come naturally, but too often their true value is not recognized, and they fail to receive the recognition they deserve.

Giving them this recognition would involve shifting the definition of authenticity away from primordialism and toward what Jonathan Friedman, following Edward Sapir, calls an ethics of "existential authenticity," where it is "that area of social life wherein we find the shared experiences that enable models of reality to achieve an effective degree of resonance among their practitioners" (Friedman 1993, 764) that is the hallmark of cultural continuity. Focusing on the existential commitments of people in the present may enable urban Papua New Guineans to expand their imagination of what a modern Melanesian culture might be, as well as to give people moral permission to pursue it. This, like every modern project, is a disconcerting one: primordialism, once learned, is an easy way to ground identity.

Equally, opening up a space for novelty creates the possibility of a too easy authenticity in which any activity counts as cultural perdurance as long as the person doing it has the right subject position. A focus on the importance of genres of practice could serve to encourage middle-class Papua New Guineans to recognize that a feasible way of life—one presupposed by the past, entailing the future, and forced to conform successfully to the moment in which it finds itself—must be rooted in particular ways of doing things. This may mean doing more than dressing up in traditional *bilas* once or twice a year. Understanding the cultural dynamics of existential authenticity requires more work by both anthropologists and Papua New Guineans, but I believe it is a more promising path than relying on images of innocent populations that can no longer (and never really could) anchor the project of Papua New Guinean cultural modernity.

Comparative Anthropologies of Order

In the end, my ideal-typical picture of Melanesians is no doubt hopelessly overdrawn. But readers willing to accept even the most basic version of it can see that leviathans are not easily constructed or maintained in Papua New Guinea. This has proved to be a blessing and a curse for the Ipili, simultaneously increasing their feasibility by maximizing their willingness to innovate and decreasing it by making them reluctant to institutionalize the hierarchies of position and agreements of meaning that would make their monstrous creations into truly efficacious actors. In the Yakatabari negotiations, individual Ipili responded agentively to the mine's demands even as "the Ipili" as a leviathan was unable to act decisively because of the roiling divisiveness of the networks out of which it was composed.

This chapter has discussed the broader national contexts that have made the Ipili feasible, and I hope to have provided some possible answers to issues of landowner recognition in Papua New Guinea today. In closing, I want to turn now to a few tentative suggestions that might conclude the argument of the book as a whole.

This book has sought to extend the comparative range of studies of social totalities by examining the corporate form as it appears in the study of both kinship and bureaucracies. Throughout this book my imagery has intentionally been biblical, evoking the ancient Near East, early modern Europe, and contemporary studies of science in order to probe what makes or unmakes social complexity. Just as the pretensions of Bronze Age monarchs were couched in idioms of sociocosmic legitimacy, so the bureaucracies that subtend the mine in Porgera imagine—and implement—a world in which individual action recapitulates an invisible but precedent cosmological order.

Such an approach has the potential to resolve some of the issues facing the regional literature on kinship. Ethnographers such as Knut Rio and Michael Scott have taken issue with Stragnerian generalizations about the nature of

Melanesian sociality. Rio argues that "the possibility of recognizing . . . social structure is itself a value" has been "washed out of anthropology" by portrayals of Melanesian fluidity (Rio 2007: 6). Scott fears that ethnographers will overlook the fact that "some Melanesians . . . recognize irreducible elementary essences" which structure social life if they start with the assumption that "there are no static pre-constituted social identities, groups, or even societies" (Scott 2007, 340). Both propose theoretical innovations to deal with this shortcoming: a sort of cultural depth-analysis of cosmology in the case of Scott, and a retooled Dumontian theory of hierarchy in the case of Rio (Rio and Smedal 2009).

These are interesting projects, but a focus on theoretical innovation draws attention away from what is, at base, simple ethnographic dissatisfaction: Stragnerian descriptions of Melanesian heat draw on ethnography from Papua New Guinea, whereas Rio and Scott work in "Island Melanesia" (Spriggs 1997), an area where Austronesian cultural influences lead people to be more comfortable with the leviathans. To my mind, the simplest way to resolve this dispute is to ask a series of ethnographic, rather than theoretical, questions: how do concepts of order differ across Melanesia? How explicitly are they recognized and deployed, and how much do they remain implicit as an aesthetic preference in local modes of sociality? Can we move beyond dichotomies of "Austronesian" and "Non-Austronesian" to a more nuanced typology of regional approaches to order and social totalities?

Thinking past primordiality also opens up the possibility for an even broader comparative analysis of social totalities. As anthropological studies of the state and corporation develop and converge, might we not bring them into dialogue with comparative religion and archaeology? Could we not also bring these approaches into dialogue with recent literature—both academic and applied—on anarchist anthropology that focuses on people who are opposed in principle to hierarchy and order (Clastres 1987; Graeber 2009; James Scott 2009) and resist what Goldenweiser called the "icy grandeur" of Leviathan? Harold Brookfield (2011) has tentatively compared Melanesia with upland Southeast Asia. James Scott claims that people in "Zomia," as he calls this area, have anti-leviathan tendencies and chose, in principle, to lead ungoverned lives. Scott sees the anti-Leviathanlike tendencies of Zomians as based in political choice. Melanesians, on the other hand, long for unity and corporateness even as they seem never to be able to achieve it. Many have debated Scott's claims, but it should be clear that this approach has the potential to become a generalizing study of order (von Benda-Beckman 2007) whose subject matter was defined not by ethnographic area but by a focus on people's explicit ideologies of order, analogous with language ideologies (Schieffelin, Woolard, and Kroskrity 1998) and how they regulate conduct—or don't.

This argument also speaks to the burgeoning literature on indigeneity. Nearly a half-century into the movement for indigenous recognition, discussions of indigeneity still revolve around issues of autochthony, patrimony, and continuity. Even as anthropologists and indigenous people insist that cultures are always changing, government frameworks for indigenous recognition (as well as some indigenous self-understanding) continue to keep primordial fixity central to discussions of indigenous authenticity. The most interesting advances in Native and Indigenous Studies have sought to move beyond an identity politics of primordialism by drawing on the literatures of cultural studies, postmodernism, and postcolonialism. But what imaginative possibilities could be opened up if we moved Melanesian modernity to the center of analysis of indigenous cultural systems and emphasized indigenous dynamism as something that is both pre- and post-colonial? Such a viewpoint would demonstrate the legitimacy of these approaches even to more intellectually conservative scholars. It would also suggest that the true agenda of cultural sustainability is not preservation of tradition but the creation of spaces in which tradition can remain fluid, molten, and vivacious (I follow here Diaz 2011).

This book is heavily indebted to the literature on the "indigenization of modernity" (Sahlins 2000), which argues that indigenous culture is revitalized, not replaced, by globalization. Because their cosmological schemes remain intact, this literature maintains, indigenous people can apply them to contemporary circumstances to create lifeways that are both modern and customary, authentic and novel. My argument here adds a proviso: as my discussion of Ipili sociality in chapter 3 indicates, indigenous lifeways are made feasible not only by cosmological schemes but also by the culturally distinct genres of action that enact them. Acts of preservation and elaboration deploy a palette of differences whose spectrum may be less vibrant than it was in the past. Richard Wilk has argued that we live in a world of "global systems of common difference" (1995)—systems in which the variety of imaginable differences is decreasing. Paul Nadasdy makes a similar argument, claiming that interaction with bureaucratic orders requires the transformation of indigenous knowledge into a bureaucratic form (2003). This transformation in turn fundamentally alters the nature of indigenous culture.

Focusing on the *parole* of grassroots culture rather than its *langue* may require a little less optimism about "develop-man" (Sahlins 1992) than we sometimes see in the literature. Something important might very well be lost when the "how" of indigeneity changes, even if the "what" of indigeneity stays the same. If tradition is a form of change, bureaucratizing it means giving something up. I do not mean to be cynical about the possibility of difference in the globalized world, but I do think it is important that we remember other options that have been foreclosed. If Lévi-Strauss lamented the end of beautifully pristine and timeless cultures, perhaps it is time for us to return to nostalgia—but for a mode of meaning making, not a particular set of content. Alternately, a recognition of the importance of genres of practice could be used as a starting point to ask how, specifically, cultural revitalization projects might succeed.

Finally, a note on leviathans themselves. For over a decade anthropology has been shifting gears from an enthusiastic wonder at the complexities and power of corporations and states to the tried-and-true strategy of ethnographic critique—revealing the concrete locations where "the global" or "the state" is made. Such a move is salutary, of course, but it involves a danger. To anthropologists and others whose experience of global capitalism is shaped by the retail purchase of commodities—T-shirts, movies, and so forth—the current world can seem kaleidoscopic indeed. But to those who study primary industry, as I have in this book, it seems naive to believe that a defamiliarizing critique of global order is adequate. Scrutinizing the occasional points of friction that seem to interrupt an otherwise flowing world or pointing out the seams on the sides of leviathans does little to diminish their power.

Pointing out the inevitable friction inherent in globalization is not, I would argue, a sufficiently radical critique of late-1990s assumptions about the kaleidoscopic flow of globalization: merely demonstrating the chinks in Leviathan's armor still assumes his overawing power and questions our own ability, methodologically, to vie with him. Rather, we need a more thoroughgoing and self-confident decomposition of the beast back into its constituent networks, all the while recognizing the terrible traction it has on the world. Just as actor-network theory has scrutinized the specificities of scientific practice, anthropologies of economic globalization, indigenous identity, and governmentality need to provide accounts of the practices of measurement that make globalization feasible, whether that be through a history of the standardization that enables the global dissemination of goods (Levinson 2006), the personal and ethnic networks that underwrite that dissemination (Stein 2010), or the small worlds of influence that, when black-boxed, appear to be (for instance) "international markets" rather than a small group of people sitting in front of computers (Knorr Cetina 2002). New conjunctions of capitalism and technology present new challenges, it is true, but the problems they put to us are also very old ones indeed—perhaps the oldest ones of all. What I have demonstrated here is that the mining industry and other globalized institutions are comprehensible as long as we are not overawed by them. What is called for is not an approach that trembles at their sight, but an anthropology ready, willing, and able to sport with leviathans.

AFTERWORD

In August 2007 Guy Mascord was killed in his home in Port Moresby by a blow to the neck with a machete or axe and repeated stabbings to his abdomen with a knife. For people familiar with life in Papua New Guinea's capital, Mascord's death was a sad reminder of the dangers there. For the international news media, his murder made good copy: a longtime resident of Papua New Guinea, the fifty-year-old British expatriate had used magic to try to protect his house from attack. A flurry of articles appeared with titles like "Teacher Had Used Voodoo to Keep Himself Safe" (2007) and "Witchcraft Fails to Save Briton Murdered by Burglars" (Parsons 2007), and then the murder was forgotten, lost in the next iteration of the Internet's endless media cycle.

For me, Guy's death was more than just a color story. Rather, it exemplified Porgera's fall from grace, for although his murder was unconnected with the mine, his life was not: Guy had frequently been employed by the Porgera Joint Venture (PJV) as a consultant, and he had written the *Porgera Mine Sustainability Report: 2000* (Placer Dome Asia Pacific 2001). It had been Guy who had produced the compressed account of the Yakatabari negotiations with which I began chapter 1 of this book. He was a gentle, quiet English-man whose 1960s-infused interest in ethnobotany had turned into a love affair with Papua New Guinea, where he had married and settled perma-nently. His death, like the negotiations, seemed to mark a turning point in the valley's history. In the years after my initial fieldwork, the promise and hope of the mine's presence began turning into something that, like Guy's murder, seemed more and more irredeemable and grim.

Sitting around the mine's community relations offices waiting for our var-ious appointments, my Porgeran friends and I often complained about what a penny-ante company Placer Dome was and how we should get a real min-ing company to come into Porgera and make them some real money. By the time I left the field in 2001, Porgerans felt more and more convinced that they had gotten the short end of the stick. As Porgerans used mine-derived money to see the world, their relocation houses started looking punier and punier. "Development" was not materializing. They wanted more and better from the mine. The mine's "sustainability reports" with pictures of smiling boy scouts and well-scrubbed schoolchildren came to seem hypocritical and self-serving. In a culture that equated moral worth with material wealth, and instilled in people a deep sense of entitlement, nothing would satisfy the Ipili until they were living in the same kind of houses as the president of Placer Dome himself. Or maybe ones just slightly larger.

As it turned out, the Ipili got their new company. In 2006 Placer Dome was acquired by Barrick Gold. Despite our kvetching, Placer Dome had al-ways been a world-class company, and when they acquired it, Barrick be-came the largest gold mining company on the planet. Although many of the faces at the mine remained the same, changes in policy and direction slowly became apparent: the sustainability reports stopped. The relentlessly earnest emphasis on transparency was replaced by opacity, punctuated by a few glossy, data-free pamphlets filled with professions of good intentions.

Social problems were taking their toll in the valley. During my first field-work, the social upheavals that accompanied mine seemed problematic but manageable—turbulence that the valley would have to ride out on its way to a better future. There was even a frisson of excitement at the atmosphere of unpredictability. Porgera was rough, dirty, and dangerous, but it was also ex-hilarating, exciting, and fun. The Yakatabari negotiations had been undone by the personal dynamics of Porgera's small world. But as the years went by, the valley found itself struggling to keep going without any high society at all. Slowly, the fragile network of people trying to hold things together in the valley began disintegrating. Some retired, some fell from power, and others rose to greater heights of authority and spent their time in corporate offices rather than living in the valley. Soon there was no one who had a coherent vision of what the valley's future would be, and no one on the other side of the fence to contact to try to make it happen.

In the years just before and after the Barrick acquisition, things got worse in a major way. A group within Porgera—but not headed by an ethnic Ipili—called the *Akali Tange Association* released a report entitled "The Shooting Fields of Porgera Joint Venture" (Akali Tange Association 2005), which documented deaths that they believed the mine was responsible for (*akali tange* is a form of mortuary compensation). This included things like mine security guards shooting people in the back after they had trespassed on mine property. Internal politics in Enga Province had resulted in the repeal of a liquor ban in Porgera. Although more often honored in the breach than the observance, the ban had limited the presence of alcohol in the valley. After it was lifted, the presence of alcohol soared in the special mining lease territory. When I visited Porgera in 2007, I saw a former elder of the Seventh-Day Adventist Church drunk and some young children, at ten o'clock in the morning. In-migration had created a crisis as well. In 2001 people were aware that there was an acute danger that they could become strangers in their own land, overwhelmed by migrants from elsewhere, particularly Engans. In 2010 much of this danger had been realized, and the Ipilis' ability to control—much less remove—the guests they hosted had evaporated. This combined with overcrowding to exacerbate social issues.

The clearest social problem was the increase in the number of illegal miners—people who entered the open pit to work the ore there. Just as Ipili identity had always been fluid, people had often entered the open pit to look for gold. I had done so, recreationally, with friends during my fieldwork in 2000. The particulars of who was mining and where they were doing it were replaced by fears—unfounded, I believe—on the part of PJV managers that cadres of "professional" Engan and Huli miners were being bused into the valley to work the ore. The results were, first, the construction of a security fence around the open pit and, second, deaths in the pit. Some miners died from accidents—the open pit is terribly unsafe—while others were shot by security guards. A long-standing practice of illegal mining had intensified, was criminalized, and then was prosecuted—with terrible results.

When I returned to the valley in 2007, the police were in the process of burning so-called 'squatter' communities to the ground in an act which may or may not have occurred during a "state of emergency." Liquor, in-migration, sexual violence—the situation had metastasized. It seemed that everyone who had the money and ability to leave the valley had done so, or at least had gotten their children as far away from it as they could. Porgerans leveraged money and compensation to buy or marry their way into Hagen, Goroka, Port Moresby, and, in a few exceptional cases, Queensland. Scholarships, internships, preferential hiring, trust funds to pay tuition—all of them did help create a small group of educated Porgerans who went to college or studied abroad. But who could blame those people if, in their early twenties, they looked at the toxic social and natural environment of the valley and saw these educational opportunities as a ticket to Sydney rather than a call to come back and become, as their fathers had planned, the next generation of leaders in the valley?

The transition to Barrick Gold from Placer Dome also radically expanded the network available to Porgerans. A well-developed network of First World activists and Third World or indigenous hosts to Barrick mines had been opposing Barrick for years—suddenly, the Ipili had allies. In 2000, Porgera was at the end of the world. In 2010, Human Rights Watch released its report on illegal miners on paper, PDF, and for Apple's new iPad. Suddenly, there was "an app for that" when it came to Porgera's misery and squalor. Increasingly framed as "indigenous" activists speaking to a global community rather than as citizens of Papua New Guinea demanding justice from their nation, a handful of Ipili landowners traveled to Canada to protest Barrick at its annual meetings.

As the middle fell away, it became increasingly impossible for me to straddle both sides of the divide between The Ipili and The Mine. Company executives grew increasingly dismissive of Ipili people. In one widely quoted comment, a Barrick executive remarked that rape was "a cultural habit" in Porgera ("Barrick Says Chief's Comments Taken out of Context" 2011). Over lunch a senior staff member in Barrick's Port Moresby office told me the company believed the Ipili were so duplicitous that there was no word for "lie" in their language. Ipili activists seemed to be spending more and more time traveling abroad to meetings and less and less time finding concrete solutions for their local communities.

The best scholarly overview of the past decades in Porgera is Catherine Coumans's "Occupying Spaces Created by Conflict: Anthropologists, Development NGOs, Responsible Investment, and Mining" (2011). It's all there: the environmental damage, the mine's security guards who shot and killed trespassers, a subsistence crisis that was bad in the 1990s and intolerable in the 2000s, and crippling social disorder caused by massive migration from outside the valley.

With Coumans's article, debate over the valley spread to academic circles. In it, she argued that any attempt to work with the mine to make things better was, in principle, unethical. In particular, Coumans singled out the anthropologist Martha Macintyre for criticism. Macintyre, a member of the Academy of Social Sciences in Australia, served on PEAK, an independent oversight body tasked with monitoring the mine's environmental performance. In doing so, Coumans wrote, "Macintyre . . . became complicit in PEAK's implicit and explicit support for the PJV mine's responses to environmental claims and alleged abuses of human rights in the SML area" (Coumans 2011, 36). Stuart Kirsch (2011) compared anthropologists doing research in Porgera to the disgraced members of the American government's Human Terrain System who had used their anthropological expertise in order to further the U.S. wars in Iraq and Afghanistan. Eventually the president of the Wenner-Gren foundation, which had published Coumans's and Kirsch's article, wrote a letter apologizing for their treatment of Macintyre (Aiello 2011).

I chose to study Porgera because the Ipili were a success story—or at least had the potential to be one. Their struggles with the mine were empirically messy and morally ambivalent, qualities that I thought would help me get beyond dualistic stereotypes of ecologically noble savages fighting the good fight against global capital. When asked about my own feasibility—how I could possibly do the research that my dissertation required—I used to answer that both sides thought they were in the right and wanted their story told. In retrospect, this was not the whole story: in fact, I thought they were both right, and I wanted to tell both sides of the story. Some Ipili people were not very nice; some mine employees were. Some of the social problems in the valley were caused by the mine, some by decisions made by Ipili. But beyond the many problems the valley faced, there were always successes and the tantalizing possibility of more.

Over the years Porgera has become more and more the dualistic, polarized political struggle that I had originally thought I had avoided. Battles have become more intense as the price of gold has skyrocketed and the welfare of the valley has plummeted. It was supposed to get easier for me to decide who was right and who was wrong in valley politics, but as the scale and complexity of problems grew, it seems more difficult to know whom to condemn. I am amazed that as the issues in Porgera get more and more complex, people seek answers that are morally and empirically simpler and simpler.

Intellectually, the institutional guilt and structural violence at play in the valley call for a rethinking of postliberal theories of responsibility (Lavin 2008). Practically, however, I don't believe we need to read more books to see what must be done. In my last trip to Port Moresby I told a Barrick executive that I thought the valley would be better off without the mine than with it. And yet neither Barrick nor pressure groups like the Porgera Landowners Association want the mine to close. The Porgera experiment is over, and the Ipili are the losers. Although some sort of remarkable turnaround is still conceivable, I think the time has come for everyone involved to realize that a postmine valley is now the only scenario in which the Ipili have a chance, in the long run, to be feasible.

BIBLIOGRAPHY

ARCHIVAL SOURCES

National Archives of Australia, Canberra
B883 PX169 Barcode 6249646 (Neptune Blood Personnel File).

National Archives of Papua New Guinea, Port Moresby
Accession 52 Box 3025 ("Native Mining" Reports).
Accession 61 Box 458 LF 555 ("Gold Discovery Porgera").

National Library of Australia, Canberra
MS. 8346 Series 3 Diary #11 (John Black Patrol Diary).
MS 8346 Series 7, Folder 1, (John Black Strickland Syndicate Folder).

Porgera District Office Archives, Porgera
Porgera Project Coordinating Unit (PPCU) Monthly Memos

PUBLISHED SOURCES

Aiello, Leslie. 2011. "Letter from the President of the Wenner-Gren Foundation." *Current Anthropology* 52 (6): 926.

Akali Tange Association. 2005. *The Shooting Fields of Porgera Joint Venture; Now a Case to Compensate and Justice to Prevail.* Report submitted to Porgera Joint Venture.

Andambo, Timothy. 2002. "The Ipili People, Their Development of the Social Technology to Extract Rent from the Porgera Lode and Their

Use of It to Build a Viable Community." Paper presented at the World Bank workshop on local management of mineral wealth, Washington, DC, 10–11 June.

Anderson, Benedict R. 1991. *Imagined Communities: Reflections on the Origin and Spread of Nationalism*. London: Verso.

Appell, George N. 1983. "Methodological Problems with the Concepts of Corporation, Corporate Social Grouping, and Cognatic Descent Group." *American Ethnologist* 10 (2): 302–11.

Asian Development Bank. 2000. *Resettlement Policy and Practice in Southeast Asia and the Pacific: Proceedings of Workshops Held in Manila and Port Vila 1998.* Manila: Asian Development Bank.

Babadzan, Alain. 1988. "Kastom and Nation Building in the South Pacific." In *Ethnicities and Nations: Processes of Interethnic Relations in Latin America, Southeast Asia, and the Pacific,* edited by Remo Gudieri, Francesco Pellizzi, and Stanley Tambiah, 199–228. Houston: Rothko Chapel.

Baglin, Douglass. 1988. *The Jimi River Expedition, 1950: Exploration in the New Guinea Highlands.* Melbourne, Australia: Oxford University Press.

Bahrani, Zainab. 2008. *Rituals of War: The Body and Violence in Mesopotamia.* New York: Zone.

Bainton, Nicholas A. 2010. *The Lihir Destiny: Cultural Responses to Mining in Melanesia.* Acton, A.C.T.: ANU E Press.

Ballard, Chris. 1995. "The Death of a Great Land: Ritual, History, and Subsistence Revolutions in the Southern Highlands of Papua New Guinea." PhD diss., Australian National University.

Ballard, Chris. 2000. "The Fire Next Time: The Conversion of the Huli Apocalypse." *Ethnohistory* 47 (1): 205–25.

Ballard, Chris, and Glenn Banks. 1997. "The Return of the Kiap to Rural Papua New Guinea." In *Emerging From Empire? Decolonisation in the Pacific: Proceedings of a Workshop at the Australian National University December 1996,* edited by Donald Denoon, 160–64. Canberra: Australian National University.

Ballard, John. 1975. "The National Bureaucracy: An Interview with Professor John Ballard." *Administration for Development* 1 (4): 47–56.

Banks, Glenn. 1997. "Mountain of Desire: Mining Company and Indigenous Community at the Porgera Gold Mine, Papua New Guinea." PhD diss., Australian National University.

Banks, Glenn. 1999. *Keeping an Eye on the Beasts: Social Monitoring of Large-Scale Mines in New Guinea.* Canberra: Australia National University, Research School of Pacific and Asian Studies.

Banks, Glenn. 2003. "Landowner Equity in Papua New Guinea's Minerals Sector: Review and Policy Issues." *Natural Resources Forum* 27 (3): 223–34.

Banks, Glenn, and Chris Ballard. 1997a. *The Ok Tedi Settlement: Issues, Outcomes, and Implications.* Canberra: National Centre for Development Studies, Research School of Pacific Studies, Australian National University.

Banks, Glenn, and Susanne Bonnell. 1997. *Porgera Social Monitoring Program Annual Report 1996.*

Barnard, Leonard. 1969. *Banish the Night: Fighting Kur, Timango, and Other Devils in New Guinea.* Mountain View, CA: Pacific.

Barnes, John A. 1962. "African Models in the New Guinea Highlands." *Man* 62 (1): 5–9.

Barnes, John A. 1967. "Agnation among the Enga: A Review Article." *Oceania* 38 (1): 33–43.

Barnes, John A. 1969. Foreword to Robert M. Glasse, *Huli of Papua: A Cognatic Descent System,* 3–5. Paris: Mouton.

"Barrick Says Chief's Comments Taken Out of Context." 2011. Papua New Guinea *Post-Courier*, March 28.

Barth, Fredrik. 1989. *Cosmologies in the Making: A Generative Approach to Cultural Variation in Inner New Guinea.* Cambridge: Cambridge University Press.

Bashkow, Ira. 1995. " 'The Stakes for Which We Play Are Too High to Allow of Experiment': Colonial Administrators of Papua on Their Anthropological Training by Radcliffe-Brown." *History of Anthropology Newsletter* 22 (2): 2–13.

Bashkow, Ira. 2004. "A Neo-Boasian Conception of Cultural Boundaries." *American Anthropologist* 106 (3): 443–58.

Bashkow, Ira. 2006. *The Meaning of Whitemen: Race and Modernity in the Orokaiva Cultural World.* Chicago: University of Chicago Press.

Bateson, Gregory. 1932. "Social Structure of the Iatmül People of the Sepik River." *Oceania* 2 (3): 245–91.

Battaglia, Debbora. 1995. "On Practical Nostalgia: Self-Prospecting among Urban Trobrianders." In *Rhetorics of Self-Making,* edited by Debbora Battaglia, 77–96. Berkeley: University of California Press.

Baudelaire, Charles. 1964. *The Painter of Modern Life and Other Essays.* Translated and edited by Jonathan Mayne. London: Phaidon.

Beauvoir, Simone de. 1956. *The Mandarins, a Novel.* Translated by Leonard M. Friedman. New York: W.W. Norton & Company.

Beier, Ulli. 1975. "The Cultural Dilemma of Papua New Guinea." *Meanjin Quarterly* 34 (3): 302–10.

Beier, Ulli. 1978. "Squatters' Art in Port Moresby." *Gigibori* 1 (4): 1–13.

Benda-Beckmann, Keebet von, and Fernanda Pirie, eds. 2007. *Order and Disorder: Anthropological Perspectives.* New York: Berghahn Books.

Benson, Peter. 2008. "El Campo: Faciality and Structural Violence in Farm Labor Camps." *Cultural Anthropology* 23 (4): 589–629.

Biersack, Aletta. 1980. "The Hidden God: Communication, Cosmology, and Cybernetics among a Melanesian People." PhD diss., University of Michigan at Ann Arbor.

Biersack, Aletta. 1992. "Short-Fuse Mining Politics in the Jet Age: From Stone to Gold in Porgera and Mt. Kare." Paper presented at the annual meeting of the American Anthropological Association, San Francisco, CA, 5 December.

Biersack, Aletta. 1995a. "Introduction: The Huli, Duna, and Ipili People Yesterday and Today." In *Papuan Borderlands: Huli, Duna, and Ipili Perspectives on the Papua New Guinea Highlands,* edited by Aletta Biersack, 1–56. Ann Arbor: University of Michigan Press.

Biersack, Aletta. 1995b. "Heterosexual Meanings: Economy, Society, and Gender among Ipilis." In *Papuan Borderlands: Huli, Duna, and Ipili Perspectives on the Papua New Guinea Highlands,* edited by Aletta Biersack, 231–64. Ann Arbor: University of Michigan Press

Biersack, Aletta. 1996a. "Word Made Flesh: Religion, the Economy, and the Body in the Papua New Guinea Highlands." *History of Religions* 36 (2): 85–111.

Biersack, Aletta. 1996b "Making Kinship": Marriage, Warfare, and Networks among Paielas. In *Work in Progress: Essays in New Guinea Highlands Ethnography in Honour of Paula Brown Glick,* edited by Hal Levine and Anton Ploeg, 19–42. New York: Peter Lang.

Biersack, Aletta. 1998. "Horticulture and Hierarchy: The Youthful Beautification of the Body in the Paiela and Porgera Valleys." In *Adolescence in Pacific Island Societies,* edited by Gilbert Herdt and Stephen C. Leavitt, 71–91. Pittsburgh, PA: University of Pittsburgh Press.

Biersack, Aletta. 1999. "The Mount Kare Python and His Gold: Totemism and Ecology in the Papua New Guinea Highlands." *American Anthropologist* 101 (1): 68–87.

Biersack, Aletta. 2006. "Red River, Green War: The Politics of Place Along the Porgera River." In *Reimagining Political Ecology,* edited by Joseph Greenberg and Aletta Biersack, 233–80. Durham, NC: Duke University Press.

Blehr, Otto. 1963. "Action Groups in a Society with Bilateral Kinship: A Case Study from the Faroe Islands." *Ethnology* 2 (3): 269–75.

Blood, Ned [Neptune]. 1949. "Sheep Airlift in New Guinea." *National Geographic* 96 (6): 831–37.

Boas, Franz. 1962. *Anthropology and Modern Life.* New York: W. W. Norton.

Bonnell, Susanne. 1999. "The Landowner Relocation Program." In *Dilemmas of Development: The Social and Economic Impact of the Porgera Gold Mine, 1989–1994,* edited by Colin Filer, 128–59. Canberra: Asia Pacific.

Bosse, Hans. 1994. *Becoming a Papua New Guinean: A Report of a Sociologist's and Group Analyst's Research with Students at Passam National High School.* Boroko: National Research Institute.

Bradshaw, Joel. 1997. "The Population Kaleidoscope: Another Factor in the Melanesian Diversity V. Polynesian Homogeneity Debate. *Journal of the Polynesian Society,* 106 (3): 222–49.

Bredekamp, Horst. 2003. *Stratégies visuelles de Thomas Hobbes.* Paris: Éditions de la Maison des Sciences de l'Homme.

Brenneis, Donald Lawrence, and Fred R. Myers. 1984. *Dangerous Words: Language and Politics in the Pacific.* New York: New York University Press.

Brightman, Robert. 1995. "Forget Culture: Replacement, Transcendence, Relexification." *Cultural Anthropology* 10 (4): 509–46.

Brison, Karen J. 1992. *Just Talk: Gossip, Meetings, and Power in a Papua New Guinea Village.* Berkeley: University of California Press.

Britan, Gerald M., and Ronald Cohen. 1980. *Hierarchy and Society: Anthropological Perspectives on Bureaucracy.* Philadelphia: Institute for the Study of Human Issues.

Brookfield, Harold. 2011. "Scott and Others in History in the Southeast Asian Uplands: A Review Essay." *Asia Pacific Journal of Anthropology* 12 (5): 484–94.

Brown, Paula. 1962. "Nonagnates among the Patrilineal Chimbu." *Journal of the Polynesian Society* 71 (1): 57–69.

Brown, Paula. 1972. *The Chimbu: A Study of Change in the New Guinea Highlands.* Cambridge, MA: Schenkman.

Browne, Bob. 2006. *Grassroots: Best of the Good Ol' Days.* N.A.: Pacific Multimedia

Brunton, Ron. 1989. "The Cultural Instability of Egalitarian Societies." *Man* 24 (4): 673–81.

Buege, Douglas. 1996. "The Ecologically Noble Savage Revisited." *Environmental Ethics* 18 (1): 71–88.

Buroway, Michael. 1998. "The Extended Case Method." *Sociological Theory* 16 (1): 4–31.

Burton, John. 1991. Porgera census project: Report for 1990. Report for Land and Community Relations, Porgera Joint Venture.

Burton, John. 1992. "The Porgera Census Project." *Research in Melanesia* 16:129–56.

Burton, John. 1997. *C'est Qui, Le Patron? Kinship and the Rentier Leader in the Upper Watut.* Vol. 1 of *Resource Management in the Asia-Pacific Program.* Canberra: Resource Management in Asia-Pacific Project, Division of Pacific and Asian History, Research School for Pacific and Asian Studies, The Australian National University.

Burton, John. 1999. "Evidence of "the New Competencies"?" In *Dilemmas of Development: The Social and Economic Impact of the Porgera Gold Mine, 1989–1994,* edited by Colin Filer, 280–301. Canberra: Asia Pacific Press.

Callon, Michel. 1980. "Struggles and Negotiations to Define What Is Problematic and What Is Not." In *The Social Process of Scientific Investigation,* edited by Karin Knorr, Roger Krohn, and Richard Whitley, 197–219. Dordrecht: D. Reidel.

Callon, Michel. 1991. "Techno-Economic Networks and Irreversibility." In *A Sociology of Monsters: Essays on Power, Technology, and Domination,* edited by John Law, 132–61. London: Routledge.

Callon, Michel, and Bruno Latour. 1981. "Unscrewing the Big Leviathan: Or How Actors Macrostructure Reality, and How Sociologists Help Them to Do So." In *Advances in Social Theory and Methodology,* edited by Karen Knorr Cetina and Aaron Cicourel, 277–303 London: Routledge and Keegan Paul.

Campbell, Ian. 1998. "Anthropology and the Professionalisation of Colonial Administration in Papua and New Guinea." *Journal of Pacific History* 33 (1): 69–90.

Carr, E. Summerson. 2009. "Anticipating and Inhabiting Institutional Identities."
   American Ethnologist 36 (2): 317–36.

Carsten, Janet. 2000. *Cultures of Relatedness: New Approaches to the Study of Kinship.*
   Cambridge: Cambridge University Press.

Chappell, David. 2005 "'Africanization' in the Pacific: Blaming Others for Disorder
   in the Periphery?" *Comparative Studies in Society and History* 47: 286–317.

Chowning, Ann. 1969. "Recent Acculturation between Tribes in Papua-New
   Guinea." *Journal of Pacific History* 4 (1): 27–40.

Clastres, Pierre. 1987. *Society against the State: Essays in Political Anthropology.*
   Translated by Robert Hurley in collaboration with Abe Stein. New York: Zone.

Clifford, James. 1988, *The Predicament of Culture: Twentieth-Century Ethnography,
   Literature, and Art.* Cambridge, MA: Harvard University Press.

Clifford, James. 2013. *Returns: Becoming Indigenous in the Twenty-first Century.*
   Cambridge, MA: Harvard University Press.

Comaroff, John L., and Simon Roberts. 1981. *Rules and Processes: The Cultural Logic
   of Dispute in an African Context.* Chicago: University of Chicago Press.

Coumans, Catherine. 2011. "Occupying Spaces Created by Conflict: Anthropologists,
   Development NGOs, Responsible Investment, and Mining." *Current Anthropology*
   52 (S3): 29–43.

Counts, David and Dorothy Counts. 1976. "Apprehension in the Backwaters." *Oceania* 46 (4): 283–305.

Crook, Tony and Adam Reed. 1998. "Forward to Special Issue 'Innovation and Creativity: Case Studies from Melanesia'." *Cambridge Anthropology* 20 (1–2): 1–3.

Da Col, Giovanni, and David Graeber. 2011. "Foreword: The Return of Ethnographic
   Theory." *Hau* 1 (1): vi–xxxv.

Day, John. 1985. *God's Conflict with the Dragon and the Sea: Echoes of a Canaanite
   Myth in the Old Testament.* Cambridge: Cambridge University Press.

De Landa, Manuel. 2006. *A New Philosophy of Society: Assemblage Theory and Social
   Complexity.* London: Continuum.

Denoon, Donald. 2005. *A Trial Separation: Australia and the Decolonisation of Papua
   New Guinea.* Canberra: Pandanus.

Diaz, Vincente. 2011. "Voyaging for Anti-Colonial Recovery: Austronesian Seafaring,
   Archipelagic Rethinking, and the Re-Mapping of Indigeneity." *Pacific Asia Inquiry*
   2 (1): 21–32.

Diaz, Vincente M., and J. K. Kauanui. 2001. "Native Pacific Cultural Studies on the
   Edge." *Contemporary Pacific* 13 (2): 315–42.

Dinnen, Sinclair, Anita Jowitt, and Tess Cain, eds. 2003. *A Kind of Mending:
   Restorative Justice in the Pacific Islands.* Canberra: Pandanus.

Dougoud, Roberta Colombo. 2005. "'Ol I Kam Lo Hul Bilong Wotnuna' (They Come
   from the Hole of Wotnuna): How a Papua New Guinean Artefact Became Traditional." In *Tradition and Agency: Tracing Cultural Continuity and Invention,* edited
   by Ton Otto, 235–66. Aarhus: Aarhus Universitetsforlag.

Downs, Ian. 1980. *The Australian Trusteeship: Papua New Guinea, 1945–75.* Canberra: Australian Government Publishing Service.

Epstein, Arnold. 1969. *Matupit: Land, Politics, and Change among the Tolai of New Britain.* Berkeley: University of California Press.

Ernst, Thomas. 1999. "Land, Stories, and Resources: Discourse and Entification in Onabasulu Modernity." *American Anthropologist* 101 (1): 88–97.

Errington, Frederick, and Deborah Gewertz. 1986. "The Confluence of Powers: Entropy and Importation among the Chambri." *Oceania* 57 (2): 99–113.

Errington, Frederick, and Deborah Gewertz. 1995. *Articulating Change in the "Last Unknown."* Boulder, CO: Westview.

Feldman, Ilana. 2008. *Governing Gaza: Bureaucracy, Authority, and the Work of Rule, 1917–1967.* Durham, NC: Duke University Press.

Filer, Colin. 1990a. "The Bougainville Rebellion, the Mining Industry and the Process of Social Disintegration in Papua New Guinea." *Canberra Anthropology* 13 (1): 1–39.

Filer, Colin. 1990b. "Diversity of Cultures or Culture of Diversity?" In *Sepik Heritage: Tradition and Change in Papua New Guinea,* edited by Nancy Lutkehaus et al, 116–28. Durham, NC: Carolina Academic Press.

Filer, Colin.1998. "The Melanesian Way of Menacing the Mining Industry." In *Modern Papua New Guinea,* edited by Laura Zimmer-Tamakoshi, 147–78. Kirksville, MO: Thomas Jefferson University Press.

Filer, Colin. 2006. "Custom, Law and Ideology in Papua New Guinea." *Asia Pacific Journal of Anthropology* 7 (1): 65–84.

Filer, Colin. 2007. "Local Custom and the Art of Land Group Boundary Maintenance in Papua New Guinea." In *Customary Land Tenure and Registration in Australia and Papua New Guinea,* edited by James Weiner and Katie Glaskin, 135–74. Canberra: ANU EPress.

Filer, Colin, and Martha Macintyre. 2006. "Grass Roots and Deep Holes: Community Responses to Mining in Melanesia." *Contemporary Pacific* 18 (2): 215–31.

Finney, Ben R. 1973. *Big-Men and Business, Entrepreneurship and Economic Growth in the New Guinea Highlands.* Honolulu: University of Hawaii Press.

Firth, Raymond. 1963. *Elements of Social Organization.* London: Watts.

Fischer, Claude S. 2008. "Paradoxes of American Individualism." *Sociological Forum* 23 (2): 363–72.

Fischer, Michael M. J. 2007. "Culture and Cultural Analysis as Experimental Systems." *Cultural Anthropology* 22 (1): 1–65.

Fisher, Melissa, and Greg Downey. 2006. *Frontiers of Capital: Ethnographic Reflections on the New Economy.* Durham: Duke University Press.

Fleming, Daniel E. 2004. *Democracy's Ancient Ancestors: Mari and Early Collective Governance.* Cambridge: Cambridge University Press.

Foster, Robert J. 2002a. "Bargains with Modernity in Papua New Guinea and Elsewhere." In *Critically Modern: Alternatives, Alterities, Anthropologies,* edited by Bruce Knauft, 57–81. Bloomington: University of Indiana Press.

Foster, Robert J. 2002b. *Materializing the Nation: Commodities, Consumption, and Media in Papua New Guinea.* Bloomington: Indiana University Press.

Foucault, Michel. 2000. "Governmentality." In *Power: The Essential Works of Foucault 1954–1984,* edited by James D. Faubion, 201–22. New York: New Press.

Fried, Morton. 1975. *The Notion of Tribe.* Menlo Park, CA: Cummings.

Friedman, Jonathan. 1993. "Will the Real Hawaiian Please Stand: Anthropologists and Natives in the Global Struggle for Identity." *Bijdragen Tot De Taal-, Land-en Volkenkunde* 149 (4): 737–67.

Furnivall, John S. 1991. *The Fashioning of Leviathan: The Beginnings of British Rule in Burma.* Edited by Gehan Wijeyewardene. Canberra: Published in association with the Economic History of Southeast Asia Project and the Thai-Yunnan Project.

Gaddis, William. 1994. *A Frolic of His Own: A Novel.* New York: Poseidon.

Gallie, Walter. 1955. "Essentially Contested Concepts." *Proceedings of the Aristotelian Society* 56: 167–98.

Gammage, Bill. 1998. *The Sky Travellers: Journeys in New Guinea, 1938–1939.* Carlton, Australia: Melbourne University Press.

Gaonkar, Dilip Parameshwar, ed. 2001. *Alternative Modernities.* Durham, NC: Duke University Press.

Geismar, Haidy. 2005. "Reproduction, Creativity, Restriction." *Journal of Social Archaeology* 5 (1): 25.

Gibbs, Philip. 1975. "Ipili Religion Past and Present: An Account of the Traditional Religion of the Porgera and Paiela Valleys of Papua New Guinea and How It Has Changed with the Coming of the European and Christianity." MA thesis, University of Sydney.

Gilberthorpe, Emma. 2007. "Fasu Solidarity: A Case Study of Kin Networks, Land Tenure, and Oil Extraction in Kutubu, Papua New Guinea." *American Anthropology* 109 (1): 101–12.

Glasse, Robert M. 1969. *Huli of Papua: A Cognatic Descent System.* Paris: Mouton.

Goldenweiser, Alexander. 1931. *Robots or Gods: An Essay on Craft and Mind.* New York: Knopf.

Goldman, Laurence. 2003. *Hoo-Ha in Huli: Considerations on Commotion and Community in the Southern Highlands Province of Papua New Guinea.* Canberra: State, Society and Governance in Melanesia Program, Research School of Pacific and Asian Studies, The Australian National University.

Goldman, Laurence. 2007. "Incorporating Huli: Lessons from the Hides License Area." In *Customary Land Tenure and Registration in Australia and Papua New Guinea,* edited by James Weiner and Katie Glaskin, 97–115. Canberra: ANU Epress.

Goldman, Laurence, and Chris Ballard, eds. 1998. *Fluid Ontologies: Myth, Ritual, and Philosophy in the Highlands of Papua New Guinea.* Westport, CT: Bergin and Garvey.

Golub, Alex. 2001. *Gold Positive: A Brief History of Porgera 1930–1997*. Madang, Papua New Guinea: Kristen Press.

Golub, Alex. 2006. "Who Is the 'Original Affluent Society'? Ipili 'Predatory Expansion' and the Porgera Gold Mine, Papua New Guinea." *Contemporary Pacific* 18 (2): 265–92.

Golub, Alex. 2007a. "From Agency to Agents: Forging Landowner Identities in Porgera: Customary Land Tenure and Registration in Australia and Papua New Guinea." In *Customary Land Tenure and Registration in Australia and Papua New Guinea*, edited by James Weiner and Katie Glaskin, 73–96. Canberra: ANU Epress.

Golub, Alex. 2007b. "Ironies of Organization: Landowners, Land Registration, and Papua New Guinea's Mining and Petroleum Industry." *Human Organization* 66 (1): 38–48.

Gorle, Gilian. 1995. "The Theme of Social Change in the Literature of Papua New Guinea, 1969–1979." *Pacific Studies* 18 (2): 79–115.

Government of Papua New Guinea. 2002. *Papua New Guinea National Census*. Port Moresby: National Statistics Office.

Graeber, David. 2009. *Direct Action: An Ethnography*. Oakland: AK Press.

Gunkel, Hermann. 2006. *Creation and Chaos in the Primeval Era and the Eschaton: A Religio-Historical Study of Genesis 1 and Revelation 12*. Translated by K. William Whitney Jr. Grand Rapids, MI: W. B. Eerdmans.

Handler, Richard. 1986. "Authenticity." *Anthropology Today* 2 (1): 2–4.

Handler, Richard. 1988. *Nationalism and the Politics of Culture in Quebec*. Madison: University of Wisconsin Press.

Hanks, William F. 1996. *Language and Communicative Practices*. Boulder, CO: Westview.

Harrison, Simon. 1993. "The Commerce of Cultures in Melanesia." *Man* 28 (1): 139–58.

Harrison, Simon. 2007. *Fracturing Resemblances: Identity and Mimetic Conflict in Melanesia and the West*. New York: Berghahn.

Healey, Christopher J. 1990. *Maring Hunters and Traders: Production and Exchange in the Papua New Guinea Highlands*. Berkeley: University of California Press.

Healy, Allan. M. 1967. *Bulolo: A History of the Development of the Bulolo Region, New Guinea*. Canberra: Australian National University, New Guinea Research Unit.

Herdt, Gilbert H., and Michele Stephen. 1989. *The Religious Imagination in New Guinea*. New Brunswick, NJ: Rutgers University Press.

Ho, Karen. 2005. "Situating Global Capitalisms: A View from Wall Street Investment Banks." *Cultural Anthropology* 20 (1): 68–96.

Hobbes, Thomas. 1996. *Leviathan*. Edited by Richard Tuck. Rev. student ed. Cambridge: Cambridge University Press.

Hobsbawm, Eric, and Terence Ranger, eds. 1983. *The Invention of Tradition*. Cambridge: Cambridge University Press.

Holy, Ladislav. 1979. *The Segmentary Lineage Structure and Its Existential Status: Segmentary Lineage Systems Reconsidered.* Belfast: Queens University Press.

Hull, Matthew S. 2012a "Documents and Bureaucracy." *Annual Review of Anthropology* 41: 251–67.

Hull, Matthew S. 2012b. *Government of Paper: The Materiality of Bureaucracy in Urban Pakistan.* Berkeley: University of California Press.

Hutchinson, Sharon. E. 2000. "Identity and Substance: The Broadening Bases of Relatedness among the Nuer of Southern Sudan." In *Cultures of Relatedness: New Approaches to the Study of Kinship*, edited by Janet Carsten, 55–72. Cambridge: Cambridge University Press.

Hviding, Edvard, and Knut Rio. 2011. *Made in Oceania: Social Movements, Cultural Heritage and the State in the Pacific.* Wantage, UK: Sean Kingston.

Jacka, Jerry. 2002. "Cults and Christianity among the Enga and Ipili." *Oceania* 72 (3):196–214.

Jacka, Jerry. 2003. "God, Gold, and the Ground: Place-Based Political Ecology in a New Guinea Borderland." PhD diss., University of Oregon.

Jacka, Jerry. 2007. "Our Skins Are Weak: Ipili Modernity and the Demise of Discipline." In *Embodying Modernity and Postmodernity: Ritual, Praxis, and Social Change in Melanesia*, edited by Sandra Bamford, 39–67. Durham, NC: Carolina Academic Press.

Jackson, Richard. 1986. "Residential Options and Relocation Issues in Porgera." Report prepared for the Porgera Joint Venture.

Jackson, Richard, and Glenn Banks. 2002. *In Search of the Serpent's Skin: The Story of the Porgera Gold Project.* Port Moresby: Placer Niugini.

Jenness, Diamond. 1930. "The Indian's Interpretation of Man and Nature." *Proceedings and Transactions of the Royal Society of Canada* 3 (24): 57–62.

Johnson, Peter. 2012. *Lode Shedding: A Case Study of the Economic Benefits to the Landowners, the Provincial Government, and the State From the Porgera Gold Mine.* Boroko: National Research Institute.

Jorgensen, Dan. 1985. "Femsep's Last Garden: A Telefol Response to Mortality." In *Aging and Its Transformations: Moving toward Death in Pacific Societies*, edited by Dorothy Ayers Counts and David R. Counts, 203–21. Lanham, MD: University Press of America.

Jorgensen, Dan. 1994. "Locating the Divine in Melanesia: An Appreciation of the Work of Kenelm Burridge." *Anthropology and Humanism* 19 (2): 130–37.

Jorgensen, Dan. 1996. "Regional History and Ethnic Identity in the Hub of New Guinea: The Emergence of the Min." *Oceania* 66 (3): 189–210.

Jorgensen, Dan. 2001. "Who and What Is a Landowner? Mythology and Marking the Ground in a Papua New Guinea Mining Project." In *Emplaced Myth: Space, Narrative, and Knowledge in Aboriginal Australia and Papua New Guinea*, edited by Alan Rumsey and James Weiner, 101–24. Honolulu: University of Hawaii Press.

Jorgensen, Dan. 2007. "Clan-Finding, Clan-Making and the Politics of Identity in a Papua New Guinea Mining Project." In *Customary Land Tenure and Registration in Australia and Papua New Guinea*, edited by James Weiner and Katie Glaskin, 57–72. Canberra: ANU EPress.

Kalinoe, Lawrence, and James Leach. 2004. *Rationales of Ownership: Transactions and Claims to Ownership in Contemporary Papua New Guinea*. Wantage, UK: Sean Kingston.

Keesing, Roger. 1972. "Simple Models of Complexity: The Lure of Kinship." In *Kinship Studies in the Morgan Centennial Year*. Edited by Priscilla Reining, 17–31. Washington, DC: Washington Anthropological Society of Washington.

Keesing, Roger. 1989. *Creating the Past: Custom and Identity in the Contemporary Pacific*.

Kiki, Albert Maori. 1968. *Kiki: Ten Thousand Years in a Lifetime; A New Guinea Autobiography*. London: Pall Mall.

Kilduff, Martin, and Wenpin Tsai. 2003. *Social Networks and Organizations*. London: Sage.

Kinsharp, Peter. 2010. "Hela, Enga, Jiwaka and Melpa Provinces Are Names Connoting Indigenous Significance to the Native People of These Provinces. Port Moresby *Sunday Chronicle*, November 7.

Kirsch, Stuart. 2011. "Comment on 'Occupying Spaces Created By Conflict.'" *Current Anthropology* 52 (S3): 540–41.

Knauft, Bruce M. 2002. *Critically Modern: Alternatives, Alterities, Anthropologies*. Bloomington: Indiana University Press.

Knorr Cetina, Karen, and Uli Bruegger. 2002. "Global Microstructures: The Virtual Societies of Financial Markets." *American Journal of Sociology* 107 (4): 905–50.

Knorr Cetina, Karen, and Alex Preda, eds. 2005. *The Sociology of Financial Markets*. Oxford: Oxford University Press.

Koselleck, Reinhart. 2004. *Futures Past: On the Semantics of Historical Time*. New York: Columbia University Press.

Kuper, Adam. 1982. "Lineage Theory: A Critical Retrospect." *Annual Review of Anthropology* 11: 71–95.

Lambek, Michael. 2010. "Toward an Ethics of the Act." In *Ordinary Ethics: Anthropology, Language, and Action*, edited by Michael Lambek, 39–62. New York: Fordham University Press.

Langness, Lewis. 1964. "Some Problems in the Conceptualization of Highlands Social Structures." *American Anthropologist* 66 (4): 162–82.

Latour, Bruno. 1987. *Science in Action: How to Follow Scientists and Engineers through Society*. Cambridge, MA: Harvard University Press.

Latour, Bruno. 2005. *Reassembling the Social: An Introduction to Actor-Network-Theory*. Oxford: Oxford University Press.

Lavin, Chad. 2008. *The Politics of Responsibility*. Urbana: University of Illinois Press.

Lavu, Kai. 2007. *Porgera Joint Venture's Presence in the Southern Highlands Province*.

In *Conflict and Resource Development in the Southern Highlands*, edited by Nicole Haley and Ronald J. May, 129–39. Canberra: ANU E Press.

Law, John. 1986. "On the Methods of Long-Distance Control: Vessels, Navigation and the Portuguese Route to India." In *Power, Action, and Belief: A New Sociology of Knowledge?*. Edited by John Law, 234–63. London: Routledge.

Lawrence, Peter. 1964. "Social Anthropology and the Training of Administration Officers at the Australian School of Pacific Administration." *Anthropological Forum* 1 (2): 195–208.

Lawrence, Peter. 1984. *The Garia: An Ethnography of a Traditional Cosmic System in Papua New Guinea*. Manchester, UK: Manchester University Press.

Leach, James. 2006. "'Team spirit': The Pervasive Influence of Place-Generation in 'Community Building' Activities Along the Rai Coast of Papua New Guinea." *Journal of Material Culture* 11 (1–2): 87–103.

Leach, James. 2007. "Creativity, Subjectivity and the Dynamic of Possessive Individualism." In *Creativity and Cultural Improvisation*, edited by Elizabeth Hallam and Tim Ingold, 99–116. New York: Berg.

Leavitt, Stephen C. 2001. "The Psychology of Consensus in a Papua New Guinea Christian Revival Movement." In *The Psychology of Cultural Experience*. Edited by Camilla Moore and Holly Mathews, 151–72. New York: Cambridge University Press.

Lederman, Rena. 1986. *What Gifts Engender: Social Relations and Politics in Mendi, Highland Papua New Guinea*. Cambridge: Cambridge University Press.

Lederman, Rena. 1989. "Contested Order: Gender and Society in the Southern New Guinea Highlands." *American Ethnologist* 16 (2): 230–47.

Lederman, Rena. 1998. "Globalization and the Future of Culture Areas: Melanesianist Anthropology in Transition." *Annual Review of Anthropology* 27:427–49.

Levenson, Jon Douglas. 1988. *Creation and the Persistence of Evil: The Jewish Drama of Divine Omnipotence*. San Francisco: Harper and Row.

Levinson, Marc. 2006. *The Box: How the Shipping Container Made the World Smaller and the World Economy Bigger*. Princeton, NJ: Princeton University Press.

Lévi-Strauss, Claude. 1969. *The Raw and the Cooked*. Translated by John and Doreen Weightman. New York: Harper and Row.

Lévi-Strauss, Claude. 1982. *The Way of the Masks*. Translated by Sylvia Modelski. Seattle: University of Washington Press.

Lévi-Strauss, Claude. 1983. *Structural Anthropology*. Translated by Monique Layton. Chicago: University of Chicago Press.

Lévi-Strauss, Claude. 1987. *Anthropology and Myth: Lectures, 1951–1982*. Translated by Roy Willis. Oxford: Blackwell.

Lewis, Herbert S. 1998. "The Misrepresentation of Anthropology and Its Consequences." *American Anthropologist* 100 (3): 716–31.

Li, Tania Murray. 2007. *The Will to Improve: Governmentality, Development, and the Practice of Politics*. Durham, NC: Duke University Press.

Liep, John, ed. 2001. *Locating Cultural Creativity*. London: Pluto Press.

Lindstrom, Lamont. 1998. "Pasin Tumbuna: Culture and Nationalism in Papua New Guinea." In *From Beijing to Port Moresby: The Politics of National Identity in Cultural Policies*, edited by Virginia R. Domínguez and David Y. H. Wu, 141–88. Australia: Gordon and Breach.

Lindstrom, Lamont. 2008. "Melanesian Kastom and Its Transformations." *Anthropological Forum* 18 (2): 161–78.

Lindstrom, Lamont. 2011. Personhood, Cargo, and Melanesian Social Unities. In *Made in Oceania: Social Movements, Cultural Heritage, and the State in the Pacific*. Edited by Edvard Hviding and Knut Rio, 253–72. Wantage, England: Sean Kingston Publishing.

Linton, Ralph. 1936. *The Study of Man: An Introduction*. New York: D. Appleton-Century.

LiPuma, Edward. 2000. *Encompassing Others: The Magic of Modernity in Melanesia*. Ann Arbor: University of Michigan Press.

Lohmann, Roger. 2003. "The Supernatural Is Everywhere: Defining Qualities of Religion in Melanesia and Beyond." *Anthropological Forum* 13 (2): 175–85.

Lovin, Robin W., and Frank E. Reynolds. 1985. "In the Beginning." In *Cosmogony and Ethical Order: New Studies in Comparative Ethics*. Edited by Robin W. Lovin and Frank E. Reynolds, 1–35. Chicago: University of Chicago Press.

Maine, Henry Sumner. 1963. *Ancient Law: Its Connection with the Early History of Society and Its Relation to Modern Ideas*. Boston: Beacon.

Malcolm, Noel. 2007. "The Name and Nature of Leviathan: Political Symbolism and Biblical Exegesis." *Intellectual History Review* 17 (1): 29–58.

Malinowski, Bronislaw. 1922. *Argonauts of the Western Pacific: An Account of Native Enterprise and Adventure in the Archipelagoes of Melanesian New Guinea*. London: G. Routledge.

Malinowski, Bronislaw. 1988. *Malinowski among the Magi: The Natives of Mailu*. Edited with an introduction by Michael W. Young. London: Routledge.

Mangi, James. 1988. "Yole: A Study of Traditional Huli Trade." MA thesis, University of Papua New Guinea.

Markell, Patchen. 2003. *Bound by Recognition*. Princeton, NJ: Princeton University Press.

Mayer, Adrian. 1966. "The Significance of Quasi-Groups in the Study of Complex Societies." In *The Social Anthropology of Complex Societies*, edited by Michael Banton, 97–122. London: Tavistock.

McArthur, Margaret. 1967. "Analysis of the Genealogy of a Mae-Enga Clan." *Oceania* 37 (4): 281–85.

McDowell, Nancy. 1988. "A Note on Cargo Cults and Cultural Constructions of Change." *Pacific Studies* 11 (2): 121–34.

Mead, Margaret. 1938. "The Mountain Arapesh. 1: An Importing Culture." *Anthropological Papers of the American Museum of Natural History* 36, part 3.

Mead, Margaret. 1954. *Growing Up in New Guinea*. Harmondsworth, UK: Penguin.

Meggitt, Mervyn. 1957. "The Ipili of the Porgera Valley, Western Highlands District, Territory of New Guinea." *Oceania* 28 (1): 31–55.

Meggitt, Mervyn. 1958. "The Enga of the New Guinea Highlands: Some Preliminary Observations." *Oceania* 28 (4): 253–330.

Meggitt, Mervyn. 1965. *The Lineage System of the Mae-Enga of New Guinea*. Edinburgh: Oliver and Boyd.

Mennis, Mary. 1979. "Biographical Notes on Ludwig Schmidt." *Oral History* 7 (5): 74–87.

Merlan, Francesca, and Alan Rumsey. 1991. *Ku Waru: Language and Segmentary Politics in the Western Nebilyer Valley, Papua New Guinea*. Cambridge: Cambridge University Press.

Mitchell, J. Clyde. 1956. "Case and Situation Analysis." *Sociological Review* 3 (1): 187–211.

Mitchell, J. Clyde. 1974. "Social Networks." *Annual Review of Anthropology* 3: 279–99.

Mitchell, Timothy. 2006. "Society, Economy, and the State Effect." In *The Anthropology of the State: A Reader*, edited by Aradhana Sharma and Akhil Gupta, 169–86. Malden, MA: Blackwell.

Moore, Donald S. 2005. *Suffering for Territory: Race, Place, and Power in Zimbabwe*. Durham, NC: Duke University Press.

Morgan, Edmund. 1992. "The Fiction of 'The People.'" *New York Review of Books*, April 23.

Mosko, Mark. "Partible Penitents: Dividual Personhood and Christian Practice in Melanesia and the West." *Journal of the Royal Anthropological Institute* 16 (2): 215–40.

Mullaney, Thomas S. 2011. *Coming to Terms with the Nation: Ethnic Classification in Modern China*. Berkeley: University of California Press.

Munn, Nancy D. 1986. *The Fame of Gawa: A Symbolic Study of Value Transformation in a Massim (Papua New Guinea) Society*. Cambridge: Cambridge University Press.

Murphy, Robert. 1991. "Anthropology at Columbia: A Reminiscence." *Dialectical Anthropology* 16 (1):65–81.

Nadasdy, Paul. 2003. *Hunters and Bureaucrats: Power, Knowledge, and Aboriginal-State Relations in the Southwest Yukon*. Vancouver: University of British Columbia Press.

Nader, Laura. 1972. "Up the Anthropologist-Perspectives Gained from Studying Up." In *Reinventing Anthropology*. Edited by Dell Hymes, 284–311. New York: Pantheon.

Narokobi, Bernard. 1974. "The Nobility of Village Life." *Catalyst: Social Pastoral Magazine for Melanesia* 4 (4): 55–70.

Narokobi, Bernard. 1975. Foundations for Nationhood. Port Moresby: Papua New Guinea Press and Bookshop.

Narokobi, Bernard. 1983. *The Melanesian Way*. Boroko, Papua New Guinea: Institute of Papua New Guinea Studies.

Narokobi, Bernard. 2000. "Papua New Guinea's Self-Image: Through a Glass Darkly." In *Uncertain Paradise: Building and Promoting a Better Papua New Guinea*, 23–31. Madang, Papua New Guinea: Divine Word University Press.

Narokobi, Bernard, R. G. Crocombe, John May, and Paul Roche. 1989. *Lo Bilong Yumi Yet = Law and Custom in Melanesia*. Goroka, Papua New Guinea: Melanesian Institute for Pastoral and Socio-Economic Service.

Nelson, Hank. 1976. *Black, White and Gold: Gold Mining in Papua New Guinea, 1878–1930*. Canberra: Australian National University Press.

O'Collins, Maev, and Peter King. 1985. "Small Is Still Beautiful: Social Development and the Eight-Point Plan." In *From Rhetoric to Reality? Papua New Guinea's Eight Point Plan and National Goals after a Decade*, edited by Peter King, Wendy Lee, and Vincent Warakai, 367–72. Port Moresby: University of Papua New Guinea Press.

Oliver, Douglas L. 1991. *Black Islanders: A Personal Perspective of Bougainville, 1937–1991*. Honolulu: University of Hawaii Press.

Otto, Ton. 1997. "After the 'Tidal Wave': Bernard Narokobi and the Creation of a Melanesian Way." In *Narratives of Nation in the South Pacific*, edited by Ton Otto and Nicholas Thomas, 33–64. Amsterdam: Harwood Academic.

Pacific Agribusiness. 1987. *Social and Economic Impact Study: Porgera Gold Mine*. 2 vols. South Melbourne, Australia.

Parker, Bradley J., and Lars Rodseth. 2005. "Part I." In *Untaming the Frontier in Anthropology, Archaeology, and History*. Edited by Bradley J. Parker and Lars Rodseth, 23–26. Tucson: University of Arizona Press.

Parker, Gary. 2004. "The Sediment Digester." Internal Memorandum, St. Anthony Falls Laboratory, University of Minnesota, Minneapolis, Minnesota.

Parson, Chris. 2007. "Witchcraft Fails to Save Briton Murdered by Burglars." Scotsman, August 27.

Parsons, Talcott. 1961. "Editorial Foreword: The General Interpretation of Action." In *Theories of Society: Foundations of Modern Sociological Theory, Volume 1*, edited by Edward Shils, Kaspar D. Naegele, and Jesse R. Pitts, 85–97. New York: Free Press of Glencoe.

Paupa, Clement. 2001. "Akiko Makes Clean Success at Mine." Papua New Guinea *National*, September 21.

Pels, Peter. 1997. "The Anthropology of Colonialism: Culture, History, and the Emergence of Western Governmental." *Annual Review of Anthropology* 26:163–83.

Philemon, Bart. 2000. "Papua New Guinea Has No Problems." In *Uncertain Paradise: Building and Promoting a Better Papua New Guinea*, 73–81. Madang, Papua New Guinea: Divine Word University Press.

Placer Dome Asia Pacific. 1988. "Relocation Agreement." Unpublished manuscript.

Placer Dome Asia Pacific. 2001. *Porgera Mine Sustainability Report: 2000.* Unpublished report.

Ploeg, Anton. 1993. "Cultural Politics among the Siassi, Morobe Province, Papua New Guinea." *Bijdragen Tot De Taal-, Land-en Volkenkunde* 149 (4): 768–80.

Power, Anthony. 1988. "The Future of Clans in Papua New Guinea in the 21st Century." In *Ethics of Development: Choices in Development Planning,* edited by Philip J. Hughes and Charmain Thirlwall, 156–74. Port Moresby: University of Papua New Guinea Press.

Power, Anthony. 1996. "Mining and Petroleum Development under Customary Land Tenure: The Papua New Guinea Experience." In *Conference Proceedings: Mining and Mineral Resource Policy Issues in Asia-Pacific: Prospects for the 21st Century,* edited by Glenn Banks, Peter Hancock, and Donald Denoon, 135–43. Canberra: Division of Pacific and Asian History, Research School of Asian and Pacific Studies, Australian National University.

Pratt, Mary Louise. 1992. *Imperial Eyes: Travel Writing and Transculturation.* London: Routledge.

Radcliffe-Brown, A. R. 1950. "Introduction." In *African Systems of Kinship and Marriage,* edited by A.R. Radcliffe-Brown and Daryll Forde, 1–85. New York: Oxford University Press for the International African Institute.

Rajak, Dinah. 2011. *In Good Company: An Anatomy of Corporate Social Responsibility.* Stanford, California: Stanford University Press.

Reay, Marie. 1959. *The Kuma: Freedom and Conformity in the New Guinea Highlands.* Carlton, Australia: Melbourne University Press on behalf of the Australian National University.

Reilly, Benjamin. 2000. "The Africanisation of the South Pacific." *Australian Journal of International Affairs* 54 (3): 261–68.

Reilly, Benjamin. 2001. "Democracy, Ethnic Fragmentation, and Internal Conflict: Confused Theories, Faulty Data, and the "Crucial Case" of Papua New Guinea." *International Security* 25 (3): 162–85.

Rio, Knut. 2007. *The Power of Perspective: Social Ontology and Agency on Ambrym Island, Vanuatu.* New York: Berghahn Books.

Rio, Knut, and Olaf Smedal. 2009. "Hierarchy and Its Alternatives: An Introduction to Movements of Totalization and Detotalization." In *Hierarchy: Persistence and Transformation in Social Formations,* edited by Knut Rio and Olaf Smedal, 1–63. New York: Berghahn Books.

Robert, Henry M., and Sarah Corbin Robert. 2011. *Robert's Rules of Order Newly Revised.* Philadelphia: Da Capo.

Robbins, Joel and David A.B. Murray. 2002. "Introduction to Special Issue 'Reinventing *The Invention Of Culture.*" *Social Analysis* 46 (1): 1–3.

Robinson, Fritz. 1988. *Porgera Relocation Study.* Report prepared for the Porgera Joint Venture.

Rofel, Lisa. 1999. *Other Modernities: Gendered Yearnings in China after Socialism.* Berkeley: University of California Press.

Rosi, Pamela. C.1994. "Bung Wantaim: The Role of the National Arts School in Creating National Culture and Identity in Papua New Guinea." Ph.D. Diss. Bryn Mawr College.

Rumsey, Alan. 1999. "The Personification of Social Totalities in the Pacific." *Journal of Pacific Studies* 23 (1): 48–70.

Rumsey, Alan. 2000. "Agency, Personhood and the 'I' of Discourse in the Pacific and Beyond." *Journal of the Royal Anthropological Institute* 6 (1): 101–15.

Rumsey, Alan. 2010. "Lingual and Cultural Wholes and Fields" In *Experiments in Holism: Theory and Practice in Contemporary Anthropology*, edited by Ton Otto and Niles Bubandt, 127–49. Malden, MA: Wiley-Blackwell.

Rutherford, Danilyn. 2012. *Laughing at Leviathan: Sovereignty and Audience in West Papua.* Chicago: University of Chicago Press.

Rynkiewich, Michael. 2001. "Narratives of Land in Melanesia: Myths We Live By." In *Land and Churches in Melanesia*, edited by Michael Rynkiewich, 60–78. Goroka, Papua New Guinea: Melanesia Institute.

Sahlins, Marshall. 1981. *Historical Metaphors and Mythical Realities: Structure in the Early History of the Sandwich Islands Kingdom.* Ann Arbor: University of Michigan Press.

Sahlins, Marshall. 1985. *Islands of History.* Chicago: University of Chicago Press.

Sahlins, Marshall. 1991. "The Return of the Event, Again." In *Clio in Oceania: Toward a Historical Anthropology*, edited by Aletta Biersack, 37–100. Washington: Smithsonian Institute.

Sahlins, Marshall. 1992. "The Economics of Develop-man in the Pacific." *Res* 21: 13–25.

Sahlins, Marshall. 1993. "Good-bye to *Tristes Tropes*: Ethnography in the Context of Modern World History." *Journal of Modern History* 65 (1): 1–25.

Sahlins, Marshall. 1996. "The Sadness of Sweetness: The Native Anthropology of Western Cosmology." Current *Anthropology* 37 (3): 395–415.

Sahlins, Marshall. 1999. "Two or Three Things That I Know about Culture." *Journal of the Royal Anthropological Institute* 5 (3): 399–421.

Sahlins, Marshall. 2000a. *Culture in Practice: Selected Essays.* New York: Zone.

Sahlins, Marshall. 2000b. "On the Anthropology of Modernity, or, Some Triumphs of Culture over Despondency Theory." In *Culture and Sustainable Development in the Pacific*, edited by Anthony Hooper, 44–61.

Sahlins, Marshall. 2004. *Apologies to Thucydides: Understanding History as Culture and Vice Versa.* Chicago: University of Chicago Press.

Sahlins, Marshall. 2010. Intercultural Politics of Order and Change. In *Experiments in Holism: Theory and Practice in Contemporary Anthropology*, edited by Ton Otto and Niles Bubandt, 102–26. Malden, MA: Wiley-Blackwell.

Salisbury, Richard Frank. 1962. *From Stone to Steel: Economic Consequences of a*

Technological Change in New Guinea. Victoria, Australia: Melbourne University Press on behalf of the Australian National University.

Sansom, Basil. 1985. "Aborigines, Anthropologists, and Leviathan." In *Indigenous Peoples and the Nation-State*, edited by Noel Dyck, 67–94. St. John's: Memorial University of Newfoundland, Institute of Social and Economic Research.

Sartre, Jean-Paul. 1963. *Search for a Method.* Translated by Hazel E. Barnes. New York: Knopf.

Sawyer, R. Keith. 2005. *Social Emergence: Societies as Complex Systems.* Cambridge: Cambridge University Press.

Schieffelin, Bambi B., Kathryn Ann Woolard, and Paul V. Kroskrity. 1998. *Language Ideologies: Practice and Theory.* New York: Oxford University Press.

Schieffelin, Edward L. 1976. *The Sorrow of the Lonely and the Burning of the Dancers.* New York: St. Martin's.

Schmid, Christine Kocher. 1993. "Cultural Identity as a Coping Strategy towards Modern Political Structures: The Nayudos Case, Papua New Guinea." *Bijdragen Tot De Taal-, Land-en Volkenkunde* 149 (4): 781–801.

Schneider, David. 2011. "Some Muddles in the Models or, How the System Really Works." *Hau* 1 (1): 451–92.

Schwartz, Theodore. 1995. "Cultural Totemism: Ethnic Identity Primitive and Modern." In *Ethnic Identity: Creation, Conflict, and Accommodation*, edited by Lola Romanucci-Ross and George A. De Vos. 3rd ed., 48–72. Walnut Creek, CA: Alta Mira.

Scott, James C. 1998. *Seeing Like a State : How Certain Schemes to Improve the Human Condition Have Failed.* New Haven, CT: Yale University Press.

Scott, James C. 2009 *The Art of Not Being Governed: An Anarchist History of Upland Southeast Asia.* New Haven, CT: Yale University Press.

Scott, John G. 2000. *Social Network Analysis: A Handbook.* London: Sage.

Scott, Michael W. . 2007. "Neither New Melanesian History Nor New Melanesian Ethnography: Recovering Emplaced Matrilineages in Southeast Solomon Islands." *Oceania* 77 (3): 337–54.

Sharma, Aradhana, and Akhil Gupta. 2006. "Introduction: Rethinking Theories of the State in an Era of Globalization." In *The Anthropology of the State: A Reader*, edited by Aradhana Sharma and Akhil Gupta, 1–42. Malden, MA: Blackwell.

Shever, Elana. 2010. "Engendering the Company: Corporate Personhood and the 'Face' of an Oil Company in Metropolitan Buenos Aires." Political and Legal Anthropology Review 33 (1): 26–46.

Siaguru, Anthony. 2001. *In-House in Papua New Guinea with Anthony Siaguru.* Canberra: Asia Pacific.

Sillitoe, Paul. 1979. *Give and Take: Exchange in Wola Society.* Canberra: Australian National University Press.

Sillitoe, Paul. 2010. *From Land to Mouth: The Agricultural "Economy" of the Wola of the New Guinea Highlands.* New Haven, CT: Yale University Press.

Silverstein, Michael. 2004. "'Cultural' Concepts and the Language-Culture Nexus." *Current Anthropology* 45 (5): 621–52.

Silverstein, Michael. 2005. "Languages/Cultures Are Dead! Long Live the Linguistic-Cultural!" In *Unwrapping the Sacred Bundle: Reflections on the Disciplining of Anthropology*, edited by Sylvia Yanagisako and Daniel Segal, 99–125. Durham, NC: Duke University Press.

Silverstein, Michael, and Greg Urban. 1995. "The Natural History of Discourse." In *Natural Histories of Discourse*, edited by Michael Silverstein and Greg Urban, 1–20. Chicago: University of Chicago Press.

Simet, Jacob. 1980. "From a Letter to the Editor of *Gigibori*." In *Voices of Independence: New Black Writing from Papua New Guinea*, edited by Ulli Beier, 216–17. New York: St. Martin's.

Sinclair, James Patrick. 2001. *Mastamak: The Land Surveyors of Papua New Guinea*. Adelaide, Australia: Crawford House.

Skinner, Quentin. 2007 "Hobbes on Persons, Authors and Representatives." In *The Cambridge Companion to Hobbes's Leviathan*, edited by Patricia Springborg, 157–80. New York: Cambridge University Press.

Smith, Adam T. 2006. "Representational Aesthetics and Political Subjectivity: The Spectacular in Urartian Images of Performance." In *Archaeology of Performance: Theaters of Power, Community, and Politics*, edited by Takeshi Inomata and Lawrence S. Cohen, 103–34. Landhan, MD: Alta Mira Press.

Smith, M. G. 1975. *Corporations and Society: The Social Anthropology of Collective Action*. Chicago: Aldine.

Smith, Mark S. 2001. *The Origins of Biblical Monotheism: Israel's Polytheistic Background and the Ugaritic Texts*. New York: Oxford University Press.

Smith, W. Robertson. 1957. *The Religion of the Semites: The Fundamental Institutions*. New York: Meridian.

Soaba, Russell. 1985. *Maiba: A Papuan Novel*. Washington: Three Continents.

Somare, Michael. 1973. Papua New Guinea's National Aims and Economic Policies. Unpublished statement made to the Papua New Guinea House of Assembly on 2 March 1973

Somare, Michael. 1974. *Our Resources Belong to Our People: The Chief Minister, Mr. Michael Somare, Outlines Foreign Investment Policies for Papua New Guinea in An Address to the Australian Institute of Directors, March 14th, 1974*. Port Moresby: Government Printer.

Somare, Michael. 1975. *Sana: An Autobiography of Michael Somare*. Port Moresby: Niugini Press.

Somare, Michael. 2000. "Where Did We Go Wrong?" In *Uncertain Paradise: Building and Promoting a Better Papua New Guinea*, 125–30. Madang, Papua New Guinea: Divine Word University Press.

Southall, Aidan. 1970. "The Illusion of Tribe." *Journal of Asian and African Studies* 5 (1–2), 8–51.

Spriggs, Matthew. *The Island Melanesians*. Oxford, UK: Blackwell.

Stasch, Rupert. 2009. *Society of Others: Kinship and Mourning in a West Papuan Place*. Berkeley: University of California Press.

Stasch, Rupert. 2010. "The Category 'Village' in Melanesian Social Worlds: Some Theoretical and Methodological Possibilities." *Paideuma* 56:41–62.

Stasch, Rupert. 2011. "Ritual and Oratory Revisited: The Semiotics of Effective Action." *Annual Review of Anthropology* 40 (1): 159–74.

Stein, Sarah Abrevaya. 2010. *Plumes: Ostrich Feathers, Jews, and a Lost World of Global Commerce*. New Haven, CT: Yale University Press.

Stephen, Michele. 1979. "Dreams of Change: The Innovative Role of Altered States of Consciousness in Traditional Melanesian Religion." *Oceania* 50 (1): 3–22.

Stocking, George W. 1995. *After Tylor: British Social Anthropology, 1888–1951*. Madison: University of Wisconsin Press.

Strathern, Andrew. 1996. *Body Thoughts*. Ann Arbor: University of Michigan Press.

Strathern, Marilyn. 1988. *The Gender of the Gift: Problems with Women and Problems with Society in Melanesia*. Berkeley: University of California Press.

Strathern, Marilyn. 1992. "Parts and Wholes: Refiguring Relationships in a Post-Plural World." In *Conceptualizing Society*, edited by Adam Kuper, 75–106. London: Routledge.

Strong, Thomas. 2007. "'Dying Culture' and Decaying Bodies." In *Embodying Modernity and Post-Modernity: Ritual, Praxis, and Social Change in Melanesia*, edited by Sandra C. Bamford, 105–24. Durham, NC: Carolina Academic Press.

Stucki, Larry. 2009. *"The Survival of the Fittest": Copper Mines, Company Towns, Indians, Mexicans, Mormons, Masons, Jews, Muslims, Gays, Wombs*. Victoria, BC: Trafford Publishing.

Stürzenhofecker, Gabriele. 1998. *Times Enmeshed: Gender, Space, and History among the Duna of Papua New Guinea*. Stanford, CA: Stanford University Press.

Taylor, James. 1939. *Hagen-Sepik Patrol Report*. Unpublished report to the Administration of the Trust Territory of New Guinea.

"Teacher Had Used Voodoo to Keep Himself Safe." 2007. Birmingham, *Sunday Mercury*, August 26.

Terrell, John. 2010. "Language and Material Culture on the Sepik Coast of Papua New Guinea: Using Social Network Analysis to Simulate, Graph, Identify, and Analyze Social and Cultural Boundaries between Communities." *Journal of Island and Coastal Archaeology* 5 (1): 3–32.

Terrell, John E., Terry Hunt, and Chris Gosden. 1997. "The Dimensions of Social Life in the Pacific: Human Diversity and the Myth of the Primitive Isolate." *Current Anthropology* 38 (2): 155–95.

Turton, David. 1979. "A Journey Made Them: Territorial Segmentation and Ethnic Identity Among the Mursi: Segmentary Lineage Systems Reconsidered." In *Segmentary Lineage Systems Reconsidered*, edited by Ladislav Holy, 119–43. Belfast,

Northern Ireland: Department of Social Anthropology, Queen's University of Belfast.

Viveiros de Castro, Eduardo. 2004. "Perspectival Anthropology and the Method of Controlled Equivocation." *Tipití* 2 (1): 3–22.

Viveiros de Castro, Eduardo. 2008. "Intensive Filiation and Demonic Alliance." In *Deleuzian Intersections: Science, Technology, Anthropology*, edited by Casper Bruun Jensen and Rödje Kjetil, 219–54. New York: Berghahn Books.

Waiko, John. 1985. "Na Binandere, Imo Averi? We Are Binandere, Who Are You?" *Pacific Viewpoint* 26 (1):9–29

Wagner, Roy. 1975. *The Invention of Culture*. Englewood Cliffs, NJ: Prentice-Hall.

Wagner, Roy. 1978. *Lethal Speech: Daribi Myth as Symbolic Obviation*. Ithaca, NY: Cornell University Press.

Wagner, Roy. 1991. "The Fractal Person." In *Big Men and Great Men: Personifications of Power in Melanesia*, edited by Maurice Godelier and Marilyn Strathern, 159–73. Cambridge: Cambridge University Press.

Ward, Alan. 2002. "Land Reform: 1971–3." Paper given at the workshop "Hindsight: A Workshop for Participants in the Decolonisation of Papua New Guinea" 3 November 2002, Canberra, Australia.

Wassmann, Jürg. 1995. *Historical Atlas of Ethnic and Linguistic Groups in Papua New Guinea, Volume 3*. Basel, Switzerland: Wepf.

Watson, James B. 1970. "Society as Organized Flow: The Tairora Case." *Southwestern Journal of Anthropology* 26 (2): 107–24.

Weber, Max. 1968. *Economy and Society: An Outline of Interpretive Sociology*. Edited by Guenther Roth and Claus Wittich. Translated by Ephraim Fischoff and others. New York: Bedminster.

Weiner, James F. 1988. *The Heart of the Pearl Shell: The Mythological Dimension of Foi Sociality*. Berkeley: University of California Press.

Weiner, James F. 2006. "Eliciting Customary Law." *Asia Pacific Journal of Anthropology* 7 (1): 15–25.

Weiner, James. 2007. "The Foi Incorporated Land Group: Group Definition and Collective Action in the Kutubu Oil Project Area, Papua New Guinea." In *Customary Land Tenure and Registration in Australia and Papua New Guinea: Anthropological Perspectives*, edited by James Weiner and Katie Glaskin, 117–35. Canberra: ANU E Press.

Weiner, James F., and Katie Glaskin. 2007. *Customary Land Tenure and Registration in Australia and Papua New Guinea: Anthropological Perspectives*. Canberra: ANU Press. Web.

Welker, Marina., Damani J. Partridge, and Rebecca Hardin. 2011. "Corporate Lives. New Perspectives on the Social Life of the Corporate Form: An Introduction to Supplement 3." *Current Anthropology* 52 (S3): 3–16.

Wesch, Michael. L. 2006. "Witchcraft, Statecraft, and the Challenge of 'Community' in Central New Guinea." PhD diss., University of Virginia.

West, Paige. 2012. *From Modern Production to Imagined Primitive: The Social World of Coffee From Papua New Guinea.* Durham, N.C.: Duke University Press.

White, Richard. 1991. *The Middle Ground: Indians, Empires, and Republics in the Great Lakes Region, 1650–1815.* Cambridge: Cambridge University Press.

Wiessner, Pauline Wilson, Akii Tumu, and Nitze Pupu. 1998. *Historical Vines: Enga Networks of Exchange, Ritual, and Warfare in Papua New Guinea.* Washington: Smithsonian Institution.

Wilk, Richard. 1995. "The Local and the Global in the Political Economy of Beauty: From Miss Belize to Miss World." *Review of International Political Economy* 2 (1): 117–34.

Williams, F. E. 1930. *Orokaiva Society.* London: Oxford University Press, 1930.

Wohlt, Paul. B. 1978. *"Ecology, Agriculture and Social Organization: The Dynamics of Group Composition in the Highlands of Papua New Guinea."* Ph.D. Diss. University of Minnesota.

Wolf, Eric. 1982. *Europe and the People Without History.* Berkeley: University of California Press.

Wolf, Eric. 1988. "Inventing Society." *American Ethnologist* 15 (4): 752–61.

Yoffee, Norman. 2001. "The Evolution of Simplicity." *Current Anthropology* 42 (5): 765–67.

Yoffee, Norman. 2004. *Myths of the Archaic State Evolution of the Earliest Cities, States and Civilizations.* New York: Cambridge University Press.

Yoffee, Norman, and Jeffrey Baines. 1998. "Order, Legitimacy, and Wealth in Ancient Egypt and Mesopotamia." In *Archaic States*, edited by Gary N. Feinman and Joyce Marcus, 199–260. Santa Fe, NM: School of American Research Press.

INDEX